CGI Programming in C & Perl

Thomas Boutell

ADDISON-WESLEY

An imprint of Addison Wesley Longman, Inc.

Reading, Massachusetts • Harlow, England • Menlo Park, California
Berkeley, California • Don Mills, Ontario • Sydney
Bonn • Amsterdam • Tokyo • Mexico City

Library of Congress Cataloging-in-Publication Data

Boutell, Thomas
    CGI Programming in C & Perl / Thomas Boutell.
        p. cm.
    Includes index.
    ISBN 0-201-42219-0
    1. World Wide Web servers--Computer programs. 2. C (Computer program language)
    3. Perl (Computer program language) 4. CGI (Computer network protocol) I Title.
TK5105.888.B69 1996
005.75--dc20
                                   96-1587
                                       CIP

Credits

cgi-lib.pl CGI library © 1995-1996 by Steven E. Brenner. The original and updated versions may be obtained from http://www.bio.cam.ac.uk/web/form.html.

The gd graphics library was written by Thomas Boutell for the QUEST Protein Database Center and was funded by the NIH National Center for Research Resources (NIH P41-RR02188).

GD.pm graphics library © 1996 by Lincoln Stein.

Moonmilk Mandalas © 1996 by Ranjit Bhatnagar. Email: ranjit@gradient.cis.upenn.edu.

Sponsoring Editor: Kim Fryer
Project Manager: Sarah Weaver
Production Coordinator: Erin Sweeney
Cover design: Watts Design?
Set in 11 point Giovanni by Greg Johnson, Art Directions

4 5 6 7 8 9 MA 02 01 00 99

4th Printing February 1999

To my parents

Contents

Acknowledgments

This book would not have been possible without the generous advice, support, and tolerance of my friends, family, and colleagues.

For their love and support, I would like to thank my family, most especially my wife, M.L. Grant, and my parents, Linda and William Boutell.

I also wish to acknowledge the patience and skill of my editor, Kim Fryer.

While writing this book, I have profited from the expertise of scores of people on the Internet. I humbly apologize for any omissions. Following is a partial list of those who helped to make this book possible: Kristen Ankiewicz, Tim Berners-Lee, Ranjit Bhatnagar, Steven Brenner, Rob Glaser, Marc Hedlund, Bob Kennewick, Tom Lane, Jerry Latter, Kate McDonnell, Pat Monardo, Corp Reed, and Lincoln Stein. I would also like to thank the denizens of Nerdsholm, the regulars of the #www and #linux IRC channels, and the resident grouches of the newsgroups talk.bizarre and comp.infosystems.www.authoring.cgi.

World Wide Web Documents

Since the beginning of the World Wide Web ("Web" or "WWW") at CERN[1] a few short years ago, the potential of this new online medium has been obvious. Web authors can create interlinked hypertext documents to provide information to users on a wide range of topics. Users, in turn, can access that information from anywhere in the world, meaning that a vast array of information is available in user-friendly form on a global scale.

The delivery of Web documents (also known as Web pages) appears transparent to the user, but several pieces of software are needed to make this happen. Each user operates a WWW browser program, such as NCSA Mosaic[2] or Netscape.[3] WWW documents are delivered by WWW server programs, such as the NCSA httpd[4] (hypertext transfer protocol daemon). Browsers and servers communicate through the Internet protocol suite, which connects many computers throughout the world (see Figure 1–1).

Web documents are usually written in HTML[5] (Hyper Text Markup Language), a simple markup language that attempts to describe the logical structure of the text. While "what you see is what you get" HTML editors have begun to emerge, the Web did not wait for such tools to become a popular medium. The simplicity of HTML makes it straightforward for users to write HTML themselves by using ordinary text editors. An instance of the more general SGML markup system,[6] it has been proven sufficient for creating an astonishingly diverse range of documents that are connected in a multitude of ways.

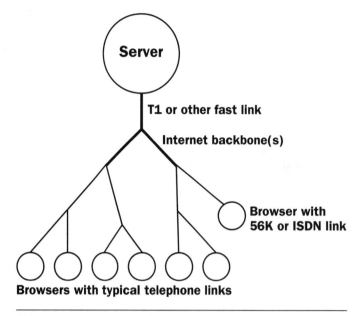

FIGURE 1–1 Flow of information in the World Wide Web

Most often, HTML is stored in static files on the server's hard drive. Such simple, static hypertext documents can convey a great deal of information, but eventually their limitations become clear. For example, what if the author wishes to provide *dynamic information*—information that changes over time? Or accept purchase information from the user? Or provide a search facility that permits a database to be explored? Dynamic resources of this sort have been around almost as long as the Web itself. Perhaps the most well-known early example, and still one of the most functional and useful, is the world map server at Xerox PARC[7] (see Figure 1–2). How to create such "interactive," dynamically generated Web documents is the subject of this book.

The Universe of Web Documents

There are many types of Web documents. Although HTML pages predominate, most pages feature inline images, which are Web documents in their own right. Content types (document types) commonly found on the Web include HTML pages; GIF-, PNG-, and JPEG-format images; Sun-, Windows-, and Mac-format sounds; and AVI-, Quicktime-, and MPEG-format video.

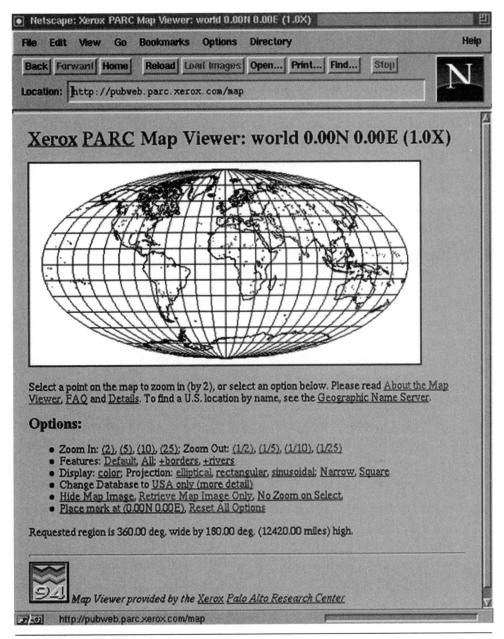

FIGURE 1-2 The world map server at Xerox PARC

How these content types are presented to the user varies. Most often, document types other than HTML pages appear to be subsidiary parts of the HTML page. From the server's perspective, however, all Web documents are equal in that they all require the server to respond to a unique request. The server may handle that request by delivering a file found on the server system or by executing another program to generate the resource requested on the fly.

For the purposes of this discussion, the distinction between a document delivered from a file and a document generated "on the fly" is crucial. The first is a *static document,* such as an HTML page stored normally in the file system. The second is a *dynamic document,* which has an interactive and/or time-sensitive nature and generally cannot be stored in the file system in advance.

Static Documents: Fixed Pages

Static documents are typically delivered from the file system of the Web server. The Web server software locates the file on the hard drive, opens it directly, and delivers it to the client (browser).

Static documents are best used to present information that doesn't change or information that needs to be updated by hand. For example, static HTML documents are well suited to the task of placing Shakespeare's plays on the Web,[8] since the text is unlikely to change!

Another example is a page showcasing recent works of an artist. The content is likely to change on a regular basis; however, the layout of the page itself is an artistic decision. So updates of the page are best left to a human artist. Even so, such pages often take advantage of dynamic features to provide variety and fast change in the content of the otherwise static page.[9]

Static documents cannot accept complex input from the user. However, they can contain links to other documents. This capability provides a simple form of interactivity. It can even be used to explore databases, although only if the author has anticipated the possible ways in which the user may wish to explore the database and has thus provided appropriate links (see Figure 1–3 for a simple example). When databases are very small, this approach can be effective. As such systems grow, however, they are quickly overwhelmed by the complex maintenance required to keep them up-to-date. Eventually, a system that generates the documents dynamically from a database becomes desirable.

Static documents have advantages. Creating them is straightforward for the author; documents are written once and stored on the server. Another

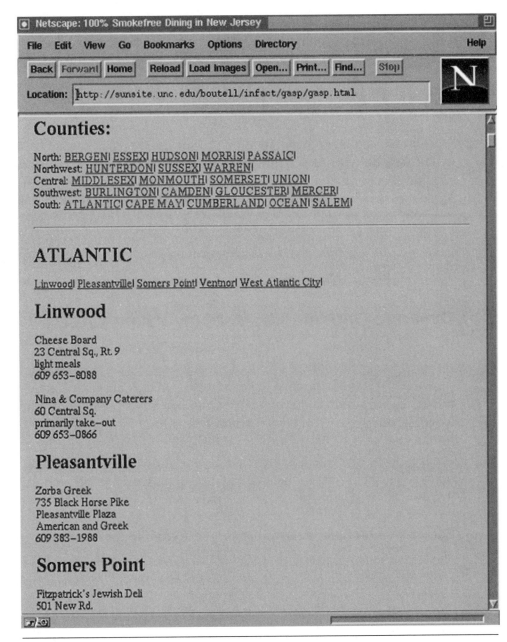

FIGURE 1–3 The GASP database of smoke-free restaurants

advantage is that they can be delivered quickly. When documents can be served from files, the Web server program can handle the request internally, without having to execute a different program.

However, static documents are limited in their expressiveness. They cannot reflect dynamically changing information. Also, when used alone they cannot accept input from the user, except in the sense that the user can choose a link to another document. Yet even that interaction requires the help of a dynamic program if an imagemap is involved. Figure 1–4 shows the process by which static documents are served.

Note, however, that even apparently static documents may take advantage of certain helpful types of dynamic documents. For example, a dynamic facility to allow searching of the text would be a useful addition to a repository of Shakespeare's plays. Also, imagemaps that direct the user to different documents depending on the portion of an image that is clicked (see Figure 1–5) are implemented as dynamic documents. A special program executes on the server to dynamically determine and deliver the correct document based on where the user clicks.

Dynamic Documents: Documents on the Fly

Dynamic documents, unlike static documents, require the server to generate the document on the fly. While static documents can be read from an existing file, dynamic documents may never exist on disk at all! Dynamic documents, for example, can be generated from databases of all kinds, from video capture systems, and from scientific instruments such as weather monitoring systems. Such documents are often transmitted directly to the client as they are created, without ever being stored in the file system. In other cases, they consist largely of fixed content, with a small amount of dynamic content generated when the page is actually delivered.

Server-side Include: One Approach to Dynamic Documents

The HTML system makes it easy to link documents to each other. However, it is sometimes desirable to assemble a single large HTML document from

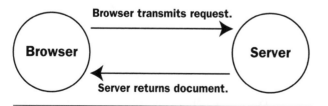

FIGURE 1–4 Delivering a static document

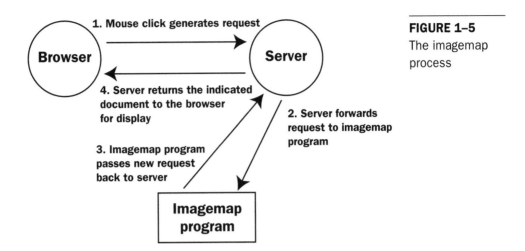

FIGURE 1–5
The imagemap
process

several smaller documents. Many Web authors ask why a Web document cannot simply include another document by reference rather than physically containing a copy of the second document. The current version of HTML does not allow for this. However, nothing prevents Web servers from providing their own extended version of HTML in which such included sections are permitted, as long as the server takes care of the task of including the second document and delivers the complete HTML document to the browser. This approach is called as the *server-side include* mechanism (see Figure 1–6).

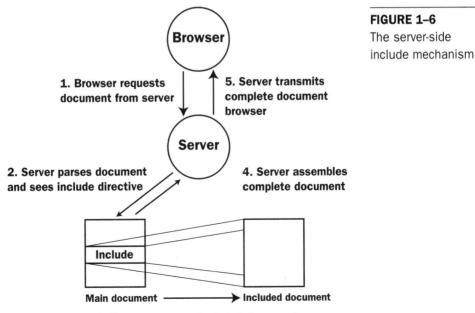

FIGURE 1–6
The server-side
include mechanism

If a static document simply were to include another static document, that first document would not be a dynamic document. However, most server-side include mechanisms also permit the output of a particular program to be included in the document or simply permit the document included by reference to be a dynamic document in its own right. A document that takes advantage of this is indeed dynamic.

Unfortunately, the server-side include mechanism has performance problems associated with it that have induced many Web server operators to disallow it. Also, server-side include is not well-standardized among Web servers. Accordingly, it is not the primary focus of this book.

CGI: The Most Common Approach

Most often, dynamic documents are completely dynamic, at least from the server's perspective. That is, they are generated entirely by an outside program executed by the server. In essence, the outside program receives any user input associated with the document as its standard input, and outputs the generated document to standard output, along with important type information identifying the nature of the document.

A standard has emerged for the construction of such completely dynamic documents by external programs installed on the server system. That standard is the Common Gateway Interface (CGI),[10] and it regulates the environment in which such programs will execute (see Figure 1–7).

CGI Programming Languages

Dynamic documents can be generated by programs written in nearly any programming language. In practice, however, some languages make better choices than others for this purpose, for reasons such as efficiency, simplicity, and security. Practical CGI languages for which useful libraries and other tools have been written include C,[11] Perl,[12 to 13] Tcl,[14] Python,[15] and REXX.[16]

This book focuses on C and Perl, with a particular emphasis on C. C and Perl are both widely available and widely used on all popular server platforms. C is emphasized primarily because of its performance advantages; under most circumstances, CGI programs written in C are the most efficient. Perl is also given extensive treatment because it is easy to use and enjoys widespread popularity for CGI applications.

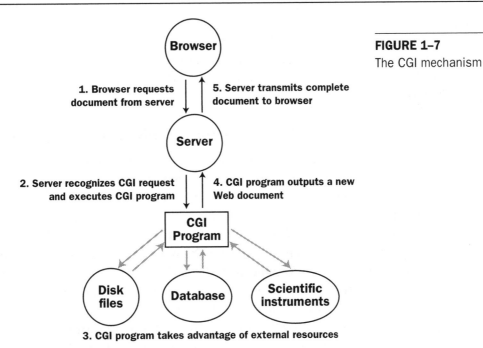

FIGURE 1–7
The CGI mechanism

CGI by Example

A CGI program can take advantage of any resource available to the server computer to generate its output. It can also accept input from the user by accepting the contents of a form filled out by the user. These two basic capabilities have led to a wide variety of applications.

One CGI application examined in detail in this book is the World Birthday Web,[17] a database I designed to allow Web users worldwide to register their own birth dates and discover others who share the same birthdate. Tens of thousands of individuals have taken advantage of the system, which continues to function smoothly.

While the World Birthday Web is in the entertainment category, it has universal appeal, and the techniques employed in its implementation are readily applicable to practical applications such as stock market analysis. In fact, a prototype CGI-based stock market analysis system is presented in Chapter 14, "World Wide Web Wall Street—An Advanced CGI Application."

Installing CGI Programs: "A Privilege, Not a Right"

CGI programs introduce a security risks. As a result, many Internet service providers (ISPs) do not allow their customers to write and install their own

CGI programs, even if they do provide users with Web space for static documents. In practice, users usually must establish their own Web server. The problem of obtaining CGI access is discussed in detail in Chapter 3, "Obtaining CGI Access."

The cgic and cgi-lib Libraries: Improved APIs for CGI Programming

One problem that often comes up in the design of CGI programs is the duplication of effort among programmers. Several libraries have been developed to take care of common CGI programming tasks in Perl, but until recently there have been few such general-purpose CGI libraries for C. This book provides extensive coverage of my cgic library, which takes care of the common tasks faced by all C programmers who attempt CGI. To illustrate the techniques involved, programs in the early chapters of the book tackle such CGI challenges as the parsing of form submissions directly. Later chapters take advantage of the cgic library for C programmers and Steven Brenner's cgi-lib library for Perl programmers. Both are introduced in Chapter 8, "Using cgic and cgi-lib: Complete CGI Solutions."

Product-specific APIs: CGI Alternatives

Many server products offer product-specific APIs that attempt to improve on the performance of the common-denominator CGI system. Most of these systems are specific to a particular server or even to a particular server and operating system.

This book focuses primarily on the standard CGI system because of its wide availability and general utility. However, CGI alternatives are discussed in more detail in Chapter 15, "What's Next: CGI and Beyond."

Conclusion

The need to deliver dynamic information and respond to user input in ways that go beyond the capabilities of static, "canned" HTML pages has led to considerable interest in CGI programming and related dynamic document-generation techniques. So the primary subject of this book is how best to construct programs that take advantage of the CGI standard to deliver dynamic, exciting multimedia documents from a variety of input sources. Chapter 2 introduces and describes the CGI standard itself.

References

1. W3 Consortium, "About the World Wide Web."
   [URL:http://www.w3.org/hypertext/WWW/]

2. National Center for Supercomputing Applications, "The NCSA Mosaic Home Page."
   [URL:http://www.ncsa.uiuc.edu/SDG/Software/Mosaic/NCSAMosaicHome.html]

3. Netscape Communications Corporation, "Netscape Navigator."
   [URL:http://home.netscape.com/comprod/netscape_nav.html]

4. NCSA HTTPd Development Team, "NCSA HTTPd."
   [URL:http://hoohoo.ncsa.uiuc.edu/docs/Overview.html]

5. W3 Consortium, "HyperText Markup Language (HTML): Working and Background Materials."
   [URL:http://www.w3.org/hypertext/WWW/MarkUp/MarkUp.html]

6. W3 Consortium, "SGML and the Web."
   [URL:http://www.w3.org/hypertext/WWW/MarkUp/SGML/]

7. Steve Putz, "About the Xerox PARC Map Viewer," Xerox PARC.
   [URL:http://www.xerox.com/PARC/docs/mapviewer.html]

8. William Shakespeare, "The Collected Works of Shakespeare," edited by Matty Farrow.
   [URL:http://www.gh.cs.usyd.edu.au/~matty/Shakespeare/index.html]

9. Kristen Ankiewicz, "Ankiewicz Galleries."
   [URL:http://www.cybercom.net/~kristen/]

10. W3 Consortium, "Overview of CGI."
    [URL:http://www.w3.org/hypertext/WWW/CGI/Overview.html]

11. Brian Kernigan and Dennis Ritchie, *The C Programming Language, Second Edition.* (New York: Prentice Hall, 1988) ISBN: 0-13-110362-8.

12. Larry Wall and Randal Schwartz, *Programming Perl.* (Sebastopol, CA: O'Reilly and Associates, 1993) ISBN: 0-937175-64-1.

13. Tom Christiansen, "Perl 5 References."
    [URL:http://www.perl.com/]

14. John K. Ousterhout, *TCL and the Tk Toolkit*. (Reading, MA: Addison-Wesley, 1994) ISBN: 0-201- 63337-X.

15. Guido van Rossum, "Python Frequently Asked Questions." [URL:http://www.cis.ohio-state.edu/hypertext/faq/usenet/python-faq/part1/faq.html]

16. Eric Giguere, "Rexx Frequently Asked Questions." [URL:http://www.hursley.ibm.com/rexx/rexxfaq.htm]

17. Thomas Boutell, "The World Birthday Web." [URL:http://www.boutell.com/birthday.cgi/]

The CGI Standard

The CGI standard is intended to provide a consistent interface between Web servers and programs that extend their capabilities. As discussed in Chapter 2, Web servers are able to deliver static documents from files without the assistance of other programs. However, dynamic content, database interfaces, and responsiveness to user input are all desirable and cannot be accomplished by static documents alone.

This chapter gives an overview of the CGI standard, examining both its definition and its reasons for existence. Topics introduced in this chapter are covered in more detail and with full examples in later chapters. So keep this in mind if you find portions of the chapter difficult to follow.

The Need for a Standard

Dynamic documents have been around almost as long as the Web itself. From the first days of the Web, programmers have found ways to generate Web pages on the fly. Early systems of this sort often involved custom servers—servers developed solely to deliver a particular type of dynamic content. The simplicity of the original HTTP[1] (HyperText Transfer Protocol) specification made this approach practical, and it is sometimes still employed today when efficiency is of paramount concern.

As Web servers gained in sophistication, it soon became apparent that it was not practical to replicate the advanced security, logging, communications, and load-management features of a modern server for every application that required dynamic documents. So Web server developers began to provide interfaces through which external programs could be executed, usually in response to a request for a document in a designated portion of the document tree. The NCSA httpd (HTTP daemon) was the first Web server to provide such an interface.[2]

These first external-program interfaces represented a significant advance but did not solve the standardization problem. The various Web servers followed separate standards for the development of external programs, so it was impossible to write a single external program that would be useful with all servers.

The Goals of CGI

The CGI standard was developed jointly by NCSA (the National Center for Supercomputing Applications) and CERN (the European Laboratory for Particle Physics) in response to the need for a consistent external-program interface.[3] In addition to a consistent, standard interface, the CGI standard seeks to provide reasonable guarantees that user input, particularly form submissions, will not be lost due to the limitations of the server operating system. The CGI standard also attempts to provide the external program with as much information as possible about the server and the browser, in addition to any information that may be known about the user. Finally, the CGI standard attempts to be straightforward so as to make the development of simple CGI applications easy.

Largely, the CGI standard has achieved these goals. Other emerging approaches are sometimes more efficient, especially when tuned to specific operating systems (see Chapter 15, "What's Next: CGI and Beyond"), but the portability and simplicity of the CGI standard has led to its widespread use.

CGI does not always achieve its goal of simplicity. The parsing of form data is somewhat complex, especially when done properly and thoroughly. However, its popularity has led to the development of several freely available tools to simplify the task of CGI programming, including several Perl libraries and the cgic library for C (see Chapter 8).

CGI and the HyperText Transfer Protocol

The server executes CGI programs in order to satisfy particular requests from the browser. The browser then expresses its requests using the HyperText Transfer Protocol.[1] The server responds by delivering either a document, an error status code, and/or a redirection to a new URL according to the rules of that protocol. While CGI programs usually need not speak the HTTP directly, certain aspects of it are important to CGI.

HTTP requests can be of several types, which are called *methods*. For CGI programmers, the most important are GET and POST.

The GET method is used to request a document and does not normally submit other input from the user. If the requested URL points to a CGI program, the CGI program generates either a new document, an error code, or a redirection to another document (see "CGI Standard Output" later in this chapter). The CGI program can identify this situation by examining the REQUEST_METHOD environment variable, which in this case will contain the string GET.

In some cases, there is a certain amount of user input, which the browser submits as part of the URL. This may happen for example when the <ISINDEX> HTML tag is used or an HTML form delivers its data via the GET method. This information will then be stored in the QUERY_STRING environment variable. This approach is rather unwieldy and so should be avoided in new CGI programs.

The POST method is used to deliver information from the browser to the server. In most cases, the information sent is a form submission. The CGI program then reads the submitted information from standard input (see "CGI Standard Input" later in this chapter for the format of the data). In this case, the REQUEST_METHOD environment variable will be set to the string POST. To be certain the posted information is a form submission, the CGI prgram examines the CONTENT_TYPE environment variable to make sure it contains the string x-www-form-urlencoded. The latest Web browsers can also post other forms of data to the Web server.

After examining the submission, the program typically generates either a new document, an error code, or a redirection to another URL (see "CGI Standard Output" later in this chapter).

Other methods, such as PUT, are coming into use, but GET and POST remain the most important HTTP methods for CGI programming.

CGI Environment Variables

The HTTP daemon (server) shares a variety of information with the CGI program. This information is communicated in the form of environment variables.

In C, environment variables are normally accessed using the getenv() function. For example, the following code example retrieves the PATH_INFO environment variable. This variable contains any additional information in the URL of the user's request beyond the path of the CGI program itself and preceding a question mark, if any:

```
char *serverName;
serverName = getenv("PATH_INFO");
```

In Perl, environment variables are found in the %ENV associative array. The following Perl expression also refers to the PATH_INFO environment variable:

```
$serverName = $ENV{'PATH_INFO'} ;
```

Appendix 1 contains a complete list of the CGI environment variables. The most important are introduced as they are used in the next several chapters.

CGI Standard Output

CGI programs are normally expected to output one of three things: a valid Web document, a status code, or a redirection to another URL.

Outputting a New Document

To output a new document, a CGI program must first indicate the type of data contained in the document. For instance, the following content type header indicates that the data that follows is in HTML:

```
Content-type: text/html
```

> **VERY IMPORTANT:** TWO line breaks must follow the `Content-type` line. Otherwise, your document will be ignored. A blank line signals the end of the headers and the beginning of the document, if any.

Following the content type header, the CGI program can output any valid HTML document. Many examples of HTML documents are in this book, beginning in Chapter 4.

Information about other content types, such as `image/gif`, is presented in Chapter 10 and Appendix 2.

Returning a Status Code

If an error occurs, the CGI program may wish to output a status code rather than a document. In this case, the following MIME header whould be output:

```
Status: #### Status Message
```

where #### is replaced with any valid HTTP status code[4] and Error Message with an explanatory message for the user.

> **IMPORTANT:** The status line must be followed by **two** line breaks. Otherwise, the status code will be ignored.

No further output is necessary.

Redirecting the Browser to Another URL

It is not uncommon for a programmer to decide that a request is best handled by redirecting the user to another URL. The other URL can be on the same or another system. In the first case, the server will usually intervene and attempt to resolve the request without sending the redirection back to the browser. In the second case, the new URL is transmitted back to the browser, which then makes a connection to a new server.

To redirect the browser to another URL, output the following header:

```
Location: URL
```

where URL is replaced with any valid URL. If the URL refers to a document on the same server, `http://hostname` can be omitted, and performance gains are realized by doing so. To ensure compatibility with all servers, you are advised to begin such local URLs from the document root (begin with a / character). *Note:* Some browsers also require the header `URI:URL...` in addition to `Location:URL...`.

> **IMPORTANT:** The status line must be followed by **TWO** line breaks. Otherwise, the redirection will be ignored.

No further output is necessary. More information about this subject is presented in Chapter 12.

Perl and C code to handle output from CGI programs is presented throughout this book beginning in Chapter 4.

CGI Standard Input

Earlier external-program standards specified form data to be stored entirely in environment variables or passed on the command line, an approach that risks truncation under some operating systems when the amount of information is too great. While the CGI standard allows this approach, it also allows and encourages an approach in which the form data is passed to the external program as its standard input, meaning the data can be accessed with simple standard I/O calls such as the C functions `getc()` and `fread()`.

When no data has been submitted by the user or a form has been submitted with the `GET` method, standard input will contain no information. However, when data has been sent by the user using the `POST` method, the data will appear at standard input. Use of the `POST` method is the preferred method for form submissions. The format for form data is:

```
keyword=value&keyword=value&keyword=value
```

that is, a stream of keyword and value pairs, where keywords and values are separated by equal signs and pairs by & signs.

> **IMPORTANT:** Note that all characters that are escaped in URLs are also escaped in posted form data. That is, if characters such as &, =, and % are typed by the user and submitted as part of the request, they will appear escaped in standard input as follows:
>
> %xx
>
> where the ASCII value of the character in hex is substituted for xx. For instance, the %, ASCII value 37 decimal, 21 hexadecimal, appears as follows:
>
> %21

The CONTENT_LENGTH environment variable will always contain the total number of characters of data to be read from standard input.

Perl and C code to handle the CGI standard input stream is presented in Chapter 7, "Handling User Input: Interacting with Forms."

Conclusion

In this chapter, I introduced the basic concepts of CGI. In Chapter 3, we begin writing CGI programs.

References

1. W3 Consortium, "HyperText Transfer Protocol Specification."
   [URL:http://www.w3.org/hypertext/WWW/Protocols/Overview.html]

2. NCSA HTTPd Development Team, "Upgrading NCSA httpd."
   [URL:http://hoohoo.ncsa.uiuc.edu/docs/Upgrade.html]

3. W3 Consortium, "Overview of CGI."
   [URL:http://www.w3.org/hypertext/WWW/CGI/Overview.html]

Obtaining CGI Access

Many individuals have accounts which permit them to offer Web pages to the world. It is natural to assume that CGI programs can be installed simply by placing them in such accounts. Alas, this is not always the case.

Q *"I obtained a CGI program. I linked to it from my Web page. I clicked on the link and it downloaded the program to my screen instead of running it! Now what?"*

A This is the most common problem new CGI programmers encounter. In most cases, CGI programs cannot simply be thrown into the same directory with a collection of HTML pages and be expected to work. Also, CGI programs can never simply be run from a local drive on the user's machine without the use of a Web server.

Web servers have their own rules by which they determine which files are CGI programs and which are documents to be simply delivered to the user. CGI programmers must obey these rules in order to ensure that their CGI programs are actually executed by the server.

Q *"You keep talking about servers. Can't I compile and test CGI programs at home using just Netscape or Mosaic?"*

A No, you usually can't. As explained in Chapter 1, CGI programs and Web servers are intimately related. CGI programming is a way of extending a Web server to deliver more than it can deliver by itself.

Q *"Why is a server required?"*

A Use of a server ensures the risks associated with executing CGI programs fall on the server, which executes the CGI program and delivers the output to the browser. The risk should never fall on the user. If Web browsers were written to execute arbitrary programs as part of any Web page, viruses and other damaging programs would be trivially easy to write and no sensible person would be willing to browse the Web! CGI programs, on the other hand, can at worst wreak havoc only on the server.

Of course, being able to execute arbitrary programs on the browser would have its own advantages. Systems designed to make that approach more practical and secure are on their way. Sun Microsystems's Java[1] is one such system.

Q *"Does this mean I have to learn to program in the Unix or Windows NT environment?"*

A Yes, if you want to be able to write CGI programs for the most commonly used Web servers. You'll need to become reasonably comfortable with Unix or Windows NT. Basic Unix commands are not covered in this book, but the commands necessary to compile and install your own CGI programs are. CGI-like systems do exist for other operating systems, such as Microsoft Windows and the Apple Macintosh, but those systems are outside the focus of this book.

While it is often possible to install a Web server on your machine at home, doing this is rarely the best way to test your CGI programs, since it is likely your home machine and the server on which you will actually install your CGI programs do not run the same operating system. Windows NT is exceptional in that Unix CGI programs are usually portable to NT.

As a result, generally you must either arrange for CGI access on a commercial or educational Internet site or take the plunge and set up your own Internet site.

Purchasing CGI Access on a Commercial Server

Purchasing web access from an ISP has become common practice as that is often more cost-effective than setting up your own Internet site. There are three basic tiers of Web access available from ISPs. First are the basic

Internet accounts that providers often offer at a flat monthly rate; I call these *Web access* accounts. Second are Internet accounts that include Unix shell access, a certain amount of Web space; I call these *shell* accounts. ISPs oriented specifically toward the Web offer a third, more-advanced service and place fewer restrictions on the frequency of access to the user's offerings. I call these *virtual site* accounts because they usually seek to create the impression that the user's Web documents are coming from a completely independent site.

Web Access Accounts

Basic Internet access accounts that do not offer access to the Unix shell are useful for browsing the Web but are not suitable for CGI programming. Accounts offered by mass-market providers such as Microsoft Network,[2] Prodigy,[3] Compuserve,[4] America Online,[5] and Netcom[6] are all of this type. If you have such an account, you will need to consider purchasing a better grade of service that includes a Unix shell account with personal Web space and CGI privileges. Such accounts are often available at very reasonable prices from locally based ISPs in your area.

Shell Accounts

ISPs that offer Unix shell accounts usually also offer a limited amount of space on their Web servers in which Web pages can be kept. These accounts may also offer CGI access, but whether they do varies extensively among ISPs. Be sure to discuss this issue with your ISP. There are good reasons why a provider might choose not to include CGI access with a basic shell account. One is that doing so creates security risks. See Chapter 9, "Sending E-mail from CGI Programs," for examples of such risks.

Note that because shell accounts are typically sold at a flat monthly rate, providers of such accounts often oversell their Internet bandwidth on the assumption that most Web pages will not receive vast numbers of accesses. Often, if your Web offerings become very popular, you will be required to move them to another ISP or purchase a better grade of service. Still, basic shell accounts can be an excellent way to get started and develop your CGI programming skills.

Two providers of Unix shell accounts that do include CGI access at the time of this writing are Northwest Nexus,[7] located in the U.S. Pacific northwest, and Best Communications,[8] located in southern California. Keep in mind that an account in another locality can often be used to access another ISP by telnet if no local provider offers CGI access and Web space.

Virtual Site Accounts

Virtual site accounts are the royal road to the Web, second only to a well-connected Internet site of your own. Indeed, they seek to simulate such a site, and in many cases, providers of such accounts can arrange matters so that several companies being served from one machine can appear to have machines of their own. Most important, such accounts do not place restrictions on the popularity of your Web pages. They also often allow the privilege of installing CGI programs to be specifically purchased, thus making it highly unlikely that the privilege will be withdrawn unexpectedly. In this case, you get what you pay for. With a reputable provider, paying up front for space on a commercial-grade Web server usually ensures good service and support. Vendors offering such virtual site accounts include Northwest Nexus,[7] Best, and many other ISPs worldwide.

Installing CGI Programs on Commercial Web Servers

The exact procedure for installing CGI programs on shell acounts and virtual site accounts differs among ISPs, so the following examples should not be taken as gospel. Your provider's policies may differ. You will need to read the documentation or contact your provider's customer support to find out precisely where and how to install CGI programs to ensure they are recognized by the Web server.

halcyon.com: A Shell Account Provider with CGI Access

halcyon.com, an Internet service provided by Northwest Nexus,[7] is a good example of an ISP that offers Web space and CGI access to Unix shell account customers. Keep in mind that this information is provided *as an example only.* The configuration of halcyon may have changed by the time you read this.

On halcyon, the top of the Web server document tree presently points to the Unix directory /archive/local/. That is, a request for the URL http://www.halcyon.com/index.html would retrieve the file /archive/local/index.html from halcyon's Web server. Halcyon permits customers to create their own subdirectories of /archive/local/. My own subdirectory on halcyon is /archive/local/boutell/, which gives me the URL http://www.halcyon.com/boutell/ on that system. CGI programs, however, are not installed in personal directories. Instead, they are installed in the directory /archive/local/htbin, which is also writable by halcyon's shell account customers.

Halcyon's Web server has been configured to consider files found in the /archive/local/htbin directory to be CGI programs to be executed, as opposed to documents to simply be delivered. As a result, when a request for the URL http://www.halcyon.com/htbin/imagemap is received, halcyon's Web server executes the program imagemap found in that directory and outputs the result to the browser, instead of delivering the program itself. Table 3–1 presents several examples of the correspondence between URLs and locations in the file system on halcyon.

TABLE 3–1 Location of Web documents and CGI programs on halcyon

URL	File System Path
http://www.halcyon.com/	/archive/local/
http://www.halcyon.com/boutell/	/archive/local/boutell/
http://www.halcyon.com/htbin/imagemap	/archive/local/htbin/imagemap

> **NOTE:** In practice, a URL accessing the imagemap program would contain more information than this. For example, accessing the last URL in Table 3–1 causes the program to output an error message indicating that the map being accessed and the location at which the user clicked the image are also expected as part of the URL.

Halcyon also provides the standard Unix perl, make, and gcc tools, thereby making it possible for users to write their own Perl- and C-based CGI programs.

Common Rules for Installing CGI Programs

While all ISPs are different, there are a few configurations common enough to merit mention here.

ISPs that use the NCSA Web server or one of its derivatives, such as the Apache server or Netscape's Netscape Server, often allow a user's personal Web pages to be stored in a subdirectory named `public_html` beneath that user's home directory. If your provider allows this, you can create your own Web space directory using by executing the following Unix command from your home directory:

```
mkdir public_html
```

Make sure this directory is readable by others by executing the following command. This command grants read and execute privileges to all users but reserves write privileges for yourself.

```
chmod 755 public_html
```

You should then create a personal home page in that directory using the Unix editor of your choice. I recommend the editor `pico` for users who are unfamiliar with Unix. Type `cd public_html` to enter the subdirectory, `pico filename.html` to edit an HTML file in that directory, and cd .. to return to your home directory. The top-level URL that corresponds to your directory will be the following:

```
http://www.myprovider.com/~myname/
```

The ~ is important! This indicates that `myname` is a user name, not a subdirectory of the main document root directory of the Web server.

> **NOTE:** NCSA-style servers are often configured to recognize the file `index.html` as a home page to be delivered if no filename is specified at the end of the previous URL. See Table 3–2.

TABLE 3–2 Typical mapping of URLs to file system paths on NCSA-style servers

URL	File System Path
`http://www.site.com/boutell/`	`/etc/httpd/docs/boutell/`
`http://www.site.com/~boutell/`	`~boutell/public_html/`
`http://www.site.com/~smith/foo/note.html`	`~smith/public_html/foo/note.html`

If all of the above works smoothly, the next question is, how do you install your CGI programs? This procedure varies widely among ISPs, but NCSA-style servers are often configured to recognize any file with the extension .cgi as a CGI program.

To test this, edit the file test.cgi in your public_html directory, giving it the following contents. *Do not include any blank lines before the first line.*

```
#!/bin/sh
echo Content-type: text/html
echo
echo Hello, world.
```

> **NOTE:** This program is a simple shell script. Most programs in this book are written in C or Perl, but for test purposes, trivial CGI programs can be easily written using the Unix shell.

Next, to ensure the Web server views this file as executable, use the Unix chmod command to indicate that this is an executable program accessible by all:

```
chmod 755 test.cgi
```

This also makes the text of the file readable by other users of your ISP. If you prefer, you may wish to set the permissions to 711, which allows all users to execute the program but only yourself to read the code.

Finally, test your CGI program, by opening the following URL in your Web browser:

```
http://www.myprovider.com/~myname/test.cgi
```

You should get back the text "Hello, world" in your browser.

If It Doesn't Work

If you get an error message instead of "Hello World" in your browser, or if the text of the script itself appears in your browser, then your ISP is not set up in precisely the way assumed by this example. Your provider may expect CGI programs to be in a different location, or it may prefer to give out the privilege of CGI access on an individual basis only to users who need it. This is not surprising, and it is no cause for panic. You will need to talk to your ISP and find out where and how to install Web pages and CGI programs on your account.

Creating Your Own Internet Site

You can, of course, establish your own permanent site on the Internet. Doing this generally ensures your organization's Web presence will not be subject to the whims of an outside system administrator and guarantees your organization will have the necessary access privileges to install CGI programs. If you intend to install a Web server and deliver dynamic documents using CGI, you will probably want your Web server to run one flavor or another of the Unix operating system. The popular Linux[9] operating system, a free implementation of POSIX (the Unix operating system standard), is particularly well suited to this purpose and runs well on typical IBM-compatible hardware.

An explanation of how to install Unix and establish an Internet site is beyond the scope of this book. However, configuring an existing Web server to recognize and support CGI programs is discussed in the rest of this chapter.

Configuring Web Servers to Recognize CGI Programs

People who have Web sites of their own have the enviable privilege of dictating the configuration of CGI programs on their systems. For the purposes of this chapter, I assume your goal is to provide flexible CGI access for your own purposes as Webmaster.

Configuring the NCSA Server and Its Derivatives

This section covers the proper configuration of the NCSA and Apache World Wide Web servers to support CGI programs. Netscape's Communications and Commerce Servers are also NCSA-derived, but have their own user-friendly, Web browser-driven configuration system with which their owners will no doubt be familiar.

There are two basic ways the server can be instructed to recognize CGI scripts. The first is to designate specific directories for CGI purposes. The second is to instruct the server to recognize as a CGI program any filename with a special extension.

Designating CGI Directories

Beneath the directory in which your Web server is installed should be a subdirectory named conf. Within this directory should be a file named srm.conf. This file controls the manner in which the server translates requests for particular URLs into accesses of particular directories.

Each line in the srm.conf file consists of a keyword followed by various arguments relevant to that keyword. Typically placed at the end of the file is the keyword ScriptAlias. This keyword can be used one or more times to declare that URLs beginning with a particular prefix should be translated into requests to execute CGI programs found in a particular directory.

It is common practice to create at least one such directory, usually as a subdirectory of the directory in which the server is located. This subdirectory is usually named cgi-bin, and in fact the standard NCSA and Apache server packages include such a directory along with a collection of CGI examples.

The appropriate ScriptAlias line to activate this directory is:

```
ScriptAlias /cgi-bin/ /path/to/your/server/cgi-bin/
```

where /path/to/your/server is replaced with the full path of your server directory on your system.

> **IMPORTANT:** If you make a change to the configuration of your server, it will not take effect until you signal the server to restart. This is done using the kill -1 command. kill alone would kill the server process, but kill -1 delivers a special signal instructing the server to re-examine its configuration.

To do this, first look at the logs subdirectory of your server installation directory and examine the file httpd.pid, which will contain the process ID of the currently running server. Then signal the server as follows:

```
kill -1 pid
```

where `pid` is replaced with the process ID number found in `httpd.pid`.

To test your configuration, try to access the `calendar` script, which is normally provided as an example with the NCSA server. If your configuration matches the previous example and the sample CGI programs that came with the server are installed in the `cgi-bin` subdirectory, then the URL to access it should be

```
http://mysite.mydomain/cgi-bin/calendar
```

If the text of the script appears, instead of a calendar, then you have made an error in the server configuration. Reread this section and consult the server documentation for additional information. If a calendar for the current month appears, your server is now properly configured for CGI programming. Read on to learn how to designate a filename extension for CGI programs, if you prefer that approach, or wish to use both approaches.

Designating a Filename Extension for CGI Programs

In the `conf` subdirectory of your Web server installation directory is a file named `srm.conf`. Within this file, you can use the `AddType` keyword to designate an extension such as .cgi that will always be recognized as a CGI program, regardless of the directory in which it is encountered. Consider the following example:

```
AddType application/x-httpd-cgi .cgi
```

The first argument here is the MIME type that the server uses to refer internally to CGI programs. It is here because `AddType` can also be used to map extensions to other types, such as `image/gif` and `text/html`.

As explained in the previous section, to actually cause the change to take effect, examine the file `httpd.pid` in the `logs` subdirectory of your server installation directory to obtain the process ID of the currently running server. Then signal the server as follows:

```
kill -1 pid
```

where `pid` is replaced with the process ID number found in `httpd.pid`. To test the change, copy the standard `calendar` example CGI program from the `cgi-bin` subdirectory to another directory on the Web server, such as the document root directory where your server's top-level home page is found. Change its name to `calendar.cgi` and then access it with the following URL:

```
http://mysite.mydomain/calendar.cgi
```

Configuring the CERN/w3 Consortium Server

The CERN server, originated by CERN and now maintained by the w3 consortium (an industry consortium affiliated with MIT), is controlled by a rule file, normally named `httpd.conf`. This file is often found at the path `/etc/httpd.conf`, although you may have installed it elsewhere. In that case, your system is probably configured to start the server with the `-r` option, which specifies an alternative location for `httpd.conf`. You may need to consult the script from which your server is launched to determine the location of the rule file.

Once you have found the rule file, it is straightforward to configure the server to recognize CGI programs. Simply add a rule beginning with the `Exec` keyword. Follow that with the URL in your Web server's space beneath which you would like to be able to refer to CGI programs. Then add the directory in your local file system in which those CGI programs will be kept.

As an example, consider the following common configuration:

```
Exec /cgi-bin/ /path/to/my/server/cgi-bin/
```

Adding this rule to your rule file will configure your server to recognize all references to URLs on your server that begin with `/cgi-bin/` as requests to execute programs found in the `cgi-bin` subdirectory of your main server directory.

> **IMPORTANT:** If you change the configuration of your server, it will not take effect until you signal the server to re-examine its rule file. The CERN server provides a special command-line flag for this purpose. Just execute the following command (I assume the server binary is in your path):
>
> ```
> httpd -restart
> ```

> **NOTE:** If your rule file is not named `/etc/httpd.conf`, you will also have to specify the `-r` option and the actual location of your `httpd.conf` file in the same manner that you are likely already specifying it when launching the server at boot time.

To test your configuration, try to access the `calendar` script that is normally provided as an example with both the NCSA and the CERN servers. If your configuration matches the previous example and the sample CGI programs found in the optional `utils` collection distributed with the CERN server are installed in the `cgi-bin` subdirectory, then the URL to access it will be

```
http://mysite.mydomain/cgi-bin/calendar
```

Alternatively, if you do not have any sample CGI programs, you can use the simple CGI example provided earlier in this chapter in the section "Common Rules for Installing CGI Programs."

If the text of the script appears, instead of calendar information, you have made an error in the server configuration. Reread this section and consult the server documentation for additional information. If a calendar for the current month appears (or a query page asking what month you are interested in), your server is now configured to support CGI programs.

Conclusion

Having read this chapter, you should be in a position to obtain CGI programming access on a well-connected Web server. Now that you have the power to install and execute CGI programs, you are ready to begin developing creative and powerful dynamic documents of your own. The following chapters introduce the programming tools involved and provide many CGI examples you can install and use on your own site.

References

1. Sun Microsystems, "Java Home Page."
   [URL:http://java.sun.com/]

2. Microsoft Corporation, "MSN Welcomes You to the Internet!"
   [URL:http://www.msn.com/]

3. Prodigy, "The PRODIGY service: Welcome!"
   [URL:http://www.prodigy.com/]

4. CompuServe, "Welcome to CompuServe."
   URL:http://www.compuserve.com/]

5. America Online, "America Online."
   [URL:http://www.aol.com/]

6. Netcom, "NETCOM On-Line Communication Services, Inc."
   [URL:http://www.netcom.com/]

7. Northwest Nexus, "Northwest Nexus."
   [URL:http://www.halcyon.com/]

8. Best Communications, "Best Internet Communications, Inc."
   [URL:http://www.best.com/]

9. Linux International, "The Linux Operating System."
   [URL:http://www.linux.org/]

Some Simple CGI Examples

Perhaps the most striking feature of most CGI programs is their simplicity. Most new CGI programmers, fearing complexity, are pleased to discover how straightforward the process actually is. Once the basic problem of obtaining CGI access has been solved (see Chapter 3), writing your first CGI program is fairly painless.

Some CGI programming tasks are more difficult than others. While it is straightforward to write simple CGI programs that only generate HTML output, it is somewhat more difficult to process user input such as a form submission. Fortunately, this is made much easier by the cgic library for C and the various equivalent libraries for Perl, such as cgi-lib. This task is introduced in Chapter 7, and the libraries to simplify it are introduced in Chapter 8.

When most people think of CGI, they think only of generating HTML output. But CGI programs can also generate images and even animations dynamically. These exciting possibilities are first examined in Chapters 10 and 12.

This chapter presents two simple CGI programs that generate HTML documents when the server executes them. Neither accepts user input, but later versions introduced in the following chapters will add various types of user interaction.

In Chapter 3, a very short shell script was presented as a trivial example of CGI for test purposes. Although shell programming is indeed adequate for simple CGI programs that do not gather user input, shell scripts are notorious for becoming difficult to understand and maintain when they grow beyond a certain point. So the rest of the examples in this book are given in C and Perl.

hello: Sending HTML to the Browser

The first example is hello, a CGI program that outputs a simple HTML document to demonstrate the basic CGI programming technique. By itself, hello is not very useful, but it is a good starting point from which to develop more intriguing examples.

hello in C

Create the file hello.c with your favorite Unix editor and type in the following, or retrieve the file from the CD that accompanies this book. (See Appendix 5 for more information about the contents of the CD, alternative online sources, and a complete Unix makefile for all of the C programs in this book.)

```
/* hello.c: a CGI example by Thomas Boutell. */

/* Bring in the declarations for standard C input and output */
#include <stdio.h>

/* Declare the main function */
int main(int argc, char *argv[])
{
    /* First indicate the content type of the document; in this
        case we are outputting HTML. Note that we output
        TWO carriage returns after the content type.
        This is important! */
    printf("Content-type: text/html\n\n");

    /* Output a proper HTML document, with <head>
        and <body> tags. */

    printf("<head>\n");
```

```
        printf("<title>Hello, World</title>\n");
        printf("</head>\n");
        printf("<body>\n");
        printf("<h1>Hello, World</h1>\n");
        printf("</body>\n");

        return 0;
}
```

To compile the program, enter the following command if you are using the gcc ANSI C compiler. If you are using a different ANSI C compiler, you will need to substitute the appropriate name, perhaps cc.

```
gcc hello.c -o hello
```

If the Unix prompt returns without incident, the compilation was success-ful. If you receive an error message, either you likely made an error in typing in the program or are not using an ANSI-standard C compiler.

> **NOTE:** All C examples in this book are written in ANSI standard C. If you are using an out-of-date C compiler, such as the cc compiler included with SunOS 4.1.3 and earlier, get an ANSI C compiler or download gcc (Gnu C), which is freely avail-able on the Internet. Consult newsgroups relating to your particular version of Unix or talk to your system administrator to find out more about the availability of ANSI C on your system.

hello in Perl

Create the file hello with your favorite Unix editor and type in the follow-ing, or retrieve the file from the CD if you prefer. (See Appendix 5 for more information about sources from which the code can be obtained.) The lines beginning with a # character are comments and are optional, except for the first line, which Unix needs to determine that this program is a Perl pro-gram. *Be sure not to place any blank lines before the first line in the following:*

```
#!/usr/local/bin/perl

#hello: a simple Perl CGI example

#Note that we output two carriage returns after the
#content type. This is very important as it marks
#the end of the CGI "header" and the beginning of
```

```
#the document to be sent to the browser.

print "Content-type: text/html\n\n";
# Output a proper HTML document, with <head>
# and <body> tags. */

print "<head>\n";
print "<title>Hello, World</title>\n";
print "</head>\n";
print "<body>\n";
print "<h1>Hello, World</h1>\n";
print "</body>\n";
```

> **IMPORTANT NOTE:** The first line may have to be changed if `perl` is not located in the `/usr/local/bin` directory on your system. On a Unix system, typing `which perl` should reveal the location of `perl` on your particular system. If that command does not locate `perl`, then `perl` is probably not installed on your computer. See the USENET newsgroup `comp.lang.perl.misc` for information on acquiring `perl` for your system or talk to your system administrator.

Testing Your CGI Program

To test the program, you must install it so that it is recognized by your Web server as a CGI program. How to do this is discussed in detail in Chapter 3, "Obtaining CGI Access."

If your server has a special `cgi-bin` subdirectory for CGI scripts, which is probably the case if you administer your own server, then copy `hello` to that directory. The URL to open with your Web browser to test the program will then be

```
http://mysite.mydomain/cgi-bin/hello
```

This will cause the CGI program to be executed and should display the "Hello, World!" message with maximum emphasis (see Figure 4-1). If your server permits CGI programs to be stored in user directories, you will probably need to rename `hello` to `hello.cgi` and copy it to your personal Web directory. In this case, the URL to open will usually be:

```
http://mysite.mydomain/~myusername/hello.cgi
```

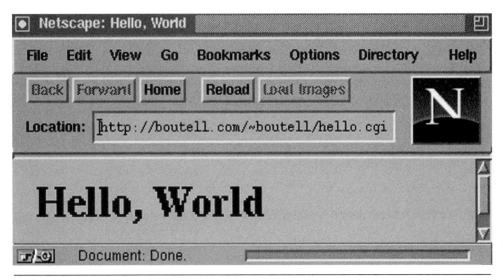

FIGURE 4-1 `hello` as displayed by Netscape

Refer to Chapter 3 for more information on the installation of CGI programs, as well as how to correctly configure Web servers to recognize CGI programs.

Using lynx as a Testing Tool

The text-based Web browser lynx can be very convenient as a testing tool, especially if it is already installed on the system on which your shell account resides. Testing with lynx also helps confirm that the HTML generated by your CGI programs is compatible with a wide range of Web browsers, not just with Netscape, Mosaic, or whatever graphical browser you may prefer. Figure 4-2 shows the output of `hello` as displayed by lynx.

> **NOTE:** If the machine you are logged onto to access your shell account is the same machine that runs the Web server, you can refer to the server by the name `localhost`. This is convenient when working on a system that is not yet permanently connected to the Internet.

FIGURE 4–2 `hello` as displayed by lynx

How the CGI Program Works

The CGI program has two important tasks to perform. First tell the browser what type of document it is about to receive, and second, of course, output the document itself.

The CGI Header: Indicating the Content Type

The program first outputs the content type, which is done by outputting the following line to standard output:

```
Content-type: text/html
```

This `Content-type` line indicates to the browser that the document to follow will consist of HTML. If the CGI program were to output plain text without HTML tags, the appropriate content type would be `text/plain`. For a GIF image, the appropriate content type would be `image/gif`. The latter possibility is explored in detail in Chapter 10. See Appendix 2 for an extensive list of content types.

Next, the program must signal to the browser that the header information describing the document is complete and the actual document itself is about to begin. Do this by *outputting an additional line break after the content type*. Failure to include this step is one of the most common mistakes made by novice CGI programmers.

Outputting the Document Body

The rest of the program simply outputs the appropriate HTML. The server passes this information on to the browser, which displays the document to the user.

The HTML document output by the `hello` program follows:

```
<head>
<title>Hello, World</title>
</head>
<body>
<h1>Hello, World</h1>
</body>
```

Leveraging Existing Programs: cuptime

`cuptime`, the second example, is a CGI program that outputs a potentially useful piece of information: the amount of time the server machine has been operating since its last reboot. `cuptime` does this by leveraging the standard Unix program `uptime`, which retrieves the needed information from the operating system. Leveraging existing Unix commands is a useful and common way to build CGI programs, although care must be taken not to execute programs in potentially dangerous ways. Such dangers can be obvious, such as executing the command `rm *`, or subtle, such as passing text input by the user to the Unix shell, thereby potentially allowing the user to gain control of the system!

This program does not involve user input, so there is no danger involved in executing an existing Unix program. However, the potential risks involved in executing such programs will be revisited in later chapters.

Flushing Output: Mysterious Glitches with Existing Programs

Often, CGI programs attempt to execute existing programs to generate part of their output. Sometimes, for no discernible reason, either the executed program appears to generate no output or its output does not appear where it should.

The operating system does not immediately transmit output the moment your program executes a `print` or `printf()` call. Instead, output is buffered to be sent in large, efficient units. This is normally a good strategy. However, surprises can occur when another program is executed and expected to contribute to the output.

To cope with this problem, you should "flush" standard output before and after calling an external program that also writes to standard output. In C, this can be accomplished with the following line of code:

```
fflush(stdout);
```

In Perl, insert the following line before the executable statements of the program:

```
require "flush.pl";
```

and execute the following statement whenever a flush is desired:

```
&flush(STDOUT);
```

cuptime in C

Create the file cuptime.c with your favorite Unix editor and type in the following. Or retrieve the file from the CD. Additional sources for the code, as well as a Unix makefile, can be found in Appendix 5.

```c
/* cuptime.c: a CGI example by Thomas Boutell. */

/* Bring in the declarations for standard C input and output */
#include <stdio.h>

/* Declare the main function */
int main(int argc, char *argv[])
{
        /* Indicate the content type */
        printf("Content-type: text/html\n\n");

        /* Output a proper HTML document, with <head>
               and <body> tags. */

        printf("<head>\n");
        printf("<title>System Uptime</title>\n");
        printf("</head>\n");
        printf("<body>\n");
        printf("<h1>System Uptime</h1>\n");
        printf("<p>\n");

        /* Make sure the preceding text has been output completely */
        fflush(stdout);
```

```
        /* Now execute the uptime program; you may need to
               change the path for your system */
        system("/usr/bin/uptime");
        /* Make sure the uptime output has been output completely */
        fflush(stdout);

        printf("</body>\n");
        return 0;
}
```

To compile the program, enter the following command if you are using the gcc ANSI C compiler. (See the first example in this chapter for comments about C compilers.)

```
gcc cuptime.c -o cuptime
```

If the Unix prompt returns without incident, the compilation was successful. If you receive an error message, you likely either made an error in typing in the program or are not using an ANSI-standard C compiler. (See the first example in this chapter for comments about ANSI standard C.)

cuptime in Perl

Create the file cuptime with your favorite Unix editor and type in the following. Or retrieve the file from the CD or any of the online sources in Appendix 5 if you prefer.

```
#!/usr/local/bin/perl

#cuptime: a simple Perl CGI example

#Bring in the standard I/O flushing subroutine. If this
#doesn't work, the Perl standard library is not installed
#properly on your system.
require "flush.pl";

#Indicate the content type
print "Content-type: text/html\n\n";

#Output the document

print "<head>\n";
print "<title>System Uptime</title>\n";
```

```
print "</head>\n";
print "<body>\n";
print "<h1>System Uptime</h1>\n";
print "<p>\n";

#Flush output &flush(STDOUT);

#Execute the uptime program system("/usr/bin/uptime");

#Flush output &flush(STDOUT);

#Now close the document
print "</body>\n";
```

Testing cuptime

To test cuptime, you must install it so that it is recognized by your Web server as a CGI program, just as you did for the first example. Then use your Web browser to access its URL. The correct URL will be identical to that for the first example, except of course the URL will end with cuptime, or uptime.cgi instead of hello or hello.cgi. See Figure 4–3 for an example of correct output.

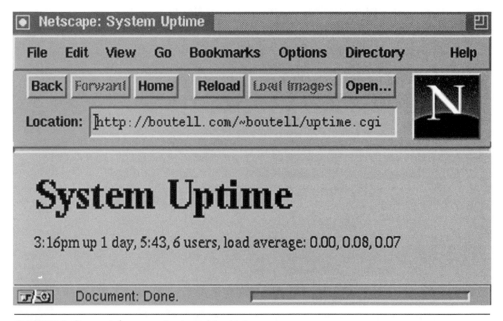

FIGURE 4–3 cuptime as displayed by Netscape

Conclusion

In this chapter, I presented two short CGI programs. Although simple, they introduce the skills that you will use to create more-powerful CGI applications. The next few chapters introduce the CGI environment variables. These variables enable you to learn more about the user and browser accessing your CGI program.

Virtual Directory Spaces: Taking Advantage of PATH_INFO

The Web is *stateless*. That is, Web servers do not keep track of who is logged in to them, and CGI programs do not converse back and forth with the user. Instead, every link on the Web begins a completely new session with a Web server. If that link points to a CGI program, then a new copy of the CGI program is executed every time that link is selected.

This naturally leads CGI programmers to wonder how they can carry on an extended session with a user in which the user is able to explore many different Web pages and follow links from one dynamically generated document to another. If the server does not "remember" what the user is doing from one link to the next, how can a CGI program do so?

There are several ways to solve this puzzle. The simplest method, yet one of the most effective, is to take advantage of the PATH_INFO environment variable. Other, more sophisticated solutions, which also depend on PATH_INFO to some extent, are discussed in Chapters 13 and 14.

PATH_INFO is part of the CGI environment that is accessible to all CGI programs. It provides the programs with information about the server, the browser, the user with which they are interacting, and the nature of the request in progress. This chapter examines CGI environment variables and discusses in particular the advantages of using PATH_INFO.

What Are Environment Variables?

Under the Unix operating system, every program exists in an environment that provides that program with important information about the computer it is running on and the user it is interacting with. The environment variables making up this environment are often familiar to Unix and MSDOS users who have used the set and setenv commands in the past to set those variables for various purposes. For example, under Unix the environment variable TERM is often set by the user's login script to indicate the type of terminal they intend to use. Also, the environment variable PATH indicates the directories that will be searched to find a program that the user wishes to execute.

How CGI Takes Advantage of Environment Variables

The CGI standard uses environment variables to store information that the CGI program can use to learn more about the server, the user, and the browser with which it is interacting.

For example, when a CGI program is executing the environment variable HTTP_USER_AGENT contains the name and version of the Web browser accessing the server if the browser has chosen to send this information.

A complete list of the CGI environment variables can be found in Appendix 1.

How CGI Environment Variables Are Accessed in C

In C programs, an environment variable is accessed using the getenv() function. This function accepts the name of an environment variable as an argument. If the environment variable is found, it returns a pointer to a null-terminated string. Otherwise, it returns a null pointer.

The following excerpt from a larger C program accesses and outputs the value of the HTTP_USER_AGENT environment variable if it is defined and UNKNOWN if it is not:

```
/* At the beginning of the function, with all
    other variable declarations */

char *httpUserAgent;

/* ... Later in the function, at any desired time: */
 httpUserAgent = getenv("HTTP_USER_AGENT");

/* This test will fail if the returned pointer is null;
    the else clause takes care of that case. */
 if (httpUserAgent) {
     printf("Value of HTTP_USER_AGENT: %s\n", httpUserAgent);
 } else {
     printf("UNKNOWN");
 }
```

Try adding this code to an existing CGI program, such as one of the examples in Chapter 4. You will want to add the code within the portion that outputs HTML to the browser and perhaps add appropriate HTML tags to format it attractively.

NOTE: It is very important to check for the null pointer case when using the value returned by the getenv() function.

How CGI Environment Variables Are Accessed in Perl

In Perl, access to CGI environment variables is achieved through the %ENV associative array. For example, consider the following Perl code:

```
$httpUserAgent = $ENV{'HTTP_USER_AGENT'} ;
print "Value of HTTP_USER_AGENT: ";
print $httpUserAgent;
print "\n";
```

Using PATH_INFO: Creating a Virtual Document Space

In Chapter 4 you read that the server recognizes CGI programs by their extension or by their presence in a designated CGI directory. That is, a URL request like this:

```
http://sitename.domain/cgi-bin/myprogram
```

is recognized by a properly configured server to be a request to execute myprogram as a CGI program.

But what about this request?

```
http://sitename.domain/cgi-bin/myprogram/september/5
```

You might expect that the server would expect to find a subdirectory named myprogram, a subdirectory of that named september, and finally a file in that directory named 5. Surprisingly, though, this is not always what happens!

The server examines the request one directory at a time. Once the server finds a CGI program at any point in the path, the rest of the request after the name of the program is cut off and placed in the environment variable PATH_INFO. See Figure 5–1 for additional examples. As a result, when the previous URL is requested, the server executes myprogram with the PATH_INFO environment variable set to /september/5.

This feature can be tremendously useful. A single CGI program can examine the contents of PATH_INFO and change its behavior accordingly and so serve many different URLs. The PATH_INFO environment variable can be used to create a "virtual directory space" in which what appear to be entire subdirectories of unique files can be generated on the fly by the CGI program as they are needed.

TABLE 5–1 URLs and PATH_INFO values

URL	PATH_INFO
http://site.com/cgi-bin/cgiprogram/main	main or /main
http://site.com/cgi-bin/cgiprogram/8/7/andrew	8/7/andrew or /8/7/andrew
http://site.com/cgi-bin/cgiprogram/	empty string or /

> **NOTE:** As shown above, some servers will not present a leading/character in PATH_INFO.

One of the most important uses of this capability is to construct new links that will cause the same CGI program to be executed, but with a different value for the PATH_INFO variable. In this way, your CGI program can present a menu of links to itself. When the user selects a link, the program will be executed again to generate a new page, presumably containing content specific to that link.

The World Birthday Web, Part I: Browsing Birthdays

The next example is a portion of a well-known CGI program on the Web called the World Birthday Web (WBW). The WBW is a database I created in a moment of whimsy in order to ensure that my birthday never passes again without notice. Coincidentally, it has ensured the same thing for a rather large number of other persons scattered around the planet.

While the WBW is not very practical in itself, it is a good example of a simple database application that is browsed and updated entirely through the Web. It is driven by a single CGI program that responds to several different URLs by generating a variety of pages and images on the fly. The complete WBW program also parses form submissions in order to add new birthday entries, a subject that is introduced in Chapter 7 and implemented for the WBW in Chapter 8.

The World Birthday Web: in C

The following is the source code for wbw1.c:

```
#define BIRTHDAY_PATH "/home/boutell/birthday_data"
#define BIRTHDAY_PROGRAM_URL "/~boutell/wbw1.cgi"
#include <stdio.h>
#include <stdlib.h>
#include <string.h>
#include <ctype.h>
#include <time.h>
```

```c
#include <sys/types.h>

/* Month names to show the user */
char *months[12] =
{
  "january", "february", "march", "april", "may", "june",
  "july", "august", "september", "october", "november", "december"
} ;

/* Month names to search for in the PATH_INFO variable */
char *months_p[12] =
{
  "/january", "/february", "/march", "/april", "/may", "/june",
  "/july", "/august", "/september", "/october", "/november", "/december"
} ;

/* Forward references */
void Browse();
void OutputMonth(int month);
void OutputDay(int month, int day);
void BirthdayOutput (int day, int month,
      char *name_s, char *url_s, char *email_s);
void BirthdayHead (char *request);
void BirthdayTail ();
void RemoveSpaces (char *dest, char *src);

int main (int argc, char *argv[])
{
      Browse();
      return 0;
}

void Browse()
{
      time_t now_t;
      int birthdayCount;
      int month, day;
      int i;
      int found = 0;
      char *pathInfo;
      FILE *in;
      char path[161];
      pathInfo = getenv("PATH_INFO");
      if (!pathInfo) {
```

```c
                strcpy(path, "/");
        } else {
                strcpy(path, pathInfo);
        }
        for (i = 0; (i < 12); i++) {
                /* See if this request matches one of the days of
                        the month. If it does, check further to see
                        if a specific day is requested. */
                int len = strlen(months_p[i]);
                if (!strncmp(path, months_p[i], len)) {
                        month = i;
                        if (path[len] == '/') {
                                int day = atoi(path+len+1);
                                if (day) {
                                        OutputDay(month, day);
                                        found = 1;
                                        break;
                                }
                        }
                        OutputMonth(month);
                        found = 1;
                        break;
                }
        }
        if (!found) {
                struct tm *now_tm;
                /* If we didn't find a request for a specific date,
                        then output today's birthdays instead. */
                /* Retrieve the current time */
                time (&now_t);
                /* Break it down into month, day, year and so on */
                now_tm = gmtime (&now_t);
                month = now_tm->tm_mon;
                day = now_tm->tm_mday;
                /* Output today's birthdays */
                OutputDay(month, day);
        }
        printf("<HR>\n");
        printf("<H2>Global Birthday Navigator (GBN)</H2>\n");
        for (i = 0; (i < 12); i++) {
                printf("<A HREF=\"%s/%s\">%s</A>\n ",
                        BIRTHDAY_PROGRAM_URL, months[i], months[i]);
        }
        printf("<A HREF=\"%s\">today</A>\n", BIRTHDAY_PROGRAM_URL);
        printf("<HR></BODY></HTML>\n");
```

```
      }

void OutputMonth(int month)
{
      int i;
      printf("Content-type: text/html\n\n");
      printf("<HTML><HEAD>\n");
      printf("<TITLE>World Birthday Web (WBW): %s</TITLE></HEAD>\n",
            months[month]);
      printf("<BODY><H1>World Birthday Web (WBW): %s</H1>\n",
            months[month]);
      printf("<H2>Please select a day of the month.</H2>\n");
      printf("<P><HR>\n");
      for (i=1; (i < 32); i++) {
            printf("<A HREF=\"%s/%s/%d\">%d</A>\n ",
                  BIRTHDAY_PROGRAM_URL, months[month], i, i);
      }
      printf("</BODY></HTML>\n");
}

void OutputDay(int month, int day) {
      FILE *in;
      char path[256];
      int birthdayCount = 0;
      printf("Content-type: text/html\n\n");
      printf("<HTML><HEAD>\n");
      printf("<TITLE>World Birthday Web (WBW)</TITLE></HEAD>\n");
      printf("<BODY><H1>");
      printf("World Birthday Web (WBW)</H1>\n");
      sprintf(path, "%s/%d/%d", BIRTHDAY_PATH, month+1, day);
      in = fopen (path, "r");
      if (in) {
            while (!feof (in)) {
                  char name_s[512], url_s[512], email_s[512];
                  char nameS[512], urlS[512], emailS[512];
                  if (!fgets (name_s, 512, in)) {
                        break;
                  }
                  RemoveSpaces (nameS, name_s);
                  if (!fgets (url_s, 512, in)) {
                        break;
                  }
                  RemoveSpaces (urlS, url_s);
                  if (!fgets (email_s, 512, in)) {
```

```
                break;
            }
            RemoveSpaces (emailS, email_s);
            if (!birthdayCount) {
                char s[81];
                sprintf(s, "%d %s",
                    day, months[month]);
                BirthdayHead (s);
            }
            birthdayCount++;
            BirthdayOutput (day, month,
                nameS, urlS, emailS);
        }
    }
    fclose (in);
    if (birthdayCount) {
        BirthdayTail ();
    } else {
        printf(
        "<em>No birthdays have been entered for this day.</em>\n");
    }
}


void RemoveSpaces(char *dest, char *src) {
    /* Remove all leading and trailing spaces. */
    char *last;

    /* First, skip to the first non-space character
        in the source string. */
    while (*src) {
        if (!isspace(*src)) {
            break;
        }
        src++;
    }

    /* Now, copy the source string to the destination string. */
    strcpy(dest, src);

    /* Now, find the last non-space character in the destination string;
        move downward through the string from the end. */
    if (!strlen(dest)) {
        return;
    }
```

```c
        last = dest + strlen(dest) - 1;
        while (last != dest) {
                if (!isspace(*last)) {
                        /* We have found the last non-space character
                                in the string, so place a final null
                                immediately after it. */
                        *(last + 1) = '\0';
                        break;
                }
                last--;
        }
}


void BirthdayOutput (int day, int month,
                char *name_s, char *url_s, char *email_s)
{
        printf("<LI>");
        if (strlen (url_s)) {
                printf("<A HREF=\"%s\">", url_s);
        }
        printf("%d %s: ", day, months[month]);
        printf("<STRONG>%s</STRONG>", name_s);
        if (strlen (email_s)) {
                printf(" <EM>%s</EM>\n", email_s);
        }
        if (strlen (url_s)) {
                printf("</A>\n");
        }
        printf("</LI>\n");
}


void BirthdayHead (char *request)
{
        printf("<H2>Birthdays for: %s</H2><UL>\n", request);
}


void BirthdayTail ()
{
        printf("</UL>\n");
        printf("<P><em>Remember, the Birthday Server");
        printf("runs on Greenwich Mean Time.</em>\n");
}
```

The World Birthday Web: in Perl

The following is the Perl source code for wbw1:

```perl
#!/usr/local/bin/perl

#You must change this path to the directory where
#you wish to keep the database entries. Make sure
#you fully specify the path from the leading /
#on down.

$birthdayPath = "/home/boutell/birthday_data";

#You must change this path to the URL at which
#the program has been installed, so it can generate
#valid links to itself.

$birthdayProgramURL = "/cgi-bin/wbw1";
 %monthIndexes = (
      "january", 0,
      "february", 1,
      "march", 2,
      "april", 3,
      "may", 4,
      "june", 5,
      "july", 6,
      "august", 7,
      "september", 8,
      "october", 9,
      "november", 10,
      "december", 12 );
  @monthNames = (
      "january",
      "february",
      "march",
      "april",
      "may",
      "june",
      "july",
      "august",
      "september",
      "october",
      "november",
      "december" );
```

```perl
#Fetch the PATH_INFO environment variable
$pathInfo = $ENV{'PATH_INFO'} ;

#Break it down into path components
@pathComponents = split(/\//,$pathInfo);

#Find the month and day, if present. Ignore any
#empty-string components in order to tolerate leading
#and trailing slashes.

$monthKnown = 0;
$dayKnown = 0;
$month = 0;
$day = 0;
#First the month
$i = 0;
while ($i <= $#pathComponents) {
      # Check for months
      $m = $monthIndexes{$pathComponents[$i]} ;
      $i++;
      if ($m) {
            $monthKnown = 1;
            $month = $m;
            last;
      }
}
#Now the day. This loop won't even get started if
#the month wasn't found, as $i will already be too large.
while ($i <= $#pathComponents) {
      # Check for days. For our purposes, a valid number
      # either evaluates as nonzero or is the string 0.
      if (($pathComponents[$i] != 0) || ($pathComponents[$i] eq '0')) {
            $dayKnown = 1;
            $day = $pathComponents[$i];
            break;
      }
      $i++;
}

print "Content-type: text/html\n\n";

print "<HTML><HEAD>\n";

if ($monthKnown && $dayKnown) {
      # Generate a page for a single day
```

```perl
            &OutputDay($month, $day);
    } elsif ($monthKnown) {
        # Generate a listing of days
        &OutputMonth($month);
    } else {
        #Generate a page for today
          local($sec, $min, $hour, $mday, $mon, $year, $wday, $yday, $isdst) =
                gmtime(time);
          &OutputDay($mon, $mday);
    }


print "<HR>\n";
print "<H2>Global Birthday Navigator (GBN)</H2>\n";
for ($i = 0; ($i < 12);
$i++) {
     print "<A HREF=\"", $birthdayProgramURL, "/",
           $monthNames[$i], "\">", $monthNames[$i], "</A>\n";
}
print "<A HREF=\"", $birthdayProgramURL, "\">today</A>\n";
print "<HR>\n";

print "</BODY></HTML>\n";

#Now the subprograms
 sub OutputDay {
     local($month, $day) = @_;
     $birthdayCount = 0;
     print "<TITLE>World Birthday Web (WBW)</TITLE></HEAD>\n";
     print "<BODY><H1>\n";
     print "World Birthday Web (WBW)</H1>\n";
     $filename = $birthdayPath . "/" . ($month + 1) . "/" . $day;
     open(file, $filename);
     while (1) {
            if (!($name = <file>)) {
                 last;
            }
            chop $name;
            if (!($url = <file>)) {
                 last;
            }
            chop $url;
            if (!($email = <file>)) {
                 last;
            }
            chop $email;
            if (!($birthdayCount)) {
```

```
                  print "<H2>Birthdays for: ",
                          ($month+1), "/", $day, "</H2>\n";
              }
              $birthdayCount++;
              print "<LI>";
              if ($url ne "") {
                  print "<A HREF=\"", $url, "\">";
              }
              print $day, " ", $monthNames[$month], ": ";
              print "<STRONG>", $name, "</STRONG> ";
              if ($email ne "") {
                  print "<EM>", $email, "</EM>";
              }
              if ($url ne "") {
                  print "</A>";
              }
              print "</LI>\n";
          }
      if ($birthdayCount) {
          print "</UL>\n";
          print "<P><em>Remember, the Birthday Server";
          print "runs on Greenwich Mean Time.</em>\n";
      }
}


sub OutputMonth {
      local($month) = @_;
      print "<TITLE>World Birthday Web (WBW): ", $monthNames[$month],
          "</TITLE></HEAD>\n";
      print "<BODY>\n";
      print "<H1>World Birthday Web (WBW): ", $monthNames[$month],
          "</H1>\n";
      print "<H2>Please select a day of the month.</H2>\n";
      print "<P><HR>\n";
      for ($i=1; ($i < 32); $i++) {
          print "<A HREF=\"", $birthdayProgramURL, "/",
              $monthNames[$month], "/", $i, "\">", $i, "</A>\n";
      }
}
```

Configuring and Compiling the WBW

Both the C and the Perl versions require you to change two values at the beginning of the program. In the C program, the two #define directives must be changed, one to indicate the directory on your file system where your data files will reside and the other to indicate the URL at which you have installed the program itself. The latter is necessary so the program can output hypertext links back to itself!

The CD as well as Appendix 5 contain a Unix Makefile for compiling the program.

Creating Data Files to Test the WBW

To try out the program, you need to create a few sample data files for various days of the year. In Chapter 8 we examine the code that allows birthdates to be submitted through the Web itself.

To test your own copy of the wbw1 program, first make sure you have made the necessary modifications mentioned in the previous section. Next, for the C version, compile the program as you compiled the earlier examples and install it in a designated CGI directory. For the Perl version, copy wbw1 to your CGI directory.

When specifying directories in CGI programs, be sure to use full paths that begin from the root directory of the entire file system. If you are not sure of the full path of a particular directory, type cd to get to the directory in question and type pwd to find out the full path.

NOTE: Depending on your server, the program may not be able to operate in a personal public_html directory even if it is renamed with a .cgi extension. This is because not all servers pass the PATH_INFO information in that case. More and more servers are handling this correctly as time goes on, including the latest NCSA servers; upgrading to the latest version of your server may help. If your server does not pass PATH_INFO to CGI programs recognized by extension, get access to a designated CGI directory on your server. If you cannot do this, you will still be able to test the program's ability to browse today's list of birthdays. It is possible to rewrite the program to use form selections for the month and date instead of the present PATH_INFO approach. Chapter 7 introduces the necessary skills to do this.

Next, you need to create data files. Create a subdirectory named 1 beneath the BIRTHDAY_PATH directory you specified; this file will contain entries for the month of January. Now create the file 5 within that directory, which will contain entries for January 5. Within that file, enter three-line records for a few sample birthdays. Do not enter any stray blank lines; each entry must consist of exactly three lines. For example:

```
Jane Smith
http://www.somewhere.com/~jsmith/
jsmith@somewhere.com
Bob Amazing
http://www.somewhere.com/~amazing/
amazing@somewhere.com
```

Of course, creating data files in this way is tedious. In Chapter 7, I introduce processing forms. Forms enable you to submit entries directly through your Web browser, and in Chapter 8 a version of the WBW with this feature is presented.

Now when you access the wbw1 CGI program with your Web browser, you should be presented with the "today's birthdays" page. Navigate to January 5, and you should see the two example entries, as shown in Figure 5–1.

How the Program Works

Unlike the earlier examples, this program is moderately large. This is partly because it has to handle several distinct jobs by examining PATH_INFO to determine what the user wants. So far, there are three possible pieces of data the user could be asking for:

1. Today's birthdays

2. A menu of days in a particular month

3. Birthdays on a particular day

The program must first determine which of these has been requested. wbw1 does this by retrieving the value of the PATH_INFO environment variable and parsing it by using the standard C string manipulation functions, or, in Perl, by splitting it using the split() function.

For instance, the C function strncmp(char *s1, char *s2, int n) compares the first n characters of s1 and s2. If they are the same, strncmp returns zero. This is used to check whether the user has requested a particular month.

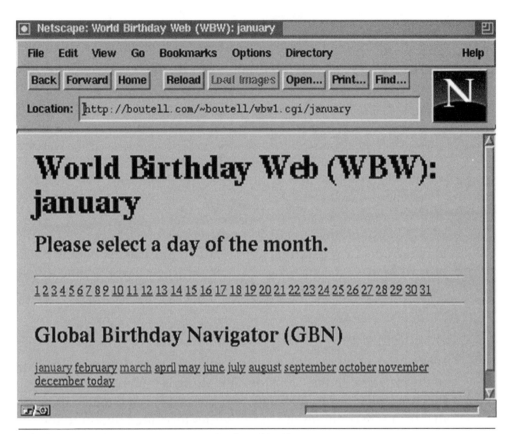

FIGURE 5–1 The January page, as displayed by Netscape

If a specific month is desired, the program next checks whether the next character in PATH_INFO after the month is a / character. If so, the program examines the portion of the string remaining after the / and converts it to an integer using the atoi(char *s) function. If a nonzero day of the month is found, the program invokes the OutputDay(int month, int day) function to output birthdays for that particular day. If not, or if no / character is found, the program invokes the OutputMonth(int month) function to output a list of links back to the same CGI program, one for each day of the month.

Perl is particularly well suited to processing text, and the Perl code for this task is more elegant. The split() function is used to split PATH_INFO into an array of strings, one for each portion of the path. A while loop locates the month information, if present. It ignores empty path components to tolerate leading slashes and examines nonempty components to find out if they are defined in the associative array %monthIndex. A similar while loop locates the day information if there are more path components.

> **NOTE:** Perl supports the concept of associative arrays. Like arrays in other languages, Perl arrays can be indexed by integers. However, unlike in other languages, Perl arrays can also be indexed by strings. wbw1.pl takes advantage of this by creating an array in which the value of the index september, for instance, is assigned to be 8 (where january equals zero). This is one of the most powerful features of Perl.

In both versions, the OutputDay function is somewhat more complicated than the OutputMonth function because it must access the file system in order to retrieve the birthdays for that particular day. The function first assembles the path of the file containing entries for that particular day as follows:

```
BIRTHDAY_PATH/month/day
```

Where BIRTHDAY_PATH is replaced with the value defined at the beginning of the program. In the C version, this string is built using the sprintf() C function, which writes formatted output to a string in much the same way that the more common printf() writes formatted output to the console. In the Perl version, strings are simply concatenated end to end using the . operator.

Data files in the WBW are arranged simply. There are numbered subdirectories, one for each month, beginning with 1 for January. And within each subdirectory, there is a file for each day of the month.

In the C version, the fopen() function is used to open the data file for reading. The program then uses the fgets() function to retrieve each line of the file. Each birthday is represented by three lines, which makes up a record in the database that consists of a user name, a URL, and an e-mail address. The RemoveSpace(char *dest, char *src) function, which is provided in the program, is used to clean up entries by removing white space at the beginning and end.

In Perl, databases more commonly store all the fields for a particular record in the database on one line and use a specific character to separate them. The WBW does not follow this approach, but the Perl code to read entries from it is still reasonably elegant. Each field is read by assigning to a string variable from the file handle. If the assignment fails, the program assumes that the end of the file has been reached.

When PATH_INFO Isn't Enough

In more-complex applications, the amount of information the next execution of the program may need to receive may be too large to place in a URL for retrieval as PATH_INFO. One reasonable approach in such cases is to create a uniquely and randomly named data file on the server that contains information about the user's interactions with the CGI program so far and then pass only the name of that file as part of the URL. Of course, the program must also have a strategy to delete such data files after a certain period of time. This approach is implemented in Chapter 13.

It is also possible to pass information in hidden fields in a form; see Chapter 7 for an introduction to processing form data. However, many older browsers you may encounter do not properly support hidden fields.

Recently, a new approach known as the HTTP cookie mechanism has emerged. See Netscape Corporation's proposal[1] for more information.

Conclusion

In this chapter, I presented an example of a CGI program that outputs links to itself. This is a very important aspect of CGI programming that nearly all significant CGI applications take advantage of.

This chapter has also introduced the usefulness of the CGI environment variables. The next chapter examines several additional variables that you can use to learn as much as possible about the user's identity.

References

1. Netscape Communications Corporation, "Client Side State: HTTP Cookies."
   [URL:http://www.netscape.com/newsref/std/cookie_spec.html]

Identifying the User: More CGI Environment Variables

Identifying the user is a natural desire among CGI programmers. If the user's identity is known, the program can make intelligent decisions as to whether that user is permitted to access particular pieces of information. The program can even personalize the page for each user.

Unfortunately, identifying the user isn't easy. While there are CGI environment variables available that provide limited information about the user's identity, there are limits to the amount of genuine security available. It is sometimes possible for one user to pretend to be another. The password-authentication schemes currently available on the Web are not as secure as they must become in the future.

Still, a significant amount of information about the user and the user's machine is available. This chapter explores the uses and limitations of that information.

More Environment Variables

One piece of information about the user that is nearly always available is the Internet address of the user's computer. If the user's ISP has configured its Domain Name Service (DNS) in a reasonably intelligent manner, the host name of the user's machine will be available. That information is found in the REMOTE_HOST environment variable. Table 6–1 provides examples of typical REMOTE_HOST values.

TABLE 6–1 Typical REMOTE_HOST values

```
foocom5.foocom.com
grue.com
toe.cs.bigschool.edu
```

Unfortunately, not all ISPs configure their DNS properly for all accounts. In particular, many users connect to accounts that are dynamically assigned a new Internet address on each connection. Often, these accounts do not have host names that the server can determine.

However, the environment variable REMOTE_ADDR is always defined. REMOTE_ADDR contains an Internet IP address in dotted decimal notation. For instance, the machine grue.com might have the following IP address:

```
193.105.57.201
```

What REMOTE_HOST and REMOTE_ADDR Are Good For

You cannot assume that only one user connects from a particular REMOTE_ADDR. In fact, you cannot assume that a given user always connects from the same REMOTE_ADDR because the user may be assigned a different temporary address the next time he or she calls. So at first glance, it seems that the information is not very useful.

However, while REMOTE_HOST and REMOTE_ADDR are not much use in determining the user's identity with complete certainty, they are very useful when a reasonable probability is all that is needed. For instance, a CGI program that has been abused by a particular site can be modified to check a "forbidden list" of addresses or host names that are denied access to the program. The program can output a message to that effect to the user and then exit.

> **NOTE:** Large Internet providers such as America Online may employ a single proxy server for thousands of users, in which case all of those users will appear to have the same address.

Of course, it is not certain that a new connection from a particular machine is being made by the abusive user, so it is best to make the message reasonably friendly. (See Figure 6–1.)

> **NOTE:** Your server may provide other means of locking out problematic sites completely. Of course, if you are not the administrator of the server itself, you may still have use for this capability in your own programs!

Consider the following C function and Perl subprogram. Both are intended to be called at the beginning of a CGI program. The code checks a list of IP addresses (not host names) that are forbidden to access the program. If the current connection comes from one of those addresses, the function outputs

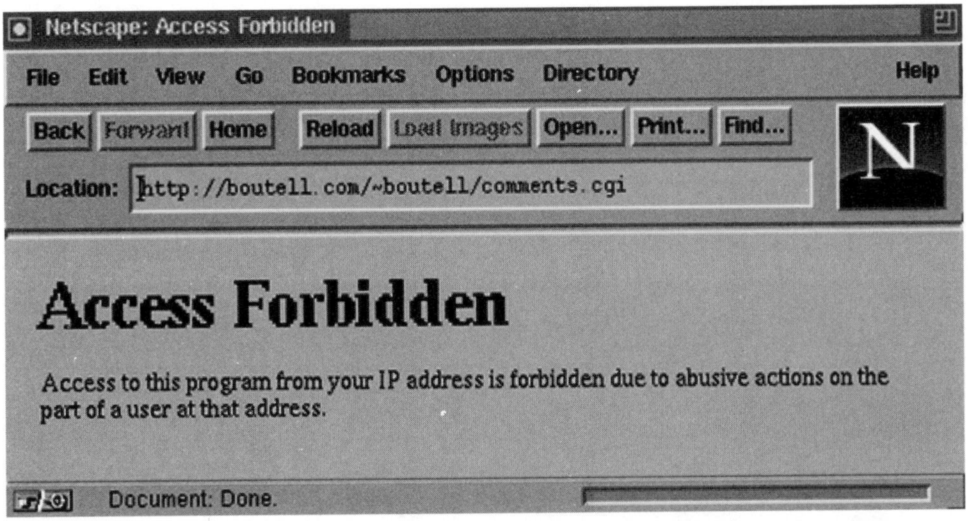

FIGURE 6–1 CheckRejectList() refusing access, as shown by Netscape

a message to that effect and terminates the program. If not, or if the address information is not available, the function returns normally.

In your own complete CGI programs, you will wish to change forbidden.txt to a complete path somewhere in your own file space. The text file should contain one IP address per line.

> **NOTE to C users:** You also will need to incorporate the RemoveSpaces function from Chapter 4 and include the string.h and stdio.h header files, if your program does not already do so.

C code for the CheckRejectList function

```
void CheckRejectList() {
    FILE *in;
    char *remoteAddress;
    remoteAddress = getenv("REMOTE_ADDR");
    if (!remoteAddress) {
        return;
    }
    in = fopen("/home/boutell/forbidden.txt", "r");
    if (!in) {
        /* Bad news — can't access the list */
        return;
    }
    while (!feof(in)) {
        char s[80];
        char address[80];
        if (!fgets(s, 80, in)) {
            break;
        }
        /* Call the RemoveSpaces function, introduced
             in Chapter 4. You will need to include
             that function from wbw1.c if you use
             this code. */
        RemoveSpaces(address, s);
        /* Check for a match. */
        if (!strcmp(remoteAddress, address)) {
            printf("Content-type: text/html\n\n");
            printf("<html>\n");
            printf("<head><title>Access Forbidden</title>\n");
            printf("</head>\n");
```

```
                printf("<body>\n");
                printf("<h1>Access Forbidden</h1>\n");
                printf("Access to this program from your IP
address\n");
                printf("is forbidden due to abusive actions on
the\n");
                printf("part of a user at that address.\n");
                printf("</body></html>\n");
                /* Make sure the message gets sent by
                        flushing standard output */
                fflush(stdout);
                /* Force an early exit from the program */
                fclose(in);
                exit(0);
            }
        }
        fclose(in);
        /* All is well; return normally */
    }
```

Perl code for the CheckRejectList subprogram

```perl
    sub CheckRejectList {
        local($remoteAddress, $candidate);
        $remoteAddress = $ENV{'REMOTE_ADDR'} ;
        if (!$remoteAddress) {
                #Can't get the address
                return 0;
        }
        if (!open(LIST, "forbidden.txt")) {
                #Bad news -- can't access the list
                return 0;
        }
        while ($candidate = <LIST>) {
                chop $candidate;
                if ($remoteAddress eq $candidate) {
                        print "Content-type: text/html\n\n";
                        print "<html>\n";
                        print "<head><title>Access Forbidden</title>\n";
                        print "</head>\n";
                        print "<body>\n";
                        print "<h1>Access Forbidden</h1>\n";
                        print "Access to this program from your IP address\n";
                        print "is forbidden due to abusive actions on the\n";
                        print "part of a user at that address.\n";
```

```
                      print "</body></html>\n";
                      #Exit prematurely
                      close LIST;
                      exit 0;
              }
      }
      #All is well, return normally
      close LIST;
}
```

REMOTE_IDENT: The Pitfalls of User Identification

The CGI environment variable REMOTE_IDENT supposedly provides the name of the user. This seems like a great piece of information to have, but in practice, it is rarely defined. Also, it is not secure.

The problem is that REMOTE_IDENT is available only if the identification protocol is turned on in your server and an identification server is available on the user's machine. Worse still, such servers are available for any system, including nonsecure systems such as Microsoft Windows. You may or may not trust the system administrators of faraway multiuser systems. But there is every reason to believe that individual users are capable of setting up their Windows machine to state any user name they find convenient.

For these reasons, it is best either to disregard REMOTE_IDENT or to use it strictly for statistical logging purposes. Fortunately, there is a better solution.

AUTH_TYPE and REMOTE_USER: Identifying the User on Your Own Terms

Most Web browsers now support at least one approach to authenticating the user's identity. The HTTP/1.0 standard includes a simple user authentication scheme whereby in which the browser can transmit a user name and password as part of the document request.

> **NOTE:** It may seem odd that the user name and password are transmitted for every request. But keep in mind that HTTP is stateless. The browser successfully avoids questioning the user for every page by simply questioning the user the first time. It sends the same name and password used for the previous request until a request is rejected, at which point, the name and password are prompted for once again.

The good news is that most servers support this scheme. Your server documentation will clarify precisely how to turn on authentication for particular subsets of the server's URL space; these can include cgi-bin directories or directories that contain .cgi files.

The bad news is that names and passwords are sent over the Web as uuencoded plaintext. This is little better and no worse than the manner in which names and passwords are transmitted when logging on to a system remotely using telnet. Theoretically, such passwords could be snooped using a packet sniffer program that watches the IP traffic on the user's or server's network or, with more difficulty, at some intervening point.

In practice, HTTP 1.0 authentication is adequate when the risk associated with failure is small and falls primarily on the server, not the customer. For example, the Nando Times electronic newspaper[1] uses HTTP 1.0 authorization to identify users for demographic purposes, thus ensuring a fairly accurate count of actual subscribers. However, HTTP 1.0 authentication is not adequate for credit card authorization purposes, due to the security concerns raises in the previous paragraph.

Once authentication has been turned on for the directory in which your program resides, users will not be able to access your program without entering a valid name and password. Once a user does successfully access the program, the name under which the user authenticated becomes available in the REMOTE_USER environment variable.

There are other types of authentication, such as the Secure Sockets Layer (SSL) and the Secure HTTP Standard (SHTTP). The AUTH_TYPE environment variable identifies which form of authorization, if any, is in use. For the HTTP 1.0 scheme described here, the value of AUTH_TYPE should be BASIC.

Applications of REMOTE_USER

The most obvious application of authentication is to keep out unauthorized users. Of course, if the server has authenticated the user and chosen to execute your CGI program, this task has already been done.

Another application of REMOTE-USER is to customize content. This feature can range from simple form letter customizations such as mentioning the user's name to advanced applications such as remembering the user's settings in a file associated with the user's authentication name. An example of customization using authentication is presented in Chapter 14, "World Wide Web Wall Street: An Advanced CGI Application."

How the User Applies for Access

If access to your application is restricted to a handful of users, authentication is not a chore: Gather names and passwords personally from those users and place them in the server's authentication file. Of course, for popular applications, this is a lot of work.

A more practical approach is to provide a form that allows the user to submit an application for an account on the system. Forms are introduced in Chapter 7, "Handling User Input: Interacting with Forms."

Once the request has been received, it is usually best for a human being to look over the application and ensure the response is plausible. However, it is entirely possible to write a CGI program not covered by authorization that accepts the application and updates the authentication file in question. This is particularly straightforward in the case of the NCSA server, which has a simple authentication file format (described in the server documentation). For further security, the name and password can be sent to the e-mail address provided by the user, instead of simply being displayed on the browser. If the benefit is small, few users will trouble themselves to arrange several unique e-mail addresses in order to gain multiple accounts.

Conclusion

In this chapter, I dealt with the sticky question of how to identify users of your CGI program. While an airtight identification is not trivial to achieve, it is certainly practical to authenticate users well enough to be reasonably certain of their identity. This is often adequate, as long as the benefits of forgery are not sufficient to justify extensive effort on the user's part. More sophisticated security schemes such as SSL and SHTTP, when in use, can be relied on more heavily to keep account names and passwords secret.

At present, CGI programs can take best advantage of the available authentication as a means of customizing content, locking out problem sites, and establishing an accurate count of users for demographic purposes. These are low-risk activities and are easily accomplished with available tools.

Now that you have the tools necessary to carry out a seamless, ongoing conversation with the user, it is time to consider the question of user input. The most powerful tool available to accept user input in CGI programs is the forms capability of HTML. Processing information submitted through forms is the subject of the next chapter.

References

1. The News and Observer Publishing Co., "Welcome to NandO.net." [URL:http://www.nando.net/]

Handling User Input: Interacting with Forms

The desire to accept input from the user is the most common reason why programmers take an interest in CGI. It is also the most difficult CGI programming task. Fortunately, there are tools available to make the process as painless as possible. Two such tools are my cgic library for C programmers and Steven Brenner's cgi-lib library for Perl programmers.

In the chapters ahead, you will see how to take advantage of those tools in order to avoid "reinventing the wheel." However, in this chapter, complete standalone programs that handle user input are presented. This is done so as to provide a better understanding of how user input is processed. If you find the details of form processing difficult to follow, keep in mind that tools to do it for you are included with this book and are covered in the following chapters.

CGI programs usually receive user input from HTML forms. Handling forms involves two actions: writing the forms and processing the actual data when it arrives. Many HTML authors go so far as to create lovely forms before realizing they haven't the slightest idea how to process the results!

Of course, this is accomplished by CGI programming. How to do this is the primary topic of this chapter. First, I also introduce you to creating forms in your HTML pages.

Creating Forms

To process form data, you'll need to first create forms. The following is an example of a simple HTML page containing a form that can be used to gather comments from the user:

```
<html>
<head>
<title>We Value Comments!</title>
</head>
<body>
<h1>We Value Comments!</h1>
<p>
<form action="comments.cgi" method="POST">
Your Name: <input type="text" name="name"><br>
Your E-Mail Address: <input type="text" name="email"><br>
Enter your comments in the area below. Please be sure to enter your
name and email address above. <br>
<textarea name="comments" rows="10" cols="60">
</textarea>
<br>
<input type="submit" value="Submit Comments">
<input type="reset" value="Clear Entries">
</form>
</body>
</html>
```

Try opening this form with your Web browser. Note that the Submit button does not do anything useful yet.

HTML forms are always enclosed by the <form> element. (Be sure to close the element with </form> at the end.) For a form to do useful work, it typically should contain one or more <input> elements.

The action field of the <form> element indicates the URL to which the input should be delivered when the form is submitted. The method field indicates exactly how the input should be delivered; the two common methods are GET and POST. While the GET method generally works, its use is discouraged because it attempts to "stuff" the input into the URL itself. Long URLs can be a problem for some browsers and servers. The POST method delivers the input separately from the URL. Most servers do not place any artificial limit on the amount of input that can be delivered via POST.

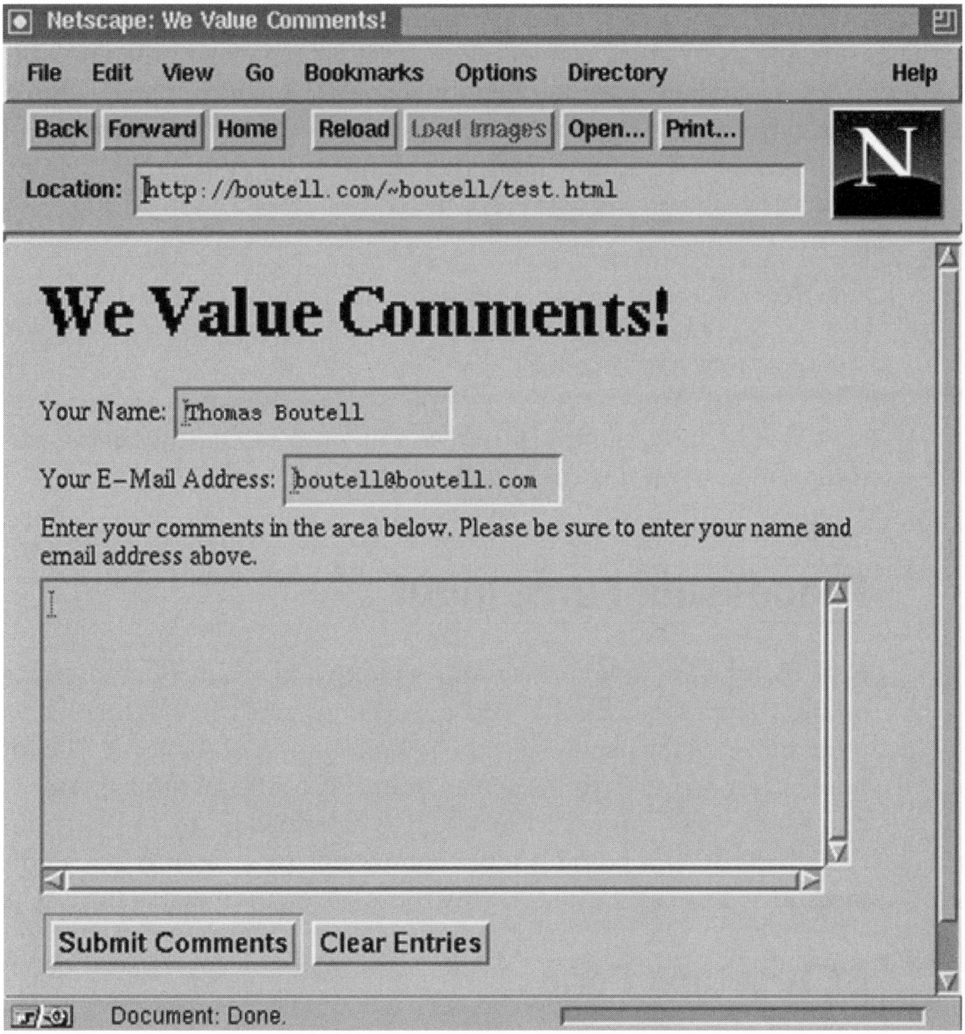

FIGURE 7–1 The comment form, as viewed by Netscape

Every <input> element has a type and a name. In this example, the text type is used, which accepts a single line of text from the user. In addition, the example uses the submit and reset types, which are used to deliver the input to the server and to clear the input fields, respectively. For these types, the value field is displayed as the name of the button.

Each <input> element should have a unique name, except for elements with the submit and reset types. Your CGI program, on the receiving end of the input, will need this information in order to determine which data corresponds to which element. The `<textarea>` element is similar to the `<input>` element, except it defines an area into which multiple lines of text may be entered. Like `<input>` elements, all `<textarea>` elements in a form should have unique names; in addition, the number of rows and columns visible to the user is specified.

> **NOTE:** This is not a limit on the total amount of text the user can enter. The `rows` and `cols`-settings determine only the size of the window displayed. The text window will scroll if necessary.

Now that we have a simple form, we will write a CGI program to process the information when it is submitted.

Processing Form Input

Note that the example form specifies the CGI program `/cgi-bin/comments` on the server as its "action." This means the server will execute that CGI program when the user selects the Submit button of the form. The information is then delivered to the server according to the method specified in the `<form>` element, either GET or POST, as described in the next section. Although the POST method is more commonly used, be sure to read the GET method section, as it explains why the POST method works the way it does.

GET-method Forms

When the GET method is used, the input is sent to the server as part of the URL. When the input reaches the CGI program, it is available in the CGI environment variable QUERY_STRING. The format of that information was first discussed in Chapter 2 and is covered in more detail here.

The data for each `<input>` element (or other form-related element) within the `<form>` element appears as part of QUERY_STRING. Each element is represented by its name as specified in the form, followed by an equal sign (the = character). If there are more elements, an ampersand (the & character) will separate them. The length of the input is indicated by the CONTENT_LENGTH environment variable, which will contain a decimal integer indicating the number of bytes in QUERY_STRING.

You may ask, *"What if there are equal signs and ampersands in the data itself? Not to mention carriage returns and spaces?"* Any valid form-handling program will encounter this situation right away, because not only ampersands and equal signs present a problem. Since the data is transmitted as part of the URL, all characters that are illegal in URLs must be escaped.

Except for spaces (see the next Note), special characters are represented by the following sequence:

```
%xx
```

where xx is a two-digit hexadecimal number specifying the ASCII code of the escaped character. For instance, the % sign itself must be sent as follows:

```
%21
```

where 21 is the hexadecimal ASCII code for the % character (2 times 16 plus 1 = 33 in decimal).

A line feed—ASCII code 10 decimal (0A hexadecimal)—is sent as follows:

```
%0A
```

It is best to assume that the hexadecimal digits A through F may appear in uppercase or lowercase.

Note that Web browsers may submit carriage returns, line feeds, or both as line separators in a <TEXTAREA> element. The example code in this chapter does not attempt to deal with this problem, but the cgic library does. If you use cgic, your code will always see a line break as a single line-feed character.

> **VERY IMPORTANT:** Because the use of spaces is so common, they are represented in a more compact fashion by the + sign. Your code must be sure to interpret the + sign as a space. Of course, spaces may also appear escaped as %20, but this shouldn't present any problems for your code.

POST-method Forms

When the POST method is used, the user's input does not appear in QUERY_STRING. Instead, it appears as standard input. This is a much better approach for most purposes.

CONTENT_LENGTH is set, just as it is for GET-method forms, and still indicates the number of bytes of form data. Your program should not read more than CONTENT_LENGTH bytes from standard input when processing a POST-method form.

As with GET-method forms, the name and value of each element are separated by the = character and elements are separated by the & character.

> **IMPORTANT:** Even though POST-method form data appears at standard input, characters are still escaped exactly the way they are escaped for GET-method forms. This means %xx still represents the single character with the ASCII code xx in hexadecimal and + still represents a space.

Accepting Comments

The code presented next accepts comments from the user when the form presented earlier in this chapter is submitted to the server using the POST method.

Accepting Comments in C

The following is the source code for comments.c:

```c
/* Change this to point to the location where you want
        comments to be kept on your system! The file
        must be writable by the Web server. */

#define COMMENT_FILE "/home/boutell/comments.txt"

#include <stdio.h>
#include <stdlib.h>

/* Global variables */

/* This example can only process up to 100 input fields in
        a single form. Of course, we know that this form
        only has a handful. Change this #define if you
        need more, or use the cgic library, which has
        no such limitations. */
```

```
#define FIELDS_MAX 100

char *names[FIELDS_MAX];
char *values[FIELDS_MAX];

int fieldsTotal = 0;

/* Makes sure this request is a form submission */
int VerifyForm();

/* Parses the submitted form data, filling the names[] and values[]
      arrays with useful information */
void ParseForm();

/* Frees the memory associated with the form data. */

void FreeForm();

/* Copies src to dst, unescaping any special characters in the
process.
      dst must be at least as large as src in order to ensure that
      there is enough space. */

void UnescapeString(char *dst, char *src);

int main(int argc, char *argv[])
{
      FILE *out;
      int i;
      int nameIndex = -1, emailIndex = -1, commentsIndex = -1;

      printf("Content-type: text/html\n\n");

      printf("<html>\n");
      printf("<head>\n");
      /* Make sure it's a POST-method form submission */
      if (!VerifyForm()) {
            printf("<title>Not a POST Form Submission</title>\n");
            printf("</head>\n");
            printf("<h1>Not a POST Form Submission</h1>\n");
            printf("This page should be accessed only by
submitting\n");
            printf("a form using the POST method. Perhaps your\n");
            printf("browser does not support forms.\n");
            printf("</body></html>\n");
```

```
        return 0;
}

/* OK, it's a form submission, so parse it. */
ParseForm();

/* Use the information */

/* Find the index of each field in the arrays */
for (i = 0; (i < fieldsTotal); i++) {
    if (!strcmp(names[i], "name")) {
        nameIndex = i;
    } else if (!strcmp(names[i], "email")) {
        emailIndex = i;
    } else if (!strcmp(names[i], "comments")) {
        commentsIndex = i;
    }
}

/* If any field is missing, complain! */
if ((nameIndex == -1) || (emailIndex == -1) || (commentsIndex == -1)) {
    printf("<title>Please fill out all the fields</title>\n");
    printf("</head>\n");
    printf("<h1>Please fill out all the fields</h1>\n");
    printf("Please fill out the name, email address, AND\n");
    printf("comment fields. Back up to the previous page\n");
    printf("to try again.\n");
    printf("</body></html>\n");
    return 0;
}

/* OK, we have all the data. Write it to a file in which
        we collect comments from users. Open to append, of course. */

out = fopen(COMMENT_FILE, "a");
fprintf(out, "From: %s <%s>\n",
    values[nameIndex], values[emailIndex]);
fprintf(out, "%s\n", values[commentsIndex]);


printf("<title>Thank you, %s</title>\n", values[nameIndex]);
printf("</head>\n");
printf("<h1>Thank you, %s</h1>\n", values[nameIndex]);
printf("Thank you for your comments.\n");
printf("</body></html>\n");
```

```
        /* Free the memory we used */
        FreeForm();
        return 0;
}

int VerifyForm()
{
        char *contentType;
        char *requestMethod;
        int bad = 0;
        /* Check the content type of the data we've received */
        contentType = getenv("CONTENT_TYPE");
        if (strcmp(contentType, "application/x-www-form-urlencoded") != 0) {
            bad = 1;
        }

        /* And make sure the POST method was used */
        requestMethod = getenv("REQUEST_METHOD");
        if (strcmp(requestMethod, "POST") != 0) {
            bad = 1;
        }

        return !bad;
}

/* Parses the submitted form data, filling the names[] and values[]
        arrays with useful information */

void ParseForm()
{
        char *contentLength = getenv("CONTENT_LENGTH");
        /* The number of characters in the data */
        int length;
        /* The buffer into which we read the data */
        char *buffer;
        /* The current position in the buffer while we search for separators */
        char *p;
        /* Determine the length of the input */
        if (!contentLength) {
            length = 0;
        } else {
            length = atoi(contentLength);
        }
        /* Allocate a buffer to store the input in. Include space
            for one extra character to make the parsing loop simpler. */
```

```
buffer = (char *) malloc(length + 1);
if (!buffer) {
      /* Uh-oh */
      return;
}
/* Read all the data from standard input */
if (fread(buffer, 1, length, stdin) != length) {
      /* Uh-oh */
      return;
}
p = buffer;
while (length) {
      /* The beginning of the current name */
      char *name;
      /* The beginning of the current value */
      char *value;

      int found;

      /* Make sure we have room for more fields. */
      if (fieldsTotal == FIELDS_MAX) {
            /* Uh-oh, can't accept any more */
            return;
      }

      name = p;

      /* First, find an equal sign. */
      found = 0;
      while (length) {
            if (*p == '=') {
                  /* End the name with a null character. */
                  *p = '\0';
                  p++;
                  found = 1;
                  break;
            }
            p++;
            length--;
      }
      if (!found) {
            /* A blank or truncated entry. Strange, but Web
                  browsers are unpredictable; be tolerant. */
            break;
      }
```

```
        value = p;
        /* Now, find an ampersand. */
        found = 0;
        while (length) {
                if (*p == '&') {
                        /* End the value with a null character. */
                        *p = '\0';
                        p++;
                        found = 1;
                        break;
                }
                p++;
                length--;
        }
        if (!found) {
                /* Assume that this is the end of the last entry. */
                *p = '\0';
        }

        /* Allocate space for the name and value in those
                arrays, then call UnescapeString to unescape
                and copy them. Be sure to allow space
                for the final null character. */
        names[fieldsTotal] = (char *) malloc(strlen(name) + 1);
        if (!names[fieldsTotal]) {
                /* Uh-oh, no memory. Return with what we do have. */
                return;
        }
        values[fieldsTotal] = (char *) malloc(strlen(value) + 1);
        if (!values[fieldsTotal]) {
                /* Uh-oh, no memory. Return with what we do have. */
                free(names[fieldsTotal]);
                return;
        }

        /* Copy the strings, un-escaping them in the process. */
        UnescapeString(names[fieldsTotal], name);
        UnescapeString(values[fieldsTotal], value);
        fieldsTotal++;
        /* Continue, finding more pairs. */
    }
    /* Free the buffer we used. */
    free(buffer);
}
```

```
void FreeForm()
{
      int i;
      for (i=0; (i < fieldsTotal); i++) {
            free(names[i]);
            free(values[i]);
      }
}

void UnescapeString(char *dst, char *src)
{
      /* Loop over the characters in the string until we
            encounter the null character at the end,
            which tests false. */
      while (*src) {
            char c;
            c = *src;
            /* Handle spaces escaped as + signs */
            if (c == '+') {
                  c = ' ';
            } else if (c == '%') {
                  /* Handle % escapes */
                  char hexdigits[3];
                  int ascii;
                  src++;
                  if (!*src) {
                        /* Digits missing! Ignore escape */
                        break;
                  }
                  hexdigits[0] = *src;
                  src++;
                  if (!*src) {
                        /* Digits missing! Ignore escape */
                        break;
                  }
                  hexdigits[1] = *src;
                  /* Add a terminating null... */
                  hexdigits[2] = '\0';
                  /* Now use the C standard library function sscanf()
                        to read the hex value */
                  sscanf(hexdigits, "%x", &ascii);
                  /* And convert it back to a character */
                  c = ascii;
            }
            *dst = c;
```

```
            src++;
            dst++;
        }
        *dst = '\0';
}
```

Accepting Comments in Perl

The following is the Perl source code for comments:

```perl
#!/usr/local/bin/perl

#Change this path!

$COMMENT_FILE = "/home/boutell/comments.txt";

# The associative array $values will contain the data.

print "Content-type: text/html\n\n";
print "<html>\n";
print "<head>\n";

# Make sure it's a POST-method form submission
if (! &VerifyForm()) {
    print "<title>Not a POST Form Submission</title>\n";
    print "</head>\n";
    print "<h1>Not a POST Form Submission</h1>\n";
    print "This page should be accessed only by submitting\n";
    print "a form using the POST method. Perhaps your\n";
    print "browser does not support forms.\n";
    print "</body></html>\n";
    exit 0;
}

#OK, it's a form submission, so parse it.
&ParseForm();

#Use the information

#If any field is missing, complain!
if ((! $values{"name"} ) ||
    (! $values{"email"} ) ||
    (! $values{"comments"} ))
{
```

```
        print "<title>Please fill out all the fields</title>\n";
        print "</head>\n";
        print "<h1>Please fill out all the fields</h1>\n";
        print "Please fill out the name, email address, AND\n";
        print "comment fields. Back up to the previous page\n";
        print "to try again.\n";
        print "</body></html>\n";
        exit 0;
}

#OK, we have all the data. Write it to a file in which
#we collect comments from users. Open to append, of course.

$fname = ">>" . $COMMENT_FILE;
open(OUT $fname);

print OUT "From: ", $values{"name"} , " <", $values{"email"} , ">\n";
print OUT $values{"comments"} , "\n";
close(OUT);

print "<title>Thank you, ", $values{"name"} , "</title>\n";
print "</head>\n";
print "<h1>Thank you, ", $values{"name"} , "</h1>\n";
print "Thank you for your comments.\n";
print "</body></html>\n";
exit 0;
sub VerifyForm
{
        local($bad, $contentType, $requestMethod, $result);
        $bad = 0;
        # Check the content type of the data we've received
        $contentType = $ENV{"CONTENT_TYPE"} ;
        if ($contentType ne "application/x-www-form-urlencoded") {
            $bad = 1;
        }
        # And make sure the POST method was used
        $requestMethod = $ENV{"REQUEST_METHOD"} ;
        if ($requestMethod ne "POST") {
            $bad = 1;
        }

        $result = ! $bad;
}
sub ParseForm
{
```

```
local($fields, $name, $value, $data);
#Split standard input into fields
read(STDIN, $data, $ENV{"CONTENT_LENGTH"} ;
@fields = split(/&/, V$data);

#Split the fields into names and values, creating
#an associative array indexed by the names

foreach $item (@fields) {
        ($name, $value) = split(/=/, $item);
        $name = &UnescapeString($name);
        $value = &UnescapeString($value);
        $values{$name} = $value;
}
}

#Unescape any special characters in a string
sub UnescapeString
{
    local($s) = $_[0];
local($pos, $ascii);
# Replace the + sign with spaces
$s =~ s/\+/ /g;
# Seek out and replace %xx hexadecimal escapes
$pos = 0;
while (($pos = index($s, "%", $pos)) != -1) {
        $ascii = hex(substr($s, $pos + 1, 2));
        substr($s, $pos, 3) = pack("c", $ascii);
}
$s;
}
```

Installing and Testing the Program

To try out this program for the C version, just compile and install it. For the Perl version, install the program in your CGI area just as you installed the earlier examples. For either version, make sure you set COMMENT_FILE properly; you may need to create that file in advance.

Note: It is very important to ensure the comment file you set in the source code exists and is writable by the Web server. Otherwise, the program will not be able to record comments. Remember, the Web server usually does not run with the same set of privileges you do. If the Web server does not run as root, you may need to create the file in advance by using the `touch` command and then grant write permissions to all users using the `chmod` command:

```
touch comments.txt
chmod 777 comments.txt
```

Of course, this is not an ideal solution. It is much easier to create secure Web offerings if you own your own server.

Once you have installed the program, set the action of the form presented earlier in this chapter to the URL at which you have installed the program. Open that HTML page, fill out the form, and select the SUBMIT element. If all goes well, the form will be processed and the comments you entered will be appended to COMMENT_FILE for you to examine at your leisure.

Existing Comment-form and Guestbook Packages

This example comment form is provided primarily to teach the techniques of form processing. It is worth mentioning that existing comment-form and guestbook packages are available to solve this particular problem in more detail.

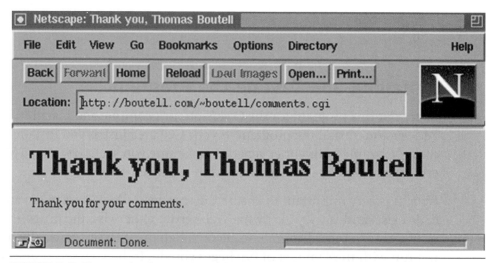

FIGURE 7–2 The result after a successful use of the comment form

Jim Hoagland's getcomments[1] is a particularly excellent package written in Perl. Additional comment-handling packages are listed in the World Wide Web FAQ.[2]

Conclusion

Providing for user input is perhaps the most important application of CGI programming. Without a CGI program to accept the input, HTML forms are useless. In this chapter, we implemented standalone programs in both C and Perl that process form submissions. Implementing and understanding these standalone programs provides a vantage point from which to evaluate the various CGI programming libraries available.

In the next chapter, I examine the cgic library. cgic is a complete CGI processing library in C that does far more than the standalone programs presented here. I will also look at Steven Brenner's cgi-lib, a similar library for Perl programmers.

References

1. Jim Hoagland, "getcomments."
   [URL:http://seclab.cs.ucdavis.edu/~hoagland/getcomments/]

2. Thomas Boutell, "The World Wide Web FAQ."
   [URL:http://www.boutell.com/faq/]

Using cgic and cgi-lib: Complete CGI Solutions

U p to this point, the CGI programming examples in this book have stood alone. For you to create serious CGI applications, however, it is best to take advantage of an existing library of code. Doing this saves time and avoids duplication of effort. Also, most of the available CGI libraries have received feedback from many programmers. While this does not guarantee perfection, more testing in the field greatly increases the odds that the bugs have been worked out. For these reasons, the rest of the book takes advantage of existing CGI libraries instead of reinventing the wheel. This chapter introduces the two libraries that are used in the book.

For C examples, my cgic library is used. You may have noticed that the C examples given so far in this book, for the most part, are substantially longer than their Perl counterparts. This is partly a fact of life in a language that doesn't have a true string type. However, using a CGI library can cut down on the amount of work dramatically. This library provides a collection of functions to make CGI programming in C a lot simpler. It also includes a number of functions often absent from CGI libraries, particularly in the areas of validation and debugging. For instance, cgic can be used to retrieve numbers within specified bounds or to ensure that a multiple-choice response is in fact one of the allowed responses. It also can capture CGI environments and reload them later while running in a debugger. cgic is included on the CD and is also available through the Web. See Appendix 5 for more information about the CD and alternative sources for its contents.

For Perl examples, Steven Brenner's cgi-lib is used. cgi-lib, distributed as the Perl package `cgi-lib.pl`, is a straightforward Perl-based CGI solution that takes care of parsing form parameters. It also handles the most common types of HTTP headers and provides simple calls to output error messages. cgi-lib is also included on the CD. See Appendix 5 for more information about the CDs contents.

Both libraries handle certain frustrating details transparently. For instance, both cgic and cgi-lib can figure out whether a form was submitted using the GET method or the POST method and both can yield the same results with either method. It is still best to stick to the POST method, however, since there is no guarantee that the Web browser and Web server will properly handle extremely long URLs.

The cgic Library: A Better API for CGI

CGI programmers often write the same code over and over. The cgic library attempts to reduce this repetition by taking care of the tasks common to all CGI programs. It also simplifies tasks that are often implemented in buggy ways. For example, `getenv()` often returns a null pointer, and CGI programmers have to check for this result every time `getenv()` is used. cgic provides the full set of CGI environment variables, which are already copied into valid, null-terminated C strings with logical names.

As such, cgic has two primary goals: reducing the amount of code that must be reinvented in every CGI program and reducing the likelihood of bugs in CGI programs.

Replacing main() with cgiMain()

Because cgic takes care of a number of tasks that must be performed at the beginning of the CGI program, cgic provides the `main()` function for you. You may wonder, then, if you don't write `main()`, where does your program begin?

Your code is expected to provide a `cgiMain()` function. cgic will call that function from `main()` after parsing form submissions and reading environment variables. In this way, there is no possibility the programmer will forget to call a parsing function or forget to call a memory-cleanup function at the end. The main() function of cgic takes care of those tasks before and after calling cgiMain(). Your own cgiMain() function simply takes advantage of the cgic environment variables, such as cgiRemoteAddr, and the cgic form query functions, such as cgiFormInteger() and cgiFormString(). Typically, to generate output, your code would first invoke cgiHeaderContentType() and then send the desired output to cgiOut using the fprintf() function. Of course, other output functions such as fwrite can also be used.

A Simple cgic Example

The first cgic example, which follows, is cgicmnts. This simple CGI program takes advantage of cgic to accept comments, just as the comments.c program in Chapter 7 did. The cgic version, however, is much shorter!

This program must be linked with the object file that results from the compilation of cgic.c. On most Unix systems, this is straightforward. The version of cgic included on the CD compiles to produce a library, and cgic programs need only be linked to that library. Also, the file cgic.h must be in the include file search path. See Appendix 5 for more information about the contents of the CD, as well as a Unix Makefile covering all of the sample C programs provided in this book. The Makefile provided next is shown as a less-cluttered example.

A Simple Makefile for cgic Applications

```
#A list of all the programs we are interested in compiling,
#as our first target
all: cgicmnts

#Change this to the ANSI C compiler on your system if you do not have
gcc CC=gcc

#Rule to create object files from C source files
#The cgic104 distribution must be in an adjacent directory!

.c.o: $<
        ${CC}  $< -c -I../cgic104

#Rule to create cgicmnts from the object files that compose it
cgicmnts: cgicmnts.o
        ${CC}  cgicmnts.o -o cgicmnts -L../cgic104 -lcgic
```

The second line of each rule in the Makefile should be set off by a tab, not by spaces. This indicates to the make utility that this second line contains the action to be performed. The first line contains the target to be created, followed by a colon and a list of the files that compose it. If either file is changed, make will recognize this and will recreate the target by executing the action.

To compile the program, first ensure that the cgic104 distribution is in an adjacent directory. Then type make. Your compiler should be invoked to compile the cgicmnts module, after which it will be invoked again to link the cgicmnts.o to the cgic library.

Later, if you modify cgicmnts.c, save it, and type make again, make will determine which steps need to be repeated. This is one of the great things about make: it saves unnecessary compiling time.

The following is the source code for cgicmnts.c:

```c
#include "cgic.h"

/* CHANGE THIS to point to a reasonable location on your system */
#define COMMENT_FILE "/home/boutell/comments.txt"

int cgiMain() {
        /* Large enough buffers for any reasonable real name
                and email address. */
        char name[256];
        char email[256];

        /* The comments themselves may be quite large, so we'll
                allocate space once we know how large they are. */
        char *comments;

        /* Space needed for the comments string. */
        int needed;

        /* Keep the results so we can complain if fields are missing. */
        int rName, rEmail, rComments;

        FILE *out;

        /* Output the usual MIME header. */
```

```
            cgiHeaderContentType("text/html");

            /* Start the HTML document. */
            fprintf(cgiOut,
                    "<HTML>\n<HEAD>\n");

            /* cgiFormStringNoNewlines()
                    will never overflow buffers or write a
                    non-terminated string. Also, even if
                    the user's browser is defective, it will
                    not return any carriage returns or line feeds. */

            rName = cgiFormStringNoNewlines("name", name, sizeof(name));
            rEmail = cgiFormStringNoNewlines("email", email,
    sizeof(email));

            /* cgiFormStringSpaceNeeded the number of bytes of
                    space guaranteed to be adequate for the
                    string in question, including the terminating null. */

            rComments = cgiFormStringSpaceNeeded("comments", &needed);

            /* Now check for missing fields. */
            if ((rName == cgiFormNotFound) || (rEmail == cgiFormNotFound)
    ||
                    (rComments == cgiFormNotFound))
            {
                    /* If any field is missing, complain! */
                    fprintf(cgiOut,
                            "<title>Please fill out all the fields</title>\n");
                    fprintf(cgiOut,
                            "</head>\n");
                    fprintf(cgiOut,
                            "<h1>Please fill out all the fields</h1>\n");
                    fprintf(cgiOut,
                            "Please fill out the name, email address, AND\n");
                    fprintf(cgiOut,
                            "comment fields. Back up to the previous page\n");
                    fprintf(cgiOut,
                            "to try again.\n");
                    fprintf(cgiOut, "</body>\n</html>\n");
                    return 0;
            }

            /* So far, so good. Allocate space for the comments. Since
```

```
            we are dynamically allocating the space, we will
            need to free the space later. */
    comments = (char *) malloc(needed);

    /* In this case, we do want to allow new lines,
            so we call cgiFormString. cgiFormString
            will guarantee that line breaks are always
            represented simply by line feeds, even if
            the user's browser does something creative. */

    cgiFormString("comments", comments, needed);

    /* OK, write the comments to disk. */

      out = fopen(COMMENT_FILE, "a");
      fprintf(out, "From: %s <%s>\n", name, email);
      fprintf(out, "%s\n", comments);

    /* Say thanks. */
      fprintf(cgiOut, "<title>Thank you, %s</title>\n", name);
      fprintf(cgiOut, "</head>\n");
      fprintf(cgiOut, "<h1>Thank you, %s</h1>\n", name);
      fprintf(cgiOut, "Thank you for your comments.\n");
      fprintf(cgiOut, "</body></html>\n");

    /* Free the memory we used for the comments. */
    free(comments);

    /* We're done. */
    return 0;
}
```

Testing cgicmnts

Testing cgicmnts is straightforward: Just install it exactly like the comments example in the last chapter. (Change the action of the form to point to the new program, of course.)

Also note that you may have to create the comments.txt file in advance and set its permissions, exactly as in the last chapter, if you have not already done so as part of that example.

The World Birthday Web, Part II: Using cgic

The next example returns to the World Birthday Web program introduced in Chapter 5. In addition to using cgic, this version can accept new entries through the use of forms.

Also, instead of creating a large virtual document space with PATH_INFO, it allows the user to select the month from a pull-down menu and fill in the day in a text entry field. PATH_INFO is still used, however, to determine which of the several forms on the WBW page was submitted. This can also be done using named Submit buttons, such as <input type="submit" name="Form1">. However, not all browsers support that feature reliably.

This approach does have a few disadvantages. In particular, there is no unique URL for each individual birthdate. So a user cannot easily bookmark a date of interest. For this particular application, this is not a major problem. However, applications that are to include that feature should keep in mind the PATH_INFO-based approach of Chapter 5. Also note that if the program is modified slightly to specify a GET-method form instead of a POST-method form, then the request for the day will be part of the URL, and so bookmarking it should work! Do not change the method for the birthday-submission form, however, as that form submits a significant amount of data.

Giving the User a Choice: Presenting Menus in Forms

Creating a menu in a form is a way to express the user's options more clearly than a simple text entry box might. Rather than the user's entering several illegal values, only to be informed of their illegality after the form is submitted, the user is presented only with the legal choices.

The <select> element is used to create single-choice menus. Within this element, any number of <option> elements can appear that indicate the individual choices. The name field of the <select> element acts as the name of the entire menu. When an option is selected, any text following that option is sent to the server as the value associated with the menu. If desired, one option can be given the SELECTED field as well, which takes no argument. In this case, that option will be sent to the server by default.

More information about menus and other form elements is presented in Chapter 11.

When the form data arrives at the CGI program, there are several ways the program can retrieve it. If a small number of acceptable values exist, it is convenient to use the cgiFormSelectSingle() function of cgic, which accepts an array of strings indicating the acceptable choices. If there are many options with numeric names, such as a list of days of the month, the cgiFormIntegerBounded() function is a simpler solution that still filters out illegal responses made from modified copies of the form.

Compiling wbw2

To combine wbw2, first, modify the Makefile mentioned previously to add an entry for wbw2 or use the Makefile included in Appendix 5 and on the CD. Next, modify the BIRTHDAY_PATH and BIRTHDAY_PROGRAM_URL settings for your own system. Finally, type make wbw to compile the program.

The following is the source code of wbw2.c:

```
#define BIRTHDAY_PATH "/CHANGE_THIS_PATH/birthday_data"
#define BIRTHDAY_PROGRAM_URL "/CHANGE_THIS_URL/wbw2.cgi"

#include <string.h>
#include <time.h>
#include <sys/types.h>

#include "cgic.h"

/* Month names to show the user */
char *months[12] =
{
  "january", "february", "march", "april", "may", "june",
  "july", "august", "september", "october", "november", "december"
} ;

/* Forward references */
void DayRequested();
void TodayRequested();
void AcceptSubmission();
void PresentOptions();
```

```
void OutputDay(int month, int day);
void BirthdayOutput (int day, int month,
      char *name_s, char *url_s, char *email_s);
void BirthdayHead (char *request);
void BirthdayTail ();
void RemoveSpaces (char *dest, char *src);

int cgiMain ()
{
      cgiHeaderContentType("text/html");
      fprintf(cgiOut,
            "<HTML>\n<HEAD>\n");
      /* Look for requests for particular days
            and submissions of new entries. If
            the PATH_INFO indicates neither,
            display today's birthdays. In all
            three cases, present the user's
            next choices afterward. */

      if ((!strcmp(cgiPathInfo, "/day")) ||
            (!strcmp(cgiPathInfo, "day"))) {
            DayRequested();
      } else if ((!strcmp(cgiPathInfo, "/submit")) ||
            (!strcmp(cgiPathInfo, "submit"))) {
            AcceptSubmission();
      } else {
            TodayRequested();
      }
      PresentOptions();
      fprintf(cgiOut,
            "</BODY>\n</HTML>\n");
      return 0;
}

void TodayRequested()
{
      int month, day;
      struct tm *now_tm;
      time_t now_t;
      /* If we didn't find a request for a specific date,
            then output today's birthdays instead. */
      /* Retrieve the current time */
      time (&now_t);
      /* Break it down into month, day, year and so on */
      now_tm = gmtime (&now_t);
```

```
        month = now_tm->tm_mon;
        day = now_tm->tm_mday;
        /* Output today's birthdays */
        OutputDay(month, day);
}

void DayRequested()
{
        int month, day;

        /* The month will be one of the twelve possible strings, of course. */
        cgiFormSelectSingle("month", months, 12, &month, 0);

        /* The day is an integer, so just use cgiFormIntegerBounded(). */
        cgiFormIntegerBounded("day", &day, 1, 31, 1);

        /* Output birthdays */
        OutputDay(month, day);
}

void AcceptSubmission()
{
        int month, day;
        char name[256];
        char url[256];
        char email[256];
        char path[256];
        FILE *out;

        /* Keep the results so we can complain if fields are missing. */
        int rMonth, rDay, rName, rEmail, rUrl;

        /* The month will be one of the twelve possible strings, of course. */
        cgiFormSelectSingle("month", months, 12, &month, 0);

        /* The day is an integer, so just use cgiFormIntegerBounded(). */
        cgiFormIntegerBounded("day", &day, 1, 31, 1);

        /* Now the user's name, url and email address. */
        rName = cgiFormStringNoNewlines("name", name, sizeof(name));
        rUrl = cgiFormStringNoNewlines("url", url, sizeof(url));
        rEmail = cgiFormStringNoNewlines("email", email, sizeof(email));

        if ((rName == cgiFormNotFound) ||
                (rMonth == cgiFormNotFound) || (rDay == cgiFormNotFound))
```

```
          {
                /* Complain. */
                fprintf(cgiOut,
                    "<title>Missing Fields</title></head>\n");
                fprintf(cgiOut,
                    "<body><h1>Missing Fields</h1>\n");
                fprintf(cgiOut,
                    "Please fill out your name, your month of birth,\n");
                fprintf(cgiOut,
                    "and your day of birth, at a minimum.\n");
                return;
          }

          /* All is well; add the data to the database. */
          sprintf(path, "%s/%d/%d", BIRTHDAY_PATH, month+1, day);
          out = fopen (path, "a");
          if (!out) {
                /* We can't access the data file to add to it. */
                fprintf(cgiOut,
                    "<title>Can't Access Data File</title></head>\n");
                fprintf(cgiOut,
                    "<body>\n<h1>Can't Access Data File</h1>\n");
                fprintf(cgiOut,
                    "Please contact the administrator.\n");
                return;
          }
          fprintf(out, "%s\n%s\n%s\n", name, url, email);
          fclose(out);
          fprintf(cgiOut,
                "<title>WBW: Birthday added successfully.</title></head>\n");
          fprintf(cgiOut,
                "<body>\n<h1>WBW: Birthday added successfully.</h1>\n");
}

void OutputDay(int month, int day) {
      FILE *in;
      char path[256];
      int birthdayCount = 0;
      fprintf(cgiOut,
          "<title>WBW: birthdays for %d %s</title></head>\n",
          day, months[month]);
      fprintf(cgiOut,
          "<body>\n<h1>WBW: birthdays for %d %s</h1>\n",
          day, months[month]);
```

```
        sprintf(path, "%s/%d/%d", BIRTHDAY_PATH, month+1, day);
        in = fopen (path, "r");
        if (in) {
                while (!feof (in)) {
                        char name_s[512], url_s[512], email_s[512];
                        char nameS[512], urlS[512], emailS[512];
                        if (!fgets (name_s, 512, in)) {
                                break;
                        }
                        RemoveSpaces (nameS, name_s);
                        if (!fgets (url_s, 512, in)) {
                                break;
                        }
                        RemoveSpaces (urlS, url_s);
                        if (!fgets (email_s, 512, in)) {
                                break;
                        }
                        RemoveSpaces (emailS, email_s);
                        if (!birthdayCount) {
                                char s[81];
                                sprintf(s, "%d %s",
                                        day, months[month]);
                                BirthdayHead (s);
                        }
                        birthdayCount++;
                        BirthdayOutput (day, month,
                                nameS, urlS, emailS);
                }
        }
        fclose (in);
        if (birthdayCount) {
                BirthdayTail ();
        } else {
                fprintf(cgiOut,
                "<em>No birthdays have been entered for this day.</em>\n");
        }
}

void BirthdayOutput (int day, int month,
        char *name_s, char *url_s, char *email_s)
{
        fprintf(cgiOut, "<LI>");
        if (strlen (url_s)) {
                fprintf(cgiOut,
                        "<A HREF=\"%s\">", url_s);
```

```
        }
        fprintf(cgiOut, "%d %s: ", day, months[month]);
        fprintf(cgiOut, "<STRONG>%s</STRONG>", name_s);
        if (strlen (email_s)) {
                fprintf(cgiOut, " <EM>%s</EM>\n", email_s);
        }
        if (strlen (url_s)) {
                fprintf(cgiOut, "</A>\n");
        }
        fprintf(cgiOut, "</LI>\n");
}

void BirthdayHead (char *request)
{
        fprintf(cgiOut, "<H2>Birthdays for: %s</H2><UL>\n", request);
}

void BirthdayTail ()
{
        fprintf(cgiOut, "</UL>\n");
        fprintf(cgiOut, "<P><em>Remember, the Birthday Server ");
        fprintf(cgiOut, "runs on Greenwich Mean Time.</em>\n");
}

void PresentOptions()
{
        int i;
        fprintf(cgiOut, "<p>\n");
        fprintf(cgiOut, "<hr>\n");
        fprintf(cgiOut, "<h2>Global Birthday Navigator (GBN)</h2>\n");

        /* Make sure that PATH_INFO will distinguish this form from others */
        fprintf(cgiOut, "<form action=\"%s/day\" method=\"POST\">\n",
                BIRTHDAY_PROGRAM_URL);

        fprintf(cgiOut, "Month:\n");
        fprintf(cgiOut, "<select name=\"month\">\n");
        for (i=0; (i < 12); i++) {
                fprintf(cgiOut, "<option>%s\n", months[i]);
        }
        fprintf(cgiOut, "</select>\n");

        fprintf(cgiOut,
                "Day: <input size=\"3\" type=\"text\" name=\"day\"> \n ");
```

```
        fprintf(cgiOut, "<input type=\"submit\"> <input type=\"reset\">\n");
        fprintf(cgiOut, "</form>\n");
        fprintf(cgiOut, "<hr>\n");
        fprintf(cgiOut, "<h2>Universal Birthday Form (UBF)</h2>\n");

        /* Make sure that PATH_INFO will distinguish this form from others */
        fprintf(cgiOut, "<form action=\"%s/submit\" method=\"POST\">\n",
            BIRTHDAY_PROGRAM_URL);

        fprintf(cgiOut, "Month:\n");
        fprintf(cgiOut, "<select name=\"month\">\n");
        for (i=0; (i < 12); i++) {
            fprintf(cgiOut, "<option>%s\n", months[i]);
        }
        fprintf(cgiOut, "</select>\n\n");

        fprintf(cgiOut,
            "Day: <input size=\"3\" type=\"text\" name=\"day\"><p>\n");

        fprintf(cgiOut, "Name: <input type=\"text\" name=\"name\"><p>\n");
        fprintf(cgiOut, "URL: <input type=\"text\" name=\"url\"><p>\n");
        fprintf(cgiOut, "Email: <input type=\"text\" name=\"email\"><p>\n");
        fprintf(cgiOut, "<input type=\"submit\" value=\"Submit Birthday\"> \n");
        fprintf(cgiOut, "<input type=\"reset\">\n");

        fprintf(cgiOut, "</form>\n");
}

void RemoveSpaces(char *dest, char *src) {
        /* Remove all leading and trailing spaces. */
        char *last;

        /* First, skip to the first non-space character
            in the source string. */
        while (*src) {
            if (!isspace(*src)) {
                break;
            }
            src++;
        }

        /* Now, copy the source string to the destination string. */
```

```
strcpy(dest, src);

/* Now, find the last non-space character in the destination string;
     move downward through the string from the end. */
if (!strlen(dest)) {
    return;
}
last = dest + strlen(dest) - 1;
while (last != dest) {
    if (!isspace(*last)) {
        /* We have found the last non-space character
             in the string, so place a final null
             immediately after it. */
        *(last + 1) = '\0';
        break;
    }
    last--;
}
}
```

Testing wbw2

wbw2 should be installed in exactly the same manner as wbw1 by using the same data files. However, be sure to use the chmod command to make the top directory in which wbw2 keeps its database writable by the Web server or by all users. To ensure the entire subdirectory tree of data becomes writable, use the following command:

```
chmod -R 777 birthday_data
```

assuming you have named that directory birthday_data. If you have control of your own server, it is of course preferable to simply make sure the directory and its contents are owned by the user ID under which the Web server is run.

To test wbw2, simply install it in the same directory that wbw1 was installed in and access it by using the same URL. Change the name of the program at the end of the URL, of course. (See Figure 8–1.)

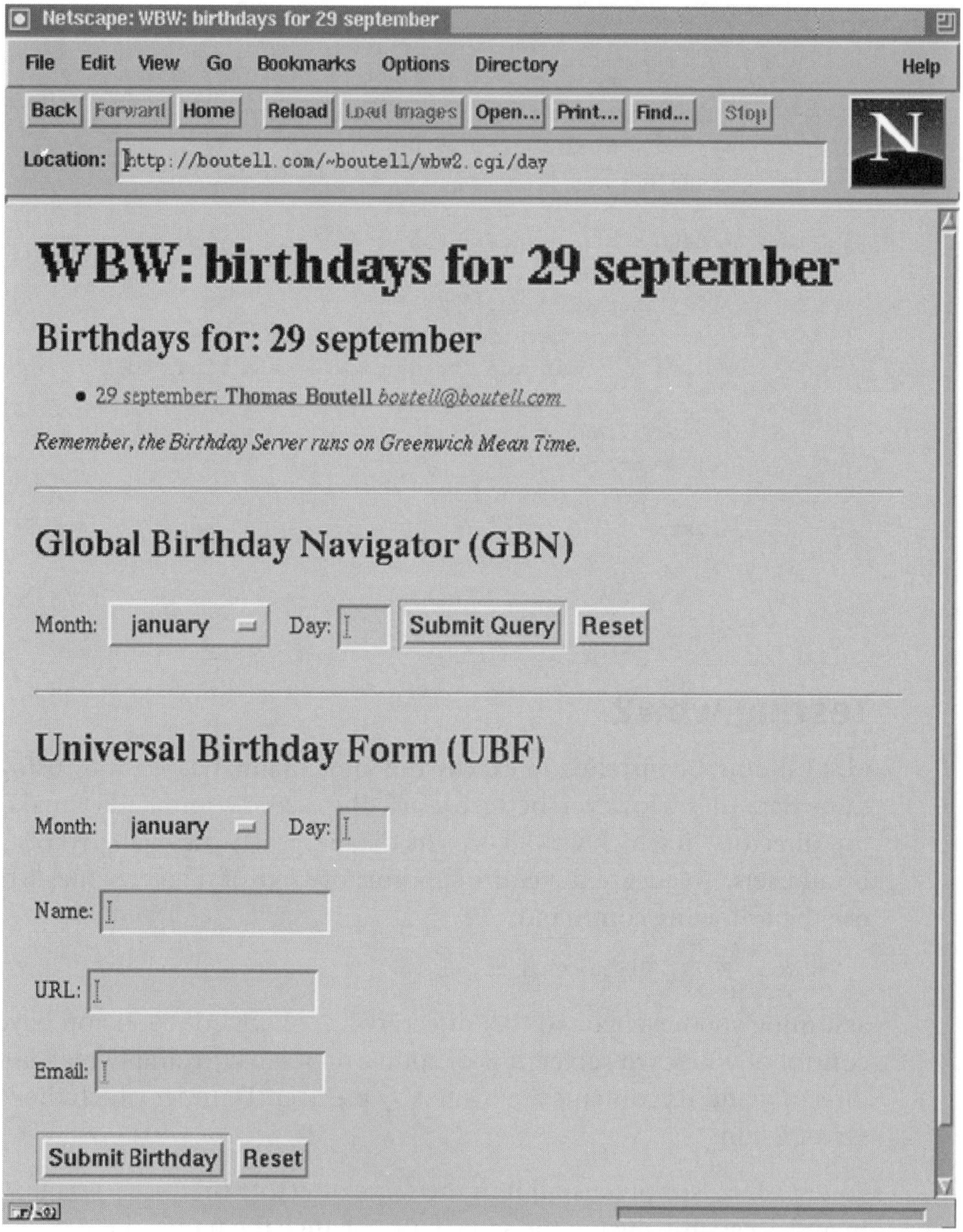

FIGURE 8–1 The data entry forms of wbw2

cgi-lib: Simplifying CGI for Perl Programmers

Steven Brenner's cgi-lib takes care of form parsing, the most complex CGI programming task. In addition, it provides error-reporting routines and a simple output routine that may prove helpful in debugging your Perl-based CGI programs. cgi-lib consists of a single file, `cgi-lib.pl`. Advanced Perl programmers will also want to examine the CGI.pm library, by Lincoln Stein, which is included on the CD. See Appendix 5 for more information.

A Simple cgi-lib Example

The first cgi-lib example is `clcmnts`. This example accepts comments submitted via a form, just as the comments example in Chapter 7 did. But the cgi-lib version is dramatically shorter.

The following is the Perl source code for `clcmnts`:

```perl
#!/usr/local/bin/perl

#Change this path!

$COMMENT_FILE = "/CHANGE/THIS/PATH/comments.txt";
require "cgi-lib.pl";

print "Content-type: text/html"\n\n;
print "<html>\n";
print "<head>\n";

#Parse the form arguments. Indicate that we want
#the results to appear in "values".
&ReadParse(*values);

#Use the information

#If any field is missing, complain!
if ((! $values{"name"} ) ||
    (! $values{"email"} ) ||
    (! $values{"comments"} ))
{
    print "<title>Please fill out all the fields</title>\n";
    print "</head>\n";
    print "<h1>Please fill out all the fields</h1>\n";
```

```
        print "Please fill out the name, email address, AND\n";
        print "comment fields. Back up to the previous page\n";
        print "to try again.\n";
        print "</body></html>\n";
        exit 0;
    }

    #OK, we have all the data. Write it to a file in which
    #we collect comments from users. Open to append, of course.

    $fname = ">>" . $COMMENT_FILE; open(OUT, $fname);

    print OUT "From: ", $values{"name"} , " <", $values{"email"} , ">\n";
    print OUT $values{"comments"} , "\n"; close(OUT);

    print "<title>Thank you, ", $values{"name"} , "</title>\n";
    print "</head>\n";
    print "<h1>Thank you, ", $values{"name"} , "</h1>\n";
    print "Thank you for your comments.\n";
    print "</body></html>\n";
    exit 0;
```

Installing clcmnts

clcmnts should be installed in the same location to which the Perl comments example in Chapter 7 was installed. The form should be modified to point to clcmnts as its action instead.

The file cgi-lib.pl, available on the CD as well as from other sources, must be present in the same directory with clcmnts or somewhere in the Perl search path on your system. See Appendix 5 for details regarding the contents of the CD-ROM.

The World Birthday Web, Part III: Using cgi-lib

The next example is the last installment of the World Birthday Web program introduced in Chapter 5. In addition to using cgi-lib, this version can accept new entries and navigate the database through the use of forms. The Perl version is quite similar to its C counterpart, presented earlier in this chapter.

You may wish to refer to that section for an overview of the pluses and minuses of this forms-based approach.

As with `clcmnts`, the file `cgi-lib.pl` must be present in the same directory with wbw2 or somewhere in the Perl search path on your system. This file is available on the CD and from other sources. See Appendix 5 for more information regarding the contents of the CD.

wbw2 should be installed exactly as wbw1 was installed. The URL to begin accessing it is the same, except for the name of the program.

Perl's associative arrays provide an obvious and powerful way to handle forms, so there is not much difference between this program and what could have been accomplished by pasting in the form-handling subprograms given in Chapter 7. That is, the Perl routines presented in that chapter are quite similar to cgi-lib in what they do. However, using a well-known cgi library such as cgi-lib is reason to have confidence that the code has been thoroughly debugged by many programmers!

The following is the source code for wbw2:

```perl
#!/usr/local/bin/perl

#Change these to locations appropriate for your system!

$birthdayPath = "/home/boutell/birthday_data";
$birthdayProgramUrl = "/~boutell/wbw2.cgi";
require "cgi-lib.pl";
%monthIndexes = (
      "january", 0,
      "february", 1,
      "march", 2,
      "april", 3,
      "may", 4,
      "june", 5,
      "july", 6,
      "august", 7,
      "september", 8,
      "october", 9,
      "november", 10,
      "december", 11 );
@monthNames = (
      "january",
      "february",
```

```perl
         "march",
         "april",
         "may",
         "june",
         "july",
         "august",
         "september",
         "october",
         "november",
         "december" );

print "Content-type: text/html\n";
print "<HTML>\n<HEAD>\n";

#Look for requests for particular days
#and submissions of new entries. If
#the PATH_INFO indicates neither,
#display today's birthdays. In all
#three cases, present the user's
#next choices afterward.

$pathInfo = $ENV{"PATH_INFO"} ;

#Clobber the leading / , if any

$pathInfo =~ s/ \///;

#Handles the content type
print &PrintHeader;

#Fetch the values
&ReadParse(*values);
if ($pathInfo eq "day") {
     &DayRequested();
} elsif ($pathInfo eq "submit") {
     &AcceptSubmission();
} else {
     &TodayRequested();
}
&PresentOptions();
print "</BODY>\n</HTML>\n"; exit 0;

sub TodayRequested
{
```

```
        #Output today's birthdays
        local($sec, $min, $hour, $mday, $mon, $year, $wday, $yday, $isdst) =
                gmtime(time);
        &OutputDay($mon, $mday);
}


sub DayRequested
{
        local($monthName, $month, $day);
        $monthName = $values{"month"} ;
        $month = $monthIndexes{$monthName} ;
        $day = $values{"day"} ;
        if ($day < 1) {
                # Constrain the day to a reasonable value
                $day = 1;
        }
        print $day, " ", $month, "\n";
        &OutputDay($month, $day);
}


sub AcceptSubmission
{
        local($monthName, $month, $day, $name, $url, $email, $path, $out);

        $monthName = $values{"month"} ;
        $month = $monthIndexes{$monthName} ;
        $day = $values{"day"} ;
        if ($day < 1) {
                $day = 1;
        }
        $name = $values{"name"} ;
        $url = $values{"url"} ;
        $email = $values{"email"} ;

        if ($name eq "")
        {
                # Complain.
                print "<title>Missing Fields</title></head>\n";
                print "<body>\n<h1>Missing Fields</h1>\n";
                print "Please fill out your name, your month of birth,\n";
                print "and your day of birth, at a minimum.\n";
                return;
        }
```

```
        # All is well; add the data to the database.
        $path = ">>" . $birthdayPath . "/" . ($month + 1) . "/" . $day;
        if (!open (OUT, $path)) {
                # We can't access the data file to add to it.
                print "<title>Can't Access Data File</title></head>\n";
                print "<body>\n<h1>Can't Access Data File</h1>\n";
                print "Please contact the administrator.\n";
                return;
        }
        print OUT $name, "\n", $url, "\n", $email, "\n";
        close(OUT);
        print "<title>WBW: Birthday added successfully.</title></head>\n";
        print "<body>\n<h1>WBW: Birthday added successfully.</h1>\n";
}

sub OutputDay {
        local($month, $day) = @_;
        $birthdayCount = 0;
        print "<TITLE>WBW: Birthdays for ", $day, " ",
                $monthNames[$month], "</TITLE></HEAD>\n";
        print "<BODY><H1>WBW: Birthdays for ", $day, " ",
                $monthNames[$month], "</H1>\n";
        $filename = $birthdayPath . "/" . ($month + 1) . "/" . $day;
        open(file, $filename);
        while (1) {
                if (!($name = <file>)) {
                        last;
                }
                chop $name;
                if (!($url = <file>)) {
                        last;
                }
                chop $url;
                if (!($email = <file>)) {
                        last;
                }
                chop $email;
                if (!($birthdayCount)) {
                        print "<H2>Birthdays for: ",
                                ($month+1), "/", $day, "</H2>\n";
                }
                $birthdayCount++;
                print "<LI>";
                if ($url ne "") {
                        print "<A HREF=\"", $url, "\">";
```

```perl
        }
        print $day, " ", $monthNames[$month], ": ";
        print "<STRONG>", $name, "</STRONG> ";
        if ($email ne "") {
            print "<EM>", $email, "</EM>";
        }
        if ($url ne "") {
            print "</A>";
        }
        print "</LI>\n";
    }
    if ($birthdayCount) {
        print "</UL>\n";
        print "<P><em>Remember, the Birthday Server";
        print "runs on Greenwich Mean Time.</em>\n";
    } else {
     print "<em>No birthdays have been entered ";
        print "for this day.</em>\n";
    }
}


sub PresentOptions
{
    local($i);
    print "<p>\n";
    print "<hr>\n";
    print "<h2>Global Birthday Navigator (GBN)</h2>\n";

    # Make sure that PATH_INFO will distinguish this form from
others
    print "<form action=\"", $birthdayProgramUrl,
        "/day\" method=\"POST\">\n";

    print "Month: \n";
    print "<select name=\"month\">\n";
    for ($i=0; ($i < 12); $i++) {
        print "<option>", $monthNames[$i], "\n";
    }
    print "</select>\n";

    print "Day: <input size=\"3\" type=\"text\" name=\"day\">\n ";

    print "<input type=\"submit\"> <input type=\"reset\">\n";
    print "</form>\n";
    print "<hr>\n";
```

```
print "<h2>Universal Birthday Form (UBF)</h2>\n";

#Make sure that PATH_INFO will distinguish this form from others
print "<form action=\"", $birthdayProgramUrl,
    "/submit\" method=\"POST\">\n";

print "Month: \n";
print "<select name=\"month\">\n";
for ($i=0; ($i < 12); $i++) {
    print "<option>", $monthNames[$i], "\n";
}
print "</select\n\n";

print "Day: <input size=\"3\" type=\"text\" name=\"day\"><p>\n";

print "Name: <input type=\"text\" name=\"name\"><p>\n";
print "URL: <input type=\"text\" name=\"url\"><p>\n";
print "Email: <input type=\"text\" name=\"email\"><p>\n";
print "<input type=\"submit\" value=\"Submit Birthday\"> \n";
print "<input type=\"reset\">\n";

print "</form>\n";
}
```

Conclusion

In this chapter, I introduced two powerful, off-the-shelf CGI programming libraries. Reusing solid libraries of existing code is a good strategy for any programming project. Reinventing the wheel is a poor practice, unless the wheel truly needs improvement.

The next chapter provides a brief look at how to send e-mail safely and reliably from CGI programs. It's not as easy as it sounds. There are many security risks that can trip up even experienced programmers!

Sending E-mail from CGI Programs

Sending e-mail is one of the most popular applications of CGI. While there are other ways to send e-mail through the Web, CGI provides more control over the content of the message. The task of sending e-mail is very similar to the task of accepting comments, except for several unique security concerns. Because sending e-mail via CGI is both popular and potentially risky, this chapter explores good and bad approaches.

Alternatives to Using CGI

If your goal is simply to allow users to drop you a line and you are not concerned about structuring the content of the message, consider using the `mailto:` URL instead. This approach can be very straightforward and effective, and with most browsers, the user has to configure an e-mail address only once. The downside is that older browsers do not always support `mailto:`, although such browsers are becoming increasingly rare. Of course, it may be acceptable for your purposes to simply explain this to the user and suggest that he or she send e-mail by other means if `mailto:` doesn't work for them.

The following is an example of the `mailto:` URL in use:

```
If you want, you can <a href="mailto:person@site.com">send me
mail</a>. If this link does not work for you, use your favorite email
program to send mail to person@site.com.
```

mailto: and the <FORM> Element

Some browsers support `mailto:` as the action for forms (see Figure 9–1). In this case, the information the user fills out in the form is sent in e-mail in the same format used for POST-method forms (see Chapter 7). You may

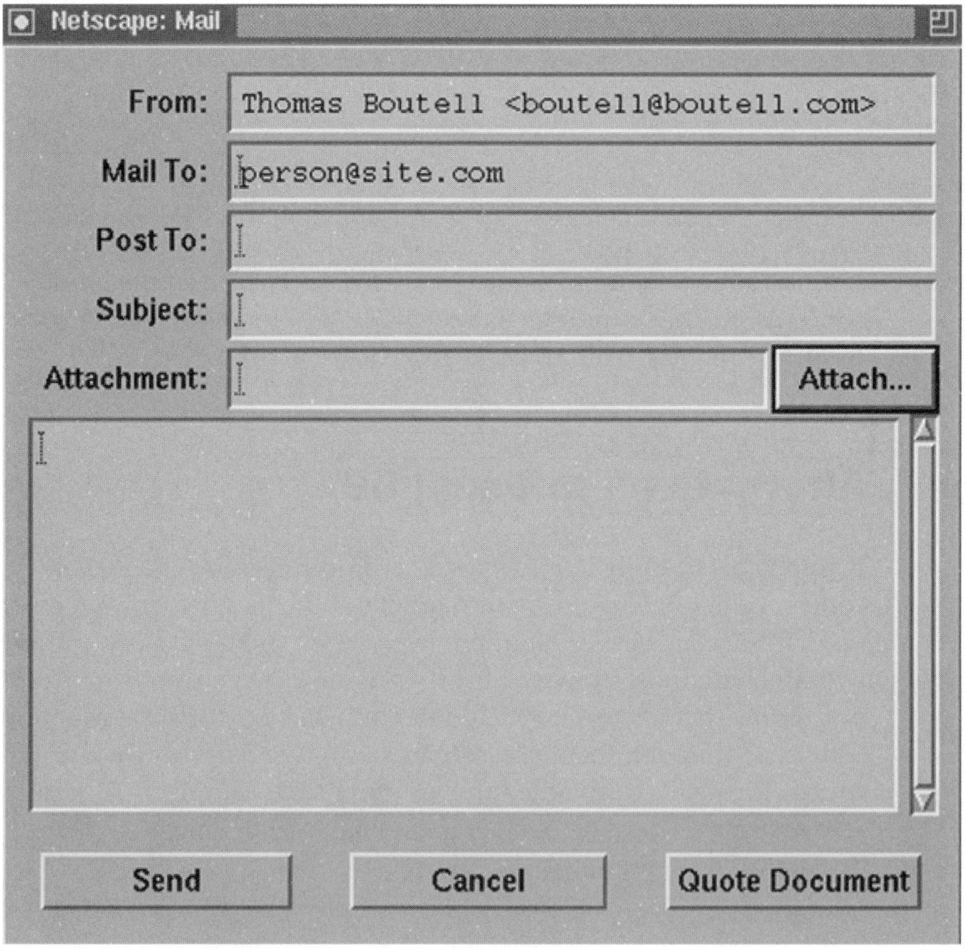

FIGURE 9–1 The Netscape `mailto:` window

find this useful if you do not have true CGI access. Unfortunately, even browsers that support the basic `mailto:` URL often do not support it as the action of a form.

When mailto: Isn't Enough

The limitations of `mailto:` become apparent when you want to structure the user's e-mail by providing blanks for particular pieces of information. For instance, a bug-report form for a software package should have blanks for the version number of the software, the user's hardware, and so on. In this way, you will more likely receive meaningful responses.

The comment forms presented in the last two chapters do a reasonable job of appending information to a file on the server system. But e-mailing it to a particular user automatically can be desirable, especially if it is part of that user's job to handle bug reports, orders, or the like. Remembering to check a special file can be a nuisance.

Security Risks of Sending E-mail with /bin/mail

Here's what most fairly experienced Unix programmers say when faced with sending e-mail:

"Hey, this is really easy. I'll just `popen()` *a copy of* `/bin/mail`, *stick the subject line in with the* `-s` *command line option, and stuff the mail into its standard input. All done. That was quick. Now I can play Netrek for a few hours."*

It's not quite that simple!

First, the `popen()` call is dangerous if anything the user submitted is sent as part of the command line. Consider what will happen if the user's subject line is

```
whatever | rm *
```

A naive mail gateway written in C might try to execute the following call as a result:

```
popen("/bin/mail -s whatever | rm *");
```

This would delete all the files in the current directory that are visible to the CGI program! Obviously, something must be done to protect against this sort of attack.

Again, even experienced programmers can fall prey to this sort of mistake. I released a simple e-mail-handling program in C that was available for over a year before I learned that on some systems users could subvert it and gain access to the Unix prompt. (I have since corrected the problem, of course!)

Cleaning up the command line doesn't solve the entire problem. Most mail programs recognize any line of text that begins with the ~ character as an escape to be followed by a special command. In particular, the sequence ~! executes the shell command that follows it! If the user sends the following e-mail to a badly written CGI program that executes /bin/mail, files will be deleted under some versions of Unix:

```
Should have been
~!rm *
More careful.
```

Because of these problems, you should avoid /bin/mail and use /lib/sendmail instead. (Sometimes sendmail is located at the path /usr/lib/sendmail or /usr/sbin/sendmail.) Sendmail is the actual mail delivery agent on most systems and is intended to be called by user-friendly mailer programs. CGI programs that send mail fall into the latter category. So do mail programs such as elm, pine, and Berkeley mail.

Sending E-mail with sendmail

The sendmail program, which is usually installed at the path /lib/sendmail or /bin/sendmail, is the best tool to use for mail delivery from your CGI program. To use it, a CGI program must open a pipe to it with the e-mail address of the recipient as the lone argument. Next, the content of the message, including any headers such as the Subject: line, should be written to the pipe. Once the pipe is closed, sendmail delivers the message. No muss, no fuss, and no dangerous security holes on most systems, as long as the name of the recipient is given by the CGI program and never by the end user.

Most of the time, only a single recipient is desired. After all, making sure the user is sending the right message to the right person is the point of creating a form instead of simply asking the user to send mail. Giving the end user a choice of acceptable recipients from a menu is fine, but the name of the recipient should be double-checked against a list kept with the CGI program. Hackers can and will create their own version of the form with creatively chosen recipient names if the CGI program blindly trusts the user's choice of recipient.

Using sendmail's -t Option for Safety

While it is possible to specify the recipient on the command line, it is safer to use the -t option. This option causes sendmail to look for a To: address line in its input. In this way, the actual sendmail command line can be kept completely free of user input, even if the user is allowed to specify the recipient. This decreases the risk that your program will fall prey to Unix security holes.

> **WARNING:** I am not aware of any version of sendmail that allows special escapes to execute programs. However, operating system vendors have been known to do dumb things. Consult the manpage for sendmail on your system and follow the USENET newsgroups comp.risks[1] and comp.security.announce closely to be sure you are aware of any security threats that may come to light.

Consider the following snippet of C code:

```
/* This is the location of sendmail on my system */
#define SENDMAIL_PATH "/lib/sendmail"
#define RECIPIENT "person@site.com"
FILE *out;
char s[256];

/* Format the command to send to the shell. */
sprintf(s, "%s %s", SENDMAIL_PATH, RECIPIENT);

/* Open the "pipe". */ out = popen(s, "w");
fprintf(out, "Subject: how's the weather?\n");

/* A carriage return to end the headers */
fprintf(out, "\n");
```

```
/* Now the body of the message */
fprintf(out, "Still raining as usual?\n");

/* Close the pipe. */
pclose(out);
```

This short example sends a less-than-useful e-mail message to the user defined by the RECIPIENT macro. A complete example appears later in this chapter.

Identifying the Sender: How Much Can Be Done?

It would be nice if the e-mail program could fill in the From: blank automatically. Unfortunately, it cannot normally be done reliably, for the reasons explained in Chapter 6, "Identifying the User: More CGI Environment Variables." *An important exception:* If authentication is being used, it is possible to keep a data file on each user that includes his or her e-mail address, which is given once when the user first signs up for your service. In that case, the REMOTE_USER environment variable can be used to look up that information. Most sites do not currently use HTTP 1.0 authentication because it is not completely secure (see Chapter 6 for details). But the popular HotWired site[2] does use it extensively, although they are now phasing it out. That site's popularity has successfully driven browser vendors to support the feature properly. Chapter 14, "World Wide Web Wall Street: An Advanced CGI Application," presents an advanced application that uses HTTP 1.0 authentication.

You can make a guess at the user's return address by using the REMOTE_HOST environment variable and providing a separate blank for the user's name. I do not recommend this. Users are comfortable typing in their full e-mail address; many give theirs to people every day. Providing a possibly incorrect guess and leaving out the user's name will only lead to confusion.

The other way around this problem is, of course, to use mailto: instead of a form. If mailto: is not acceptable, you must provide a From: blank and an E-mail Address: blank for the user to fill in and also emphasize to the user that the information is necessary.

A Complete E-mail Form: Accepting Bug Reports

bugrep is a CGI program that accepts reports of bugs in a software product. bugrep is intended to be used with the following form. Be sure to change the action to point to the location at which you install bugrep.

This HTML document employs a few HTML form tags you've not been properly introduced to, notably <select> and <option>. I talk more about these in Chapter 11.

```
<html>
<head>
<title>HubriSoft Bug Report Form</title>
</head>
<body>
<h1>HubriSoft Bug Report Form</h1>
<p> At <strong>HubriSoft</strong>, all of our software is perfect. If
you, as an imperfect mortal, mistakenly believe you have discovered a
bug, please feel free to fill out this form. Your bug report will be
delivered to the overworked, underpaid tech support engineers of
HubriSoft, who will spill electronic espresso on it.
<p>
<form action="bugrep.cgi" method="POST">
Your Name: <input type="text" name="name"><br>
Your E-Mail Address: <input type="text" name="email"><br>
Version of HubriSoft Omega Pro Used: <select name="version">
<option selected>PLEASE CHOOSE ONE
<option>1.0
<option>1.1
<option>1.2
<option>1.3
<option>2.0
</select> <br>
System Used:
<select name="system">
<option selected>PLEASE CHOOSE ONE
<option>Windows
<option>Mac
<option>Unix
</select> <br>
Please describe the alleged bug in the area below. <br>
<textarea name="bug" rows="10" cols="60"> </textarea> <br>
```

```
<input type="submit" value="Submit Bug Report">
<input type="reset" value="Clear Entries">
</form>
</body>
</html>
```

NOTE: The C version of the program must be linked with cgic. See Appendix 5 and the CD for a Unix Makefile suitable for all the C programs in this book.

bugrep Source Code: in C

The following is the source code for the C version of bugrep.

```
#include "cgic.h"

/* CHANGE THIS to point to the location of the
        sendmail binary on your system. */

#define SENDMAIL "/lib/sendmail -t"

/* CHANGE THIS to your email address. */

#define RECIPIENT "CHANGE@bar.com"

int cgiMain() {
        /* Large enough buffers for any reasonable real name
                and email address. */
        char name[256];
        char email[256];

        /* The version "number". */
        char version[32];

        /* The user's system. */
        char userSystem[32];

        /* The bug report itself may be quite large, so we'll
                allocate space once we know how large it is. */
        char *bug;

        /* Space needed for the bug string. */
        int needed;
```

```c
/* Keep the results so we can complain if fields are missing. */
int rName, rEmail, rComments, rVersion, rSystem;

FILE *out;

/* Output the usual MIME header. */
cgiHeaderContentType("text/html");

/* Start the HTML document. */
fprintf(cgiOut,
    "<HTML>\n<HEAD>\n");

/* cgiFormStringNoNewlines()
    will never overflow buffers or write a
    non-terminated string. Also, even if
    the user's browser is defective, it will
    not return any carriage returns or line feeds. */

rName = cgiFormStringNoNewlines("name", name, sizeof(name));
rEmail = cgiFormStringNoNewlines("email", email, sizeof(email));

/* A "falsified" version number would not particularly
    matter in this case, so we'll just get the string
    instead of using cgiFormSelectSingle. */
rVersion = cgiFormStringNoNewlines("version", version,
    sizeof(version));

/* The same goes for the system. */
rSystem = cgiFormStringNoNewlines("system", userSystem,
    sizeof(userSystem));

/* cgiFormStringSpaceNeeded returns the number of bytes of
    space guaranteed to be adequate for the
    string in question, including the terminating null. */

rComments = cgiFormStringSpaceNeeded("bug", &needed);

/* Now check for missing fields. Since any well-behaved browser
    will submit the default for each option menu if nothing
    was actually chosen by the user, we check for
    the "PLEASE CHOOSE ONE" strings as well as for a
    missing field. */

if ((rName == cgiFormNotFound) || (rEmail == cgiFormNotFound) ||
    (rBug == cgiFormNotFound) || (rSystem == cgiFormNotFound) ||
```

```
                (rVersion == cgiFormNotFound) ||
                (!strcmp(userSystem, "PLEASE CHOOSE ONE")) ||
                (!strcmp(version, "PLEASE CHOOSE ONE")))
        {
                /* If any field is missing, complain! */
                fprintf(cgiOut,
                    "<title>Please fill out all the fields</title>\n");
                fprintf(cgiOut,
                    "</head>\n");
                fprintf(cgiOut,
                    "<h1>Please fill out all the fields</h1>\n");
                fprintf(cgiOut,
                    "Please indicate your name, email address, software
version\n");
                fprintf(cgiOut,
                    "number, and system, and submit the form again.\n");
                fprintf(cgiOut, "</body></html>\n");
                return 0;
        }

        /* So far, so good. Allocate space for the bug. Since
                we are dynamically allocating the space, we will
                need to free the space later. */
        bug = (char *) malloc(needed);

        /* In this case, we do want to allow new lines,
                so we call cgiFormString. cgiFormString
                will guarantee that line breaks are always
                represented simply by line feeds, even if
                the user's browser does something creative. */

        cgiFormString("bug", bug, needed);

        /* OK, send email to the user responsible for bug reports. Use the
                popen() Unix function, which executes the specified program
                and writes to its standard input through a "pipe". */

          out = popen(SENDMAIL, "w");
          fprintf(out, "From: %s <%s>\n", name, email);
          fprintf(out, "To: %s\n", RECIPIENT);
        fprintf(out, "Subject: bug report\n");
        fprintf(out, "\n");
        fprintf(out,
            "This bug report was submitted via the WWW-Email gateway.\n");
        fprintf(out, "--\n\n");
```

```
    fprintf(out, "System: %s\n", userSystem);
    fprintf(out, "Version: %s\n", version);
      fprintf(out, "%s\n", bug);

    /* Always close pipes with pclose(), not fclose(). */

    pclose(out);

    /* Say thanks. */
      fprintf(cgiOut, "<title>Thank you, %s</title>\n", name);
      fprintf(cgiOut, "</head>\n");
      fprintf(cgiOut, "<h1>Thank you, %s</h1>\n", name);
      fprintf(cgiOut, "Thank you for your bug report.\n");
      fprintf(cgiOut, "</body></html>\n");

    /* Free the memory we used for the bug report. */
    free(bug);

    /* We're done. */
    return 0;
}
```

bugrep Source Code: in Perl

The following is the source code for the Perl version of bugrep.

```
#!/usr/local/bin/perl
require "cgi-lib.pl";

#Change this path if this is not the location of sendmail on your
system

$SENDMAIL = "/lib/sendmail -t";

#Change this to your email address. Single quotes used to avoid
#interpretation of the @ sign by Perl.

$RECIPIENT = 'boutell@boutell.com';

print "Content-type: text/html\n\n";
print "<html>\n";
print "<head>\n";

#Parse the form arguments. Indicate that we want
#the results to appear in "values".
```

```
&ReadParse(*values);

#Use the information

#If any field is missing, complain!  if ((! $values{"name"} ) ||
     (! $values{"email"} ) ||
     (! $values{"bug"} ) ||
     (! $values{"system"} ) ||
     (! $values{"version"} ) ||
     ($values{"system"}  eq "PLEASE CHOOSE ONE") ||
     ($values{"version"}  eq "PLEASE CHOOSE ONE"))
{
     print "<title>Please fill out all the fields</title>\n";
     print "</head>\n";
     print "<h1>Please fill out all the fields</h1>\n";
     print "Please fill out the name, email address, software version,\n";
     print "system, and bug report fields. Back up to the previous page\n";
     print "to try again.\n";
     print "</body></html>\n";
     exit 0;
}

#OK, we have all the data. Write it to a file in which
#we collect bug from users. Open to append, of course.

$fname = "|" . $SENDMAIL; open(OUT, $fname);

print OUT "To: ", $RECIPIENT, "\n";
print OUT "From: ", $values{"name"} , " <", $values{"email"} , ">\n";
print OUT "Subject: bug report\n";
print OUT "\n";
print OUT "This bug report was submitted via the WWW-Email gateway.\n";
print OUT "--\n\n";
print OUT "System: ", $values{"system"} , "\n";
print OUT "Version: ", $values{"version"} , "\n";
print OUT $values{"bug"} , "\n";
close(OUT);

print "<title>Thank you, ", $values{"name"} , "</title>\n";
print "</head>\n";
print "<h1>Thank you, ", $values{"name"} , "</h1>\n";
print "Thank you for your bug report.\n";
print "</body></html>\n";
exit 0;
```

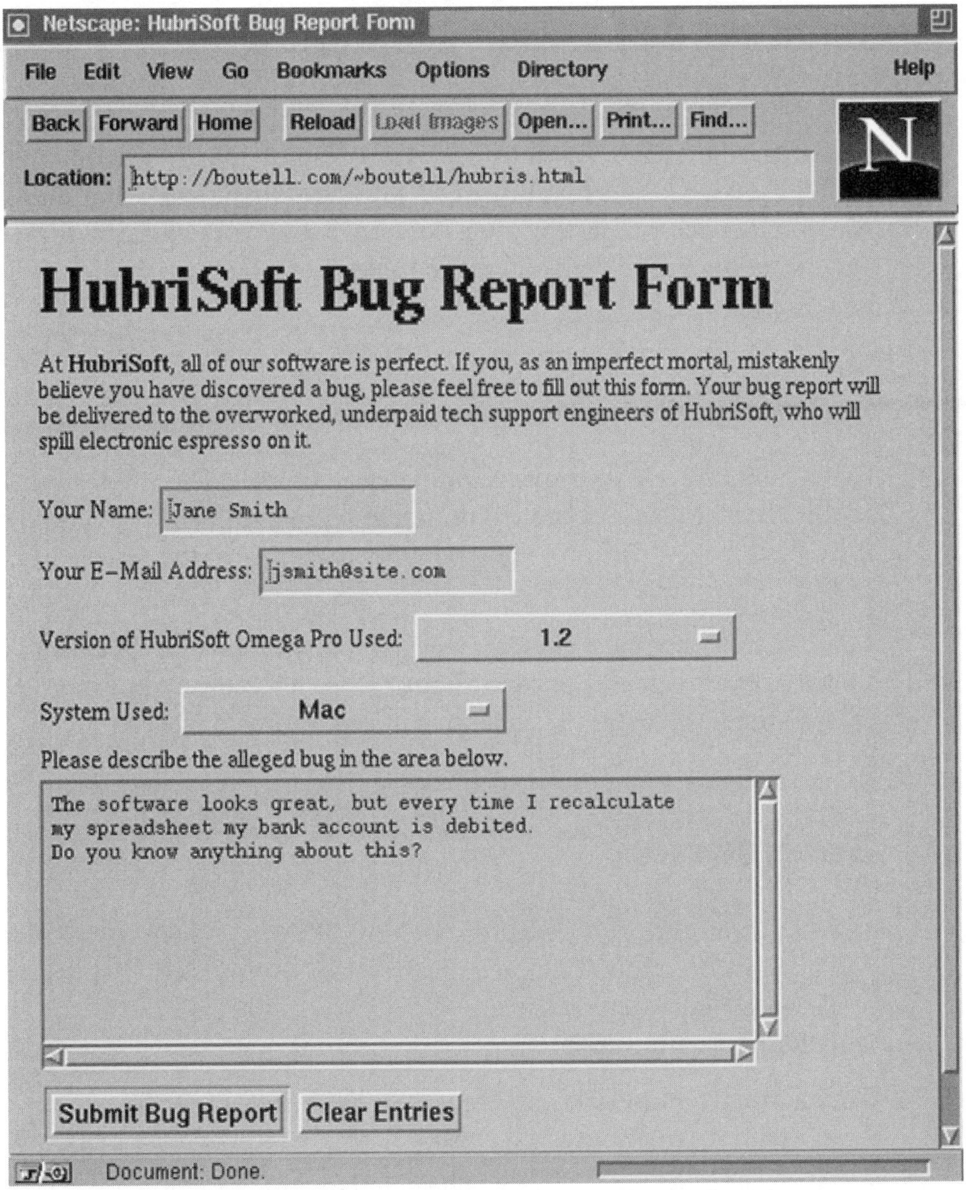

FIGURE 9–2 The HubriSoft bug report form in use

Existing CGI E-mail Packages

If you don't want to write your own, here are existing CGI e-mail packages available on the Web. The most impressive is cgiemail,[3] one of the MIT DCNS (Massachusetts Institute of Technology Distributed Computing and Network Services) CGI programs. cgiemail can work with any form and can be configured to deliver the e-mail in any format you desire.

Conclusion

CGI e-mail delivery is simple to implement, but tricky to implement safely. In this chapter I have examined both good and bad ways to go about sending e-mail from a CGI program and explored some of the security problems of CGI in the process.

I have covered the more mundane CGI applications. Now it's time to take a look at more creative applications of CGI, such as automatic image generation. In the next chapter I take a look at generating images on the fly.

References

1. ACM Committe on Computers and Public Policy, "Forum on Risks to the Public in Computers and Related Systems (comp.risks)." Moderated by Peter G. Neumann.
   [URL:news:comp.risks]

2. Hotwired Ventures LLC, "Welcome to HotWired."
   [URL:http://www.hotwired.com]

3. Massachusetts Institute of Technology Distributed Computing and Network Services, "MIT DCNS CGI Programs."
   [URL:http://web.mit.edu/afs/athena.mit.edu/astaff/project/wwwdev/www/dist/mit-dcns-cgi.html]

CHAPTER **10**

Multimedia: Generating Images in Dynamic Documents

Generating HTML on the fly is impressive, but some things cannot be expressed adequately by text alone. Sometimes it is enough to select one of many existing images to display as part of a CGI-generated page. At other times, however, even this is not enough. What is really needed is the ability to draw or modify images themselves as part of a CGI-generated Web page. Fortunately, this is not difficult to do, and the tools to accomplish it are readily available. In this chapter I will explore those tools and present a useful general-purpose piece of CGI code to generate bar charts as part of a Web page.

Pointing to Existing Images in a CGI-generated HTML Page

The simplest way to display a variety of images as part of a CGI-generated page is to generate a different <IMG SRC> tag depending on the desired image. This approach does not require the execution of a separate CGI program to generate the image. This tactic should be considered whenever the task can be accomplished using one of a reasonable number of images. The images can then be hand-drawn or computer-generated in advance.

The following short example program generates a link to a different image each time the page is accessed. To use it, you need to set the appropriate images URL in the code and place four GIF images in the directory pointed to by that URL named `image0.gif`, `image1.gif`, `image2.gif`, and `image3.gif`. A subdirectory of your personal Web pages directory is a good place to use. Make sure the files are readable by the Web server, of course.

For a Unix Makefile suitable to compile this program, see Appendix 5 as well as the CD.

Referencing Inline Images in C

The following is the source code for `refimage.c`. This program does not need to deal with forms, so it does not use the cgic library.

```c
/* Change this to the directory where your GIF images are kept.
      Make sure a final slash appears. This is NOT a file
      system path; it is the URL on your server where
      the images can be found. */

#define IMAGE_DIR_URL "/~boutell/images/"

#include <stdio.h>
#include <stdlib.h>

/* Included so we can get the current time for use
      as a random number "seed" to get a unique series
      of random numbers */
#include <time.h>

int main(int argc, char *argv[])
{
      time_t now;
      time(&now);
      char imagePath[256];
      int choice;
      srand((unsigned int)now);
      printf("Content-type: text/html\n\n");
      printf("<html>\n");
      printf("<head>\n");
```

```
printf("<title>Random Inline Images Demonstration</title>\n");
printf("</head>\n");
printf("<body>\n");
printf("<h1>Random Inline Images Demonstration</h1>\n");
printf("<p>This page contains one of four possible inline images,\n");
printf("selected at random.\n");

/* Choose a random winner from among the four images */
choice = rand() % 4;

/* Format the URL. */
sprintf(imagePath, "%s/image%d.gif", IMAGE_DIR_URL, choice);

/* Now output the <img src> tag. */
printf("<img src=\"%s\">\n", imageUrl);

printf("</body>\n");
printf("</html>\n");
return 0;
}
```

Referencing Inline Images in Perl

The following is the source code for refimage:

```
# Change this to the directory where your GIF images are kept.
# Make sure a final slash appears. This is NOT a file
# system path; it is the URL on your server where
# the images can be found.
$imageDirUrl = "/~boutell/images/";

print "Content-type: text/html\n\n";
print "<html>\n";
print "<head>\n";
print "<title>Random Inline Images Demonstration</title>\n";
print "</head>\n";
print "<body>\n";
print "<h1>Random Inline Images Demonstration</h1>\n";
print "<p>This page contains one of four possible inline images,\n";
print "selected at random.\n";

# Seed the random number generator. Uses the current time as a seed.
srand;

# Choose an image.
```

```
$choice = rand % 4;

# Format the URL.
$imagePath = $imageDirUrl . "/" . $choice . ".gif";

# Output the <img src> tag.
print "<img src=\"", $imagePath, \"">\n";

print "</body>\n";
print "</html>\n";

exit 0;
```

Random Numbers in CGI Programs

It is not uncommon for a CGI program to pick a random number for one purpose or another, as in the previous example. Often, programmers will call the rand() function in C or Perl, only to discover that their CGI program always makes the same random choice. This is because the random-number generator must first be "seeded" with a piece of information that varies from one run to the next. Otherwise, the series of "random" numbers will always be the same!

In C, a reasonable solution is to use the current time as a seed when calling the srand() function. This is demonstrated in the previous example. Perl also has an srand() function. If no argument is specified, Perl's version of srand() conveniently does exactly the same thing as my C code: It uses the current time as the seed value.

The current time is a reasonable seed value for most applications, but not if you are generating passwords or some other piece of information that has important security implications. In such cases, it is best to use some other piece of fast-changing information, such as the process ID of your program, in addition to the current time.

Astute readers may point out that the rand() function is usually not a particularly good random-number generator. This is true, but it is generally sufficient for simple applications. Generating better random numbers is a complex topic and is outside the scope of this book.

Generating Dynamic Images: MIME Types and Multimedia

The previous code is handy when one of a set of existing images will do. But it is not good enough when a new, unique image is desired. To obtain such an image, a GIF (or another type of image) must be generated on the fly in a CGI program.

There are really two issues here: how to correctly transmit the image to the user and how to generate the image.

Inline Images: How They Really Work

Repeat this mantra to yourself a few hundred times: "Every inline image is a document in its own right!"

When a browser encounters an inline image reference in the middle of a document such as this one:

```
<img src = "foo.gif">
```

It opens a *completely new connection* back to the server in order to obtain the GIF. The server, in turn, looks for that file and retrieves it in much the same way that it retrieves an HTML document. All documents are of equal importance, as far as the server is concerned. *The server doesn't even know* that the GIF is an inline image.

What does this mean for us? It means that a CGI program can generate a GIF file or other image document just as easily as it can an HTML document. All it must do is specify the correct content type before outputting the image.

A CGI Program That Delivers an Image Instead of HTML

The following short CGI program delivers a GIF-format image, rather than an HTML document.

Essentially, it is necessary to specify the correct content type for a GIF image rather than an HTML document. This is done by outputting the following content type line instead of the usual `text/html` as follows:

```
Content-type: image/gif
```

followed by two line breaks, as always.

After that point, the raw GIF image data can simply be sent to standard output, character by character. However, care must be taken to ensure the binary data is not mangled by the operating system. Developers of CGI programs for MSDOS, OS/2, Windows NT, and related operating systems should see the next note.

Delivering Images in C

The following is the source code for `dimage.c`. This program does not need to deal with forms, so it does not use the cgic library.

> **NOTE TO PC PROGRAMMERS:** Programmers of the MSDOS, MS Windows NT, MS Windows, and IBM OS/2 environments must make sure that standard output is in binary mode before attempting to transmit GIF images and other binary documents from CGI programs. It is not sufficient to open all input files in binary mode; output must also take place in binary mode. Otherwise, the operating system will attempt to translate carriage returns and line feeds and so mangle the binary file. This mode setting can be accomplished by including the include file `fcntl.h` at the beginning of the program and calling `_setmode(fileno(STDOUT), O_BINARY);` as soon as it is known that the output of the program will be a binary file. In Perl, this can be accomplished with the statement `binmode(STDOUT);`.

This program expects to find a GIF-format image at the specified location in your file system. The next example actually generates an image. It demonstrates how to deliver one properly from a CGI program.

For a Unix Makefile suitable to compile this program, see Appendix 5 as well as the CD.

```c
#include <stdio.h>

/* Make sure MSDOS is defined if you are using NT, MSDOS or OS/2! */

#ifdef MSDOS
```

```
#include <fcntl.h>
#endif /* MSDOS */

#define IMAGE_FILE "/home/boutell/images/test.gif"

int main(int argc, char *argv)
{
    int ch;
    FILE *in;
    /* The 'b' ensures that the file is opened in binary mode.
         This is very important on DOS and related systems
         such as NT and OS/2. It does no harm on other systems. */
    in = fopen(IMAGE_FILE, "rb");
    if (!in) {
         /* Uh-oh, no such image */
         printf("Status: 404 Not Found\n\n");
         printf("dimage could not find the image to send!\n");
         exit(0);
    }
    /* Make sure MSDOS is defined if you are using NT, MSDOS or
OS/2! */
#ifdef MSDOS
    _setmode(fileno(stdout), O_BINARY);
#endif /* MSDOS */
    printf("Content-type: image/gif\n\n");
    /* Now write the contents of the file to standard output */
    while (1) {
         ch = getc(in);
         if (ch == EOF) {
              break;
         }
         putc(ch, stdout);
    }
    fclose(in);
    return 0;
}
```

Delivering Images in Perl

The following is the Perl source code for dimage.

This program expects to find a GIF-format image at the specified location in your file system. The next example actually generates an image. It demonstrates how to deliver one properly from a CGI program.

```
$imageFile = "/home/boutell/images/test.gif";

if (!open(GIF, $imageFile)) {
      # All is not well
      print "Status: 404 Not Found\n\n";
      print "dimage could not find the image to send!\n";
      exit 0;
}
binmode(GIF);
# All is well
print "Content-type: image/gif\n\n";
binmode(STDOUT);
# Do reads of up to 4096 bytes at a time instead
# of reading line-by-line. This is binary data and
# line breaks may be few and far between.

while (read(GIF, $buffer, 4096)) {
      print $buffer;
}

close(GIF);

exit 0;
```

Using the dimage Program

The dimage program can be tested by installing it in your CGI directory or renaming it appropriately to ensure that your server recognizes it as a CGI program. When you access the program's URL, your Web browser will download the image and display it directly. Depending on your configuration, an external viewer may be launched to display the image instead.

Using the dimage Program from a Web Page

Be sure to try out the dimage program as a component of an HTML page that references it as an inline image. Consider the following example:

```
<html>
<head>
<title>An Inline Image Delivered by a CGI Program</title>
</head>
<body>
```

```
<h1>An Inline Image Delivered by a CGI Program</h1>
<img src="http://myserver/cgi-bin/dimage">
</body>
</html>
```

You will need to change the URL in the `<img src>` tag to refer to the correct location of the dimage program on your own server. You may use a relative URL rather than an absolute URL.

If It Doesn't Work

The dimage program should successfully transmit an image to your browser when the correct URL is accessed. If not, there are several possible reasons why. If the server reports that the CGI program could not be executed, you probably have not installed the dimage program at the correct location. If the dimage program indicates politely that the GIF file could not be found, check the IMAGE_FILE or `$imageFile` setting at the beginning of the program and change it appropriately.

URL "Extensions" (also known as, "If It STILL Doesn't Work")

One final and more problematic possibility: Some Web browsers have been known to refuse to display an image unless the URL has the right extension, such as `.gif` or `.jpeg`.

Q *"Hey! You just told me that the content type is all that matters!"*

A Yes, and I told you the truth. Web browsers that pay any attention whatsoever to the "extension" on a URL are broken. Unfortunately, they do exist. Many versions of NCSA Mosaic for Windows have this bug.

Q *"So what can I do about it?"*

A Sneak around the problem! Add `/dummy.gif` to the end of the URL after the name of your image-generating CGI program. Your server will still recognize your program and will pass `/dummy.gif` to your program in the PATH_INFO environment variable. You are free to take advantage of this information or ignore it completely.

Try this in the previous HTML document. Change the URL to

```
<img src="http://myserver/cgi-bin/dimage/dummy.gif">
```

The simple example program given previously will ignore it completely and just do the right thing. Several later examples will take advantage of PATH_INFO to determine whether a particular execution of the program is meant to generate an image or the HTML document that refers to it.

Off-the-shelf Ways to Generate Images

Q *"Great, so how do I draw a new image on the fly? I've got some stock quotes, some dew point temperatures, some widget sales figures. How can I graph this stuff?"*

A Depending on what you want to accomplish, generating images dynamically can be quite easy. The well-known free software package gnuplot[1] is available for many platforms and supports a reasonable range of plotting features (see Figure 10–1). The equally well-known netpbm[2] utilities can be used to convert, scale, combine, and otherwise manipulate images in interesting ways, all from the command line.

Command line tools like gnuplot and the netpbm utilities are very convenient, as long as your application meets two conditions:

1. The capabilities of gnuplot and netpbm are sufficient for your needs.

   This requirement is probably met if you simply need to draw a quick graph. If your intentions are more artistic and/or idiosyncratic, gnuplot may not prove sufficient.

2. The speed of gnuplot and/or the netpbm utilities is sufficient for your application.

   Speed becomes a major issue if you are generating images dynamically as a part of many pages in your site or creating an interactive application in which the user will have to wait for the images over and over. Because the netpbm utilities are very flexible, they are also not particularly fast for Web tasks, particularly the common case of adding a small amount of information to an existing GIF image in a hurry.

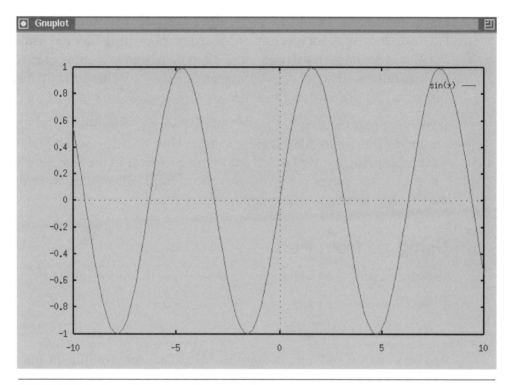

FIGURE 10–1 A graph produced by gnuplot

Using the gd Graphics Library

The gd[3] graphics library that I wrote is a handy set of functions to create, read, draw upon, and write GIF-format images. Future versions will also support the new PNG[4] image format. Although gd is written in C, wrappers are available to take advantage of it from many other languages, including Perl (version 5.0 or higher). The rest of this book uses gd extensively.

Fortunately, it is included on the CD. See Appendix 5 for more information about the contents of the CD and alternative sources for those materials.

Because gd is a general-purpose drawing library, it can be used to draw a wide variety of things. Graphs are a particularly popular application of dynamic GIFs on the Web. This chapter presents a handy graphing module you can reuse in your own projects.

The gd graphics library provides routines to create, manipulate, and destroy GIF-format images. Images can be loaded from existing files or created anew, and portions of existing images can be pasted into others to create sophisticated results. Of course, images can also be written to GIF-format files or output directly to a Web browser from a CGI program.

If you are programming in C, you will first want to compile the gd library, producing the library file `libgd.a` (under Unix). The provided Makefiles on the CD assume the gd distribution can be found in the directory `../gd1.2`, and this is in fact the way the example directories are laid out on the CD. See Appendix 5 for more information.

Using gd from Perl

To write gd programs in Perl, you need to have the following items:

1. Perl version 5.0 or later

2. The `GD.pm`[5] Perl module

Perl versions 5.0 and later support the use of existing compiled C modules from within Perl programs. This is very useful, as it allows Perl to be extended without recompiling the entire Perl interpreter. (On some platforms, dynamic linking may not be available. In those cases, Perl can be relinked to include `GD.pm`.)

The `GD.pm` module is a wrapper that provides access to the capabilities of gd from within Perl. It is included on the CD. See Appendix 5 for more information.

Basic gd Programming Techniques

The following discussion provides short examples in C. One language was chosen for ease of readability; however, the complete examples following this discussion are in both C and Perl. As you will see, there is little difference between gd code in C and gd code in Perl.

gd programs usually begin with the creation of a `gdImagePtr` object, like this:

```
/* At the beginning of the function */
gdImagePtr im;
```

```
/* Create an image 256 pixels across by 256 pixels down */
im = gdImageCreate(256, 256);
```

Next, we invoke a number of gd functions to alter the image. For instance, consider the following code:

```
/* Variable declarations; do this at the beginning of the function */
int black, red;

/* ... after creating the image ... */

black = gdImageColorAllocate(im, 0, 0, 0);
```

Here, gdImageColorAllocate() asks gd to provide a pen of the specified color for use with the image. Note, the image pointer is the first argument to nearly all gd functions in C.

The first allocated color automatically becomes the color of all background pixels in the image. Next we allocate a color to draw with as follows:

```
red = gdImageColorAllocate(im, 255, 0, 0);
```

The second through fourth arguments to gdImageColorAllocate are the red, green, and blue components of the color, respectively. Thus black is 0,0,0, while red is 255,0,0.

Now consider the following drawing command:

```
gdImageArc(im, 128, 128, 255, 255, 0, 360, red);
```

This command draws an arc in red, centered in the image, from zero through 360 degrees, with a width and height reaching the edges of the image. In other words, it draws a red circle in the middle of the image that extends to the edges (see Figure 10–2).

Drawing an image doesn't accomplish much unless there is a way to write the image to a GIF file. This is done using the gdImageGif() function as follows:

```
/* Variable declaration; put this line at the beginning of the
program */
FILE *out;

/* ... After drawing the image, but before destroying it ... */

out = fopen("test.gif", "wb");
gdImageGif(im, out);
fclose(out);
```

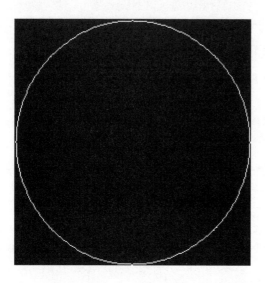

FIGURE 10–2 The red circle example

After manipulating a gd image, you need to return the memory associated with the image to the system. This is done with the following line of code:

```
gdImageDestroy(im);
```

For a complete example of a functional gd program, read on.

A Simple gd Example Program

The following program, gd short, is not a CGI program. Rather, it is a simple command-line program demonstrating the proper use of the gd library to draw a GIF image. Build and test this simple example program to make sure you have properly compiled and installed the gd library on your system.

When run successfully, gdshort should produce the file test.gif. Any GIF viewing program should have no difficulty displaying it. See Figure 10–3.

gdshort.c: in C

The following is the C source code of gdshort.c.

```
#include <stdio.h>
/* If gd.h is not in the search path for includes, specify a full
path here */
#include "gd.h"
```

```
int main(int argc, char *argv[])
{
    /* Declare a pointer to an image. This pointer acts as a "handle"
        through which the image is accessed. */
    gdImagePtr im;

    /* Color indexes. Once set, these values will be used as
        "pens" to draw on the image. */
    int black, white;

    /* The file pointer to which the file will be written. */
    FILE *out;

    /* Create the image. */
    im = gdImageCreate(100, 100);

    /* Allocate the background color (black; red, green, and blue
        values are all zero). The image is always the first argument. */
    black = gdImageColorAllocate(im, 0, 0, 0);

    /* Allocate the foreground color (white; red, green, and blue
        values are all at maximum). */
    white = gdImageColorAllocate(im, 255, 255, 255);

    /* Now draw a solid white rectangle in the middle of the image. */
    gdImageFilledRectangle(im, 25, 25, 74, 74, white);

    /* Almost done: we still have to write the image to a file.
        Note that the file is opened for writing in binary mode.
        This is crucial under DOS and related operating systems. */
    out = fopen("test.gif", "wb");

    /* Write the image to the file in GIF format. */
    gdImageGif(im, out);

    /* Close the file. */
    fclose(out);

    /* Destroy the image. This is important in order to return
        memory to the operating system properly! */
    gdImageDestroy(im);

    /* All went well. */
    return 0;
}
```

FIGURE 10–3 The solid white rectangle example

Compiling gdshort.c

To build gdshort successfully, you need to link it with the gd library. Under Unix, the following Makefile will do the trick, provided the gd library has been successfully compiled in an adjacent directory. Change LIBDIRS and INCLUDEDIRS if you have installed gd somewhere else. A Makefile for all C programs in this book is also included on the CD and in Appendix 5.

For other platforms, particularly DOS and related platforms, compile gd as a static library and add it to the list of libraries to be linked with the project you create for gdshort. Also be sure to add the directory containing gd to the list of directories to be searched for #include files.

> **NOTE:** gd was not written with the 16-bit DOS memory models in mind. Use the large memory model and modify the gd library source code to `malloc()` all arrays. Better yet, use a 32-bit compiler under Windows NT or Windows 95.

The following is a Makefile for the gdshort program.

```
#A list of all the programs we are interested in compiling,
#as our first target

all: gdshort

#Change this to the ANSI C compiler on your system if you do not have
gcc
CC=gcc

#Any additional directories in which libraries will be found
LIBDIRS=-L../gd1.2

#Any additional directories in which include files will be found
INCLUDEDIRS=-I../gd1.2
```

```
#Rule to create object files from C source files

.c.o: $<
      ${CC} $< ${INCLUDEDIRS}  -c

#Libraries to be linked against
LIBS=-lgd -lm

#Rule to create gdshort from the object files that compose it

gdshort: gdshort.o
    ${CC}  gdshort.o -o gdshort ${LIBDIRS}  ${LIBS}
```

See Chapter 8 for an introduction to Unix Makefiles.

gdshort in Perl

The following is the Perl source code for gdshort:

```perl
#!/usr/local/bin/perl

#Please note: before taking advantage of this module,
#you must install the GD.pm Perl package. See the
#GD.pm documentation for details.

use GD;

# Create the image.
$im = new GD::Image(100,100);

# Allocate the background color (black; red, green, and blue
# values are all zero). The image is always the first argument.
$black = $im->colorAllocate(0,0,0);

# Allocate the foreground color (white; red, green, and blue
# values are all at maximum).
$white = $im->colorAllocate(255, 255, 255);

# Now draw a solid white rectangle in the middle of the image.
$im->filledRectangle(25, 25, 74, 74, $white);

# Almost done: we still have to write the image to a file.
# NOTE: no special provision is made here to open the file
# in binary mode. If you are using DOS, OS/2, Windows or
# Windows NT, consult the documentation of your Perl
# interpreter for more information about opening files
```

```
# in binary mode.

# Open the file.

open(OUT, ">test.gif") || die "Can't open test.gif\n";

# Write the image to the file in GIF format.

$data = $im->gif;

print OUT $data;

# Close the file.

close(OUT);

# It is not necessary to explicitly destroy the image.
# Perl will clean up the resources automatically.

# All went well.
exit 0;
```

Drawing Graphs on the Fly

Although gd has the capability to draw almost anything, this doesn't mean that drawing an elaborate graphic from scratch is always an appealing prospect.

The following example presents a useful charting module that generates bar charts of the information passed to it, with appropriate labels on the x- and y-axes. Feel free to elaborate on this module.

This chart module is designed to accept a gd image, a set of values to be charted, a unit of measurement, and a set of labels for each entry on the x-axis. The code is intended to handle a wide range of values in a reasonable manner. For instance, if the range of values on the y-axis extends into four digits or more, values will be scaled by a factor of one thousand, one million, or more as needed. The legend displayed as part of the graph indicates the scaling factor used. This module does not, however, attempt to scale up very small values (values less than .001).

A short test program, testc, follows the charting module. This test program is a CGI program and can be referenced from a Web page by using an <IMG SRC> tag, as with any other inline image.

Declarations for the Chart Module, in C: chart.h

The following is the #include file, chart.h, for the chart module.

```
#ifndef CHART_H
#define CHART_H 1

#include "gd.h"

/* The C exclusive OR operator | can be used to combine
      any or all of these. */

#define chartBar 1
#define chartCross 2
#define chartLine 4

typedef int chartType;

/* A module to draw a chart on the specified gd image. The
      chart will occupy the entire image. The image should
      be created first with gdImageCreate(). The "units"
      string must be no longer than 100 characters! */

void chartDraw(gdImagePtr im, chartType t,
      char **labels, char *units, float *data, int points);

#endif /* CHART_H */
```

Source Code for the Charting Module, in C: chart.c

The following is the source code for the charting module.

```
#include <math.h>
#include <stdio.h>

#include "chart.h"
#include "gdfontl.h"

/* Color definitions. These can be changed here. */
```

```
#define BACKGROUND        192, 192, 192
#define BORDER            0,   0,   0
#define TEXT              0,   0,   0
#define BAR               255, 64,  64
#define LINE              64,  64,  255
#define CROSS             64,  160, 64
#define TICK              64,  64,  64

/* A module to draw a chart on the specified gd image. The
      chart will occupy the entire image. */

void chartDraw(gdImagePtr im, chartType t,
      char **labels, char *units, float *data, int points)
{
      /* Basic colors */
      int backgroundColor;
      int barColor;
      int lineColor;
      int crossColor;
      int borderColor;
      int textColor;
      int tickColor;

      /* Range of data */
      float dataMin, dataMax, dataRange;

      /* Spacing */
      int spaceX, spaceY, baseX, baseY;

      int i;

      /* Previous pixel, to draw continuous lines */
      int lastX, lastY;

      /* Points for polygons */
      gdPoint p[4];

      float lastLabel;

      int first;

      /* Divisor to use to make the display of units
            on the Y axis manageable. */
      float divisor;
```

```
/* The size of a Y-axis tick, and an accumulator
        to progress through ticks. */
float tick, tickAccum;

/* First, allocate colors. */
backgroundColor = gdImageColorAllocate(im, BACKGROUND);

/* Set this as the transparent color for the GIF. */
gdImageColorTransparent(im, backgroundColor);

borderColor = gdImageColorAllocate(im, BORDER);

textColor = gdImageColorAllocate(im, TEXT);

tickColor = gdImageColorAllocate(im, TICK);

if (!points) {
        /* Nothing to draw! */
        return;
}

if (t & chartBar) {
        barColor = gdImageColorAllocate(im, BAR);
}
if (t & chartLine) {
        lineColor = gdImageColorAllocate(im, LINE);
}
if (t & chartCross) {
        crossColor = gdImageColorAllocate(im, CROSS);
}

/* Second, find the range of the data. */
for (i=0; (i < points); i++) {
        if ((!i) || (data[i] < dataMin)) {
                dataMin = data[i];
        }
        if ((!i) || (data[i] > dataMax)) {
                dataMax = data[i];
        }
}
dataRange = dataMax - dataMin;

/* Decide how much space is available. Start with all of it... */

spaceX = gdImageSX(im);
```

```
/* The left edge is occupied by the Y axis labels and numbers,
     plus a bit of space for aesthetic purposes... */
baseX = 0;
if (units) {
     baseX += gdFontLarge->h;
}

baseX += gdFontLarge->h + 2;
/* Subtract that space from the space available for the graph... */
spaceX -= baseX;

/* Now compute the space available on the Y axis. */
spaceY = gdImageSY(im);

spaceY -= (gdFontLarge->h + 2);

baseY = 0;

/* Make sure we don't divide by zero. */
if (!dataRange) {
     dataRange = 1.0;
}

/* Discover how many Y-axis "ticks" are appropriate.
     There should be at least two and no more than twenty, and
     the step between ticks should be a power of ten. */
tick = pow(10.0, floor(log10(dataRange / 2.0)));
tickAccum = tick * ceil(dataMin / tick);

/* Decide the divisor for labels.
     Powers of 1000 are familiar
     to the user. */
divisor = 1.0;
if (abs(dataMax) > abs(dataMin)) {
     while (abs(dataMax) / divisor >= 1000.0) {
          divisor *= 1000.0;
     }
} else {
     while (abs(dataMin) / divisor >= 1000.0) {
          divisor *= 1000.0;
     }
}
/* Draw the tick lines now, so they will appear
     "behind" the graph. Also label the ticks
```

```
                        as often as is possible without crowding. */

first = 1;
while (tickAccum <= dataMax) {
        int y = spaceY - (spaceY * (tickAccum - dataMin) / dataRange)
                + baseY;
        int textY;
        char s[20];
        int w;
        /* Format the tick label, and see if there is enough
                space after the previous one to make room for
                a text label. */
        sprintf(s, "%3.2f", tickAccum / divisor);
        w = gdFontLarge->w * strlen(s);
        textY = y + w/2;
        if (first || (textY < lastLabel)) {
                /* Don't actually draw it unless it fits
                        in the image */
                if ((textY - w > baseY) &&
                        (textY < (spaceY + baseY))) {
                        gdImageStringUp(im, gdFontLarge,
                                baseX - gdFontLarge->h,
                                textY, s, textColor);
                }
                /* The extra two pixels are for aesthetic purposes */
                lastLabel = y - w/2 - 2;
                first = 0;
        }
        gdImageLine(im, baseX, y, baseX + spaceX, y, tickColor);
        tickAccum += tick;
}

/* Now draw the graph. */
for (i=0; (i < points); i++) {
        int x, y, w;
        x = spaceX * (i + 1) / (points + 1) + baseX;
        y = spaceY - (spaceY * (data[i] - dataMin) / dataRange)
                + baseY;
        if (labels) {
                int label;
                w = strlen(labels[i]) * gdFontLarge->w;
                label = x - w / 2;
                if ((!i) || (label > lastLabel)) {
                        if ((label > 0) &&
```

```
                                (label + w < baseX + spaceX)) {
                                gdImageString(im, gdFontLarge,
                                        label, baseY +
                                        spaceY + 2, labels[i],
                                        textColor);
                        }
                        lastLabel = x + w / 2 + 2;
                }
        }

        if (t & chartBar) {
                /* Compute the width, then assemble the
                        points of a polygon. */
                w = (spaceX / (points + 1));

                /* Reduce the width to two-thirds, making
                        the bars easier to tell apart. */
                w = w * 2 / 3;

                /* Set up the points. */
                p[0].x = x - w / 2;
                p[0].y = y;
                p[1].x = x + w / 2;
                p[1].y = y;
                p[2].x = x + w / 2;
                p[2].y = baseY + spaceY - 1;
                p[3].x = x - w / 2;
                p[3].y = baseY + spaceY - 1;

                /* Fill the polygon. */
                gdImageFilledPolygon(im, p, 4, barColor);
        }
        if (t & chartLine) {
                if (i) {
                        gdImageLine(im, lastX, lastY, x, y, lineColor);
                }
        }
        if (t & chartCross) {
                gdImageLine(im, x-2, y-2, x+2, y+2, crossColor);
                gdImageLine(im, x+2, y-2, x-2, y+2, crossColor);
        }
        lastX = x;
        lastY = y;
}
```

```
/* Draw the border lines at left and bottom... */
gdImageLine(im, baseX, baseY, baseX, baseY + spaceY, borderColor);
gdImageLine(im, baseX, baseY + spaceY,
        baseX + spaceX, baseY + spaceY, borderColor);

/* Label the Y axis (units) */
if (units) {
    int h;
    char label[121];
    if (divisor != 1.0) {
        sprintf(label, "%sx%.0f", units, divisor);
    } else {
        sprintf(label, "%s", units);
    }
    /* Rotated 90 degrees */
    h = gdFontLarge->w * strlen(label);
    gdImageStringUp(im, gdFontLarge,
        0, baseY + (spaceY / 2) + (h / 2),
        label, textColor);
} else {
    int h;
    char label[121];
    if (divisor != 1.0) {
        sprintf(label, "x%.0f", divisor);
    } else {
        sprintf(label, "");
    }
    /* Rotated 90 degrees */
    h = gdFontLarge->w * strlen(label);
    gdImageStringUp(im, gdFontLarge,
        0, baseY + (spaceY / 2) + (h / 2),
        label, textColor);
    }
}
```

Source Code for the Charting Test Program, in C: testc.c

The following is the source code for a simple demonstration of the chart module.

```
#include "chart.h"

#include <stdlib.h>
```

```
#include <time.h>

int main(int argc, char *argv[])
{
      gdImagePtr im;
      int points;
      float data[100];
      char *labels[100];
      int i;
      time_t t;
      int m;
      time(&t);
      srand((int) t);
      m = rand() % 1000000;
      im = gdImageCreate(400, 300);
      points = (rand() % 50);
      for (i=0; (i < points); i++) {
            data[i] = rand() % m;
            labels[i] = (char *) malloc(5);
            sprintf(labels[i], "%d", i);
      }
      chartDraw(im, chartBar | chartLine | chartCross,
            labels, "Widgets", data, points);
      printf("Pragma: nocache\n");
      printf("Content-type: image/gif\n\n");
      gdImageGif(im, stdout);
      for (i=0; (i < points); i++) {
            free(labels[i]);
      }
      gdImageDestroy(im);
      return 0;
}
```

Compiling testc

To compile testc, compile `chart.c` and `test.c` as part of the same project
and link them to the gd library. As with the first example, be sure that the
library has been compiled as a static library and that `gd.h` is in one of the
include directories searched by your compiler.

For a Makefile suitable for compiling testc or any other C program in this
book, see the CD as well as Appendix 5.

Source Code for the Chart module, in Perl: chart.pl

The following is the source code for the Perl version of the charting module.

```perl
#!/usr/local/bin/perl

# The following is a Perl version of the charting function.

# The Perl OR operator | can be used to combine
# any or all of these.

$chartBar = 1;
$chartCross = 2;
$chartLine = 4;

# A function to draw a chart on the specified gd image. The
# chart will occupy the entire image. The image should
# be created first with gdImageCreate(). The "units"
# string must be no longer than 100 characters!
#
# chartDraw should be invoked with a GD.pm image object,
# the chart type (see above), an array of X axis labels
# (which can be empty), the unit of measurement
# for the Y axis, and an array of numeric data values.

use GD;

sub chartDraw
{
        local($im, $t, *labels, $units, *data) = @_;

    $points = @data;

    # First, allocate colors.
    $backgroundColor = $im->colorAllocate(192, 192, 192);

    # Set this as the transparent color for the GIF.
    $im->transparent($backgroundColor);

    $borderColor = $im->colorAllocate(0, 0, 0);

    $textColor = $im->colorAllocate(0, 0, 0);

    $tickColor = $im->colorAllocate(64, 64, 64);
```

```perl
if (! $points) {
    # Nothing to draw!
    return;
}

if ($t & $chartBar) {
    $barColor = $im->colorAllocate(255, 64, 64);
}
if ($t & $chartLine) {
    $lineColor = $im->colorAllocate(64, 64, 255);
}
if ($t & $chartCross) {
    $crossColor = $im->colorAllocate(64, 160, 64);
}

# Second, find the range of the data.
for ($i = 0; ($i < $points); $i++) {
    if ((!$i) || ($data[$i] < $dataMin)) {
        $dataMin = $data[$i];
    }
    if ((!$i) || ($data[$i] > $dataMax)) {
        $dataMax = $data[$i];
    }
}
$dataRange = $dataMax - $dataMin;

# Decide how much space is available. Start with all of it...

@imSize = $im->getBounds();
$spaceX = $imSize[0];

# The left edge is occupied by the Y axis labels and numbers,
# plus a bit of space for aesthetic purposes...
$baseX = 0;
if ($units ne "") {
    $baseX += gdLargeFont->height;
}

$baseX += gdLargeFont->height + 2;

# Subtract that space from the space available for the graph...
$spaceX -= $baseX;

# Now compute the space available on the Y axis.
$spaceY = $imSize[1];
```

```
$spaceY -= (gdLargeFont->height + 2);

$baseY = 0;

# Make sure we don't divide by zero.
if (!$dataRange) {
    $dataRange = 1.0;
}

# Discover how many Y-axis "ticks" are appropriate.
# There should be at least two and no more than twenty, and
# the step between ticks should be a power of ten.
$tick = 10.0 ** int(log($dataRange / 2.0) / log(10.0));
$tickAccum = $tick * (int($dataMin / $tick) + 1);

# Decide the divisor for labels.
# Powers of 1000 are familiar
# to the user.
$divisor = 1.0;
if (abs($dataMax) > abs($dataMin)) {
    while (abs($dataMax) / $divisor >= 1000.0) {
        $divisor *= 1000.0;
    }
} else {
    while (abs($dataMin) / $divisor >= 1000.0) {
        $divisor *= 1000.0;
    }
}
# Draw the tick lines now, so they will appear
# "behind" the graph. Also label the ticks
# as often as is possible without crowding.

$first = 1;
while ($tickAccum <= $dataMax) {
    $y = $spaceY - ($spaceY * ($tickAccum - $dataMin) / $dataRange)
        + $baseY;
    # Format the tick label, and see if there is enough
    # space after the previous one to make room for
    # a text label.
    $s = sprintf("%3.2f", $tickAccum / $divisor);
    $w = gdLargeFont->width * length($s);
    $textY = $y + $w / 2;
    if ($first || ($textY < $lastLabel)) {
        # Don't actually draw it unless it fits
        # in the image
```

```
            if (($textY - $w > $baseY) &&
                ($textY < ($spaceY + $baseY))) {
                $im->stringUp(gdLargeFont,
                    $baseX - gdLargeFont->height,
                    $textY, $s, $textColor);
            }
            # The extra two pixels are for aesthetic purposes
            $lastLabel = $y - $w / 2 - 2;
            $first = 0;
        }
        $im->line($baseX, $y, $baseX + $spaceX, $y, $tickColor);
        $tickAccum += $tick;
    }


# Now draw the graph.
for ($i=0; ($i < $points); $i++) {
    local($x, $y, $w) = (0, 0, 0);
    $x = $spaceX * ($i + 1) / ($points + 1) + $baseX;
    $y = $spaceY - ($spaceY * ($data[$i] - $dataMin) / $dataRange)
        + $baseY;
    if ($i <= $#labels) {
        $w = length($labels[$i]) * gdLargeFont->width;
        $label = $x - $w / 2;
        if ((!$i) || ($label > $lastLabel)) {
            if (($label > 0) &&
                ($label + $w < $baseX + $spaceX)) {
                $im->string(gdLargeFont,
                    $label, $baseY +
                    $spaceY + 2, $labels[$i],
                    $textColor);
            }
            $lastLabel = $x + $w / 2 + 2;
        }
    }


    if ($t & $chartBar) {
        # Compute the width, then assemble the
        # points of a polygon.
        $w = ($spaceX / ($points + 1));

        # Reduce the width to two-thirds, making
        # the bars easier to tell apart.
        $w = $w * 2 / 3;
```

```
        # Set up the points.

        $p = new GD::Polygon;
        $p->addPt($x - $w / 2, $y);
        $p->addPt($x + $w / 2, $y);
        $p->addPt($x + $w / 2, $baseY + $spaceY - 1);
        $p->addPt($x - $w / 2, $baseY + $spaceY - 1);

        # Fill the polygon.
        $im->filledPolygon($p, $barColor);
    }
    if ($t & $chartLine) {
        if ($i) {
            $im->line($lastX, $lastY, $x, $y, $lineColor);
        }
    }
    if ($t & $chartCross) {
        $im->line($x - 2, $y - 2, $x + 2, $y + 2, $crossColor);
        $im->line($x + 2, $y - 2, $x - 2, $y + 2, $crossColor);
    }
    $lastX = $x;
    $lastY = $y;
}

# Draw the border lines at left and bottom...
$im->line($baseX, $baseY, $baseX, $baseY + $spaceY, $borderColor);
$im->line($baseX, $baseY + $spaceY,
    $baseX + $spaceX, $baseY + $spaceY, $borderColor);

# Label the Y axis (units)
if ($units ne "") {
    local($h, $label) = ( 0 , "" );
    if ($divisor != 1.0) {
        $label = sprintf("%sx%.0f", $units, $divisor);
    } else {
        $label = units;
    }
    # Rotated 90 degrees
    $h = gdLargeFont->width * length($label);
    $im->stringUp(gdLargeFont,
        0, $baseY + ($spaceY / 2) + ($h / 2),
        $label, $textColor);
} else {
```

```
            local($h, $label) = ( 0 , "" );
            if ($divisor != 1.0) {
                    $label = sprintf("x%.0f", $divisor);
            } else {
                    $label = "";
            }
            # Rotated 90 degrees
            $h = gdLargeFont->width * length(label);
            $im->stringUp(gdLargeFont,
                    0, $baseY + ($spaceY / 2) + ($h / 2),
                    $label, $textColor);
        }
    }
```

Source Code for the Chart Test Program, in Perl: testc

The following is the Perl source code for a simple demonstration of the chart module.

```
#!/usr/local/bin/perl
# "use GD.pm" is taken care of by requiring chart.pl

require "chart.pl";

srand;
$m = int(rand(1000000)) + 1;
$im = new GD::Image(400, 300);
$points = int(rand(50)) + 1;

for ($i = 0; ($i < $points); $i++) {
    $data[$i] = rand($m);
    $labels[$i] = sprintf("%d", $i);
}

chartDraw($im, $chartBar | $chartLine | $chartCross,
    *labels, "Widgets", *data);

print "Pragma: nocache\n";
print "Content-type: image/gif\n\n";
$data = $im->gif;

print $data;
exit 0;
```

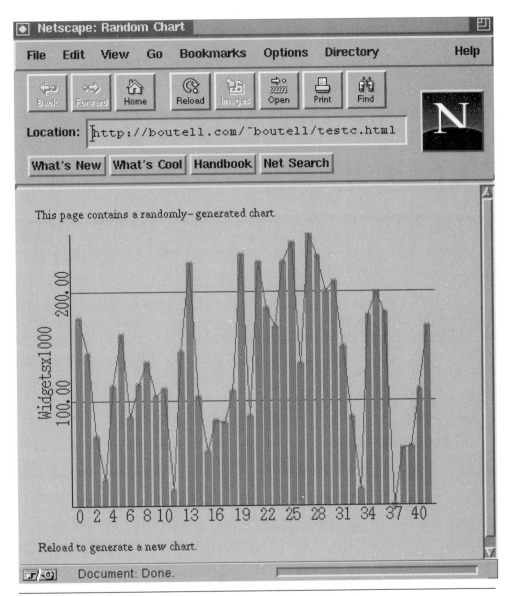

FIGURE 10–4 Bar charts drawn by gd

Testing testc

To try out testc, simply install the software as you have installed other CGI programs and reference it from an <IMG SRC> tag in an HTML page. The same page used for the dimage program example earlier in this chapter should work nicely. You should see a bar chart of randomly generated information.

The randomness, of course, comes from the test program and not from the module itself. This module will be used for more practical purposes in Chapter 14. See Figure 14–4 for an example of the chart module in use.

Conclusion

Many projects benefit from dynamically generated graphics. In this chapter I have introduced the necessary techniques and tools to generate them. The bar chart module discussed in this chapter will be reused in Chapter 14, "World Wide Web Wall Street: An Advanced CGI Application."

I have now touched on each of the major aspects of typical CGI programming. The remaining chapters explore advanced features of HTML, CGI, HTTP, and the latest Web servers and browsers. Chapter 11 revisits the subject of forms and introduces a number of useful and powerful form elements that were not discussed in Chapter 7.

References

1. Thomas Williams, Colin Kelley et al., "gnuplot."
   [URL:http://www.cs.dartmouth.edu/gnuplot_info.html]

2. Jef Poskanzer et al., "netpbm Utilities."
   [URL:ftp://wuarchive.wustl.edu/graphics/graphics/packages/NetPBM]

3. Thomas Boutell, "The gd Graphics Library."
   [URL:http://www.boutell.com/gd/]

4. Thomas Boutell et al., "The PNG Image Format."
   [URL:http://www.boutell.com/boutell/png/]

5. Lincoln Stein, "The GD.pm Perl5 Module."
   [URL:http://www-genome.wi.mit.edu/ftp/pub/software/WWW/GD.html]

CHAPTER 11

Advanced Forms: Using All the Gadgets

E arlier chapters introduced HTML forms and made considerable use of them. Many useful form elements, however, have not been introduced yet. These include single-selection menus and radio buttons, multiple-selection list boxes, and checkboxes.

Technically, HTML forms themselves are not part of the CGI standard. In practice, however, they are all but useless without a CGI program on the receiving end. Also, forms are probably the most common reason to write CGI applications.

This chapter will take advantage of the cgic library and the cgi-lib.pl library to handle the form data when it arrives at the server. Doing this also presents an opportunity to explore the more advanced features of cgic.

New Tricks with Text Elements

In past chapters, I made extensive use of `<INPUT>` tags and `<TEXTAREA>` tags. But until now, I have not fully examined the options available with these tags.

Password Entry Fields

Consider the following HTML excerpt:

```
<INPUT TYPE="password" NAME="secretstuff"> Password <br>
```

If this HTML text appears inside a <FORM> tag, the user will be presented with a single-line text field much like any other, except the browser will not display the characters the user types in that field. Most browsers display asterisks in place of the actual characters (see Figure 11–1). This is useful for secret information.

> **NOTE:** This does not mean that the information will be transmitted to the server in a secure way! This facility should not be trusted to carry crucial information, especially financial information, unless a security protocol such as the Secure Sockets Layer (HTTPS) or Secure HTTP is being used.

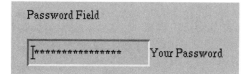

FIGURE 11–1 A password tag, as displayed by Netscape

Specifying the Width of the Text Control

Consider the following HTML:

```
<INPUT TYPE="text" SIZE="50" NAME="street"> Street <br>
```

This HTML tag displays a normal single-line text entry field, except that the tag displayed is large enough to accommodate 50 characters, provided this is practical on the display. It is also possible to specify multiline text entry fields by specifying a size of the form width, height, and you may encounter such pages. However, this approach is discouraged because the <TEXTAREA> tag does a better job of handling multiline text fields.

The SIZE attribute does not limit the actual amount of information that can be entered. It only limits the amount that is displayed at any one time. Most browsers will scroll the text field if more data is entered.

FIGURE 11–2 A wide, single-line text field, as displayed by Netscape

Limiting the Amount of Text Entered

Consider the following HTML excerpt, which elaborates on the previous example:

```
<INPUT TYPE="text" SIZE="50" MAXLENGTH="80" NAME="street"> Street <br>
```

If this HTML text appears inside a <FORM> tag, the user will be presented with a single-line text field that will not accept more than 80 characters (see Figure 11–2). The text field displays only 50 characters at a time but will scroll as necessary to accommodate more text, up to 80 characters.

> **NOTE:** Although the SIZE and MAXLENGTH attributes are useful for limiting user frustration, it is crucial that your code never blindly depend on MAXLENGTH. There have been, and doubtless will be, browsers that ignore MAXLENGTH or handle it improperly. Customized browsers can even be written maliciously to take advantage of such mistakes by submitting additional text beyond the size you expected. If you are not careful to copy only the number of bytes you have allocated space for, hackers may be able to subvert your server! Perl users and cgic users are reasonably safe from this, since Perl has variable-length strings and cgic makes it easy to limit the number of bytes read from a form field.

Specifying Defaults

A default value can be specified for any text entry field as follows:

```
<INPUT TYPE="text" VALUE="Finland" NAME="country"> Country <br>
```

When this entry tag is encountered in an HTML form, it will appear with Finland already entered in the window. This is convenient when the correct entry for a field can be guessed with reasonable accuracy or when it is helpful to start the user off with a reasonable entry, such as the following:

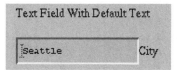

FIGURE 11–3 An input field with a default value, as displayed by Netscape

```
<INPUT TYPE="text" VALUE="http://" NAME="url"> URL (full URL please!) <br>
```

This may help to jog the user's memory as to exactly what a URL is. Then again, it may not.

Specifying Default Text for a <TEXTAREA> Tag

The <TEXTAREA> tag was introduced in Chapter 7. Also introduced were the rows- and cols- attributes, which restrict the size of the control but not the actual amount of text entered. One feature of <TEXTAREA> not yet mentioned is setting the default text.

Consider the following HTML:

```
<TEXTAREA rows="5" cols="50" name="message">
Default text
goes here; line
breaks will be
respected.
</TEXTAREA>
```

When this <TEXTAREA> tag is encountered as part of an HTML form, it will appear with 5 visible rows and 50 visible columns, but it will scroll to accommodate any amount of text. The text control will be initialized with any text found between the <TEXTAREA> and </TEXTAREA> tags.

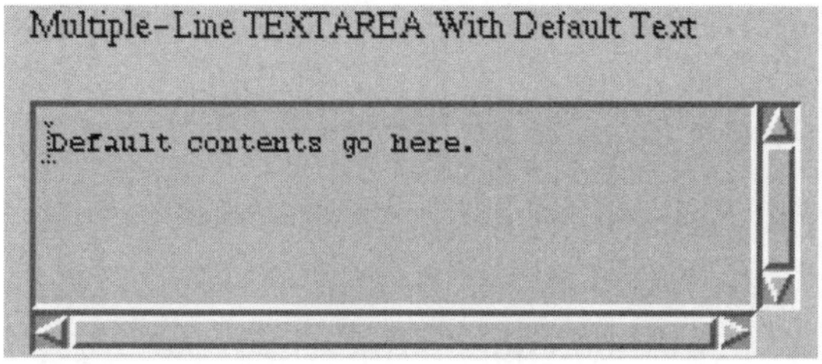

FIGURE 11–4 A <TEXTAREA> tag with default text, as shown by Netscape

Checkboxes: When "On" and "Off" Are the Only Options

While it is possible to gather all the information you might need using only text fields, some users will enter almost any random thing the interface permits them to enter. So when there are only two or a few options, it is useful to give the user a firm push in the right direction. Checkboxes nicely handle the case of two options.

Consider the following HTML excerpt:

```
<INPUT TYPE="checkbox" NAME="spam" VALUE="spam"> Send Me Junk Mail<br>
```

This checkbox is unchecked by default, as the programmer has correctly guessed that the user probably won't want to receive junk mail. Of course, the client for whom the form is being designed may feel differently. Fortunately, it is also possible to check checkboxes by default:

```
<INPUT TYPE="checkbox" CHECKED NAME="spam" VALUE="spam">
Send Fabulous Color Brochure<br>
```

You may say, "Great, but how do I find out if the radio box is checked when the form is submitted to my CGI program?"

If the checkbox is checked, the browser will submit a value for that name; otherwise, nothing will be submitted. Therefore it is sufficient simply to test whether that field name was submitted at all. Fortunately, cgic provides a convenience function for this purpose.

Consider the following C code excerpt:

```
if (cgiFormCheckboxSingle("spam") == cgiFormSuccess) {
    /* Alert the mail room; time to send a brochure... */
}
```

Testing a checkbox is also straightforward using `cgi-lib.pl`. Although it is possible to test whether the checkbox item was submitted at all, with `cgi-lib.pl` it is more familiar to most programmers to simply check whether the item has the correct value rather than an empty string.

Consider the following Perl code excerpt:

```
if ($input{'spam'} eq "spam") {
    # Alert the mail room; time to send a brochure...
}
```

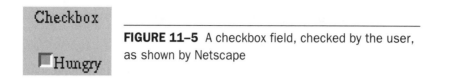

FIGURE 11–5 A checkbox field, checked by the user, as shown by Netscape

It is also valid to write this code like this:

```
if (defined($input{'spam'} )) {
    # Alert the mail room; time to send a brochure...
}
```

The `defined` function of Perl tests whether any assignment has ever been made to an associative array with a particular key.

Named Submit Buttons: A One-click Way to Make Decisions

Although it is possible to express most of the usual applications of forms without the need for more than one Submit button, occasionally you may want to have several Submit buttons with separate names. The advantage of this is that a user's selecting one of several Submit buttons can be a fast way to make a final additional choice from the form.

Consider the following set of HTML tags:

```
<INPUT TYPE="submit" NAME="up" value="Increase All Selected Values">
<INPUT TYPE="submit" NAME="down" value="Decrease All Selected Values">
```

Named Submit buttons work just like checkboxes, except the VALUE attribute is used to indicate the name that should appear on the button.

Imagemap Clicks as Submit Buttons

In rare cases you may want to accept several form settings from the user and then have the user click somewhere in an imagemap in order to submit the data. The following HTML tags should be used:

```
<INPUT TYPE="image" NAME="image">
<IMG SRC="image.gif" ISMAP>
```

When the image is clicked, the form is immediately submitted, and two separate attribute/value pairs are submitted representing the location of the imagemap click. One attribute is named image.x, the other image.y. The value is the position in pixels on the appropriate axis.

For more information about imagemaps, including the more common means of implementing imagemaps in CGI programs, see Chapter 12.

Selection Menus: When "a," "b," and "c" Are the Only Acceptable Choices

Like checkboxes, selection menus help to ensure the user makes a reasonable choice. Unlike checkboxes, selection menus allow one or more of several options to be chosen.

Usually, a selection menu allows only one option to be chosen, although this behavior can be changed. Consider the following HTML:

```
Sneaker Color <BR>
<SELECT NAME="color">
<OPTION value="gray" SELECTED> Gray
<OPTION value="black"> Black
<OPTION value="blue"> Blue
</SELECT>
```

When this group of tags is encountered as part of an HTML form, it will be presented to the user as an option menu, as a scrolled list, or perhaps as a series of radio buttons. The exact appearance will vary among browsers. Some browsers will present a different interface depending on the number of choices. On all correctly implemented browsers, however, the user will be permitted to select one, and only one, choice. If the user selects a different color, the old selection will be cleared, and so on.

You can specify in advance that an option should be selected by using the SELECTED attribute of the <OPTION> tag. This has been done in the previous case with the color gray.

You may ask what your CGI program will receive when a form containing a <SELECT> tag is submitted. One of the name/value pairs submitted for the form will have the name specified for the <SELECT> tag and the value specified for the <OPTION> tag the user has chosen, or the text of the option if no value attribute is present. cgic provides a convenience function to retrieve such choices. Consider the following C excerpt:

```
/* OUTSIDE of any function */

char *colors[] = {
    "gray",
    "black",
    "blue"
} ;

/* ... INSIDE cgiMain or some other function */

/* Declare variables (at start of function) */

int choice;

cgiFormSelectSingle("color", colors, 3, &choice, 0);

/* colors[choice] now points to the name of the chosen color */
```

This function is designed to ensure the user selects one of a limited set of acceptable choices. If the user somehow manages to enter an illegal value, perhaps by modifying a copy of the form, the default value will be chosen automatically and an appropriate error code will be returned. The programmer can pay attention to the error code or ignore it (as in this case), knowing that cgic will ensure a reasonable value is always retrieved.

Normally, this is a feature. However, in some cases, you may wish to be able to add many new <OPTION> tags to a <SELECT> tag without having to update code or update a data file scanned by the code. In such cases, you treat the <SELECT> tag just like any text entry field as follows:

```
char buffer[81];
cgiFormString("color", buffer, 81);
```

This simple call retrieves the color name the user submitted. The downside of this approach is that the submitted color is not checked for validity.

cgi-lib.pl always uses the latter approach. Consider the following line of Perl code:

```
$color = $input{'color'} ;
```

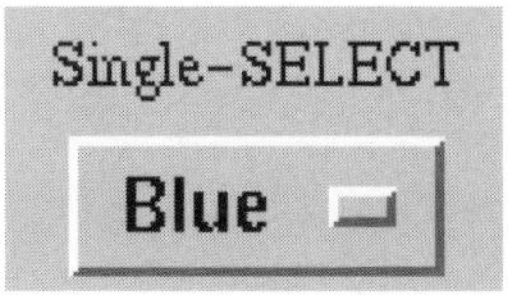

FIGURE 11–6 A small selection menu, as shown by Netscape

cgi-lib.pl does not provide a built-in way to validate selections, but this is not difficult to do with a few lines of Perl code. The acceptable values could be stored in an associative array, for instance, and the submitted value checked with a single statement.

Multiple Selections: "onions and garlic, but no cucumbers, please"

The <SELECT> tag can also be used to permit several options to be chosen at the same time. From an HTML standpoint, this is quite simple. However, from a CGI programming standpoint it is somewhat less so.

Consider the following HTML:

```
Vegetables <BR>
<SELECT name="vegetables" MULTIPLE>
<OPTION value="onions" SELECTED> Onions
<OPTION value="garlic" SELECTED> Garlic
<OPTION value="cucumbers"> Cucumbers
</SELECT>
```

The presence of the MULTIPLE attribute to the <SELECT> tag indicates that any number of options can be selected.

Multiple selections change the rules considerably. cgic provides a way to fetch several selections while still validating the selected choices, as discussed next.

Retrieving Multiple Selections in C

Consider the following excerpt from a cgic program:

```
/* Outside of any function */

char *vegetables[] = {
    "onions",
    "garlic",
```

```
            "cucumbers"
} ;

/* INSIDE cgiMain or some other function */

/* Declare variables (at start of function) */
int i, selected[3];

/* Now fetch the selections */

cgiFormSelectMultiple("vegetables",
      vegetables, 3, selected, 0);

for (i=0; (i < 3); i++) {
      printf("%s ", vegetables[i]);
      if (selected[i]) {
            printf("chosen<br>\n");
      } else {
            printf("not chosen<br>\n");
      }
}
```

As with single-selection menus, there may be times when you do not wish
to validate the responses. The cgiFormStringMultiple() function of cgic
is provided for this purpose. Consider the following code excerpt:

```
/* Declare variables at beginning of function */

/* Pointers to an array of strings. The first will
      point to the array returned by cgic. The
      second will point to the current string
      being examined in that array. */
char **strings, char **string;

cgiFormStringMultiple("vegetables", &strings);

/* Point to the first string so we can step through the strings */
string = strings;

/* The last entry in strings is a pointer to a null string. */

while (*string) {
      printf("%s chosen<br>\n", *string);
      string++;
}
```

```
/* IMPORTANT: free the array of strings when it is
      no longer of interest. Otherwise, the memory will
      not be reclaimed until the program exits. */
cgiStringArrayFree(strings);
```

Retrieving Multiple Selections in Perl

cgi-lib.pl handles multiple selections in almost the same way it handles single selections. One string contains all of the selected items. The selected items are separated by null characters.

Consider the following Perl excerpt:

```
@vegetables = split(/\0/, $input{'vegetables'} );

foreach $v (@vegetables)
{
      print $v, " chosen<br>\n";
}
```

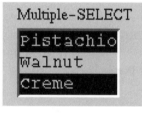

FIGURE 11–7 Multiple selections, as shown by Netscape

Radio Buttons: Another Approach to Single-choice Selections

In addition to the <SELECT> tag approach just demonstrated, you can also use a collection of <INPUT> tags with the TYPE attribute set to RADIO. The rule is simple: All radio buttons with the same NAME attribute are grouped together, and only one of those buttons can be selected at any given time. The CHECKED attribute can be set for one of the buttons in the group, thereby establishing it as the default.

Consider the following HTML:

```
<p>
Exclusive Radio Button Group: Age of Truck in Years
<input type="radio" name="age" value="1"> 1
```

```
<input type="radio" name="age" value="2"> 2
<input type="radio" name="age" value="3" checked> 3
<input type="radio" name="age" value="4"> 4
```

When this collection of tags is encountered as part of an HTML form, it will be displayed as a set of radio buttons. The text following each input tag is used as a label. This is distinct from the value submitted when that button is checked, which is indicated by the VALUE attribute. If the user checks another button, the previously chosen button is automatically unchecked.

When the form is submitted, only one name/value pair will appear for the radio button group. The name will be set to the NAME attribute shared by all of the buttons, and the value will be set to the VALUE attribute of the button that was actually chosen.

You may notice that single-choice selection menus are submitted in exactly the same way. This is correct. Also, the same techniques can be used to retrieve the information, so the code examples are not repeated here (see "Selection Menus: When "a," "b," and "c" Are the Only Acceptable Choices," earlier in this chapter).

cgic does provide a separate function for radio buttons, but it is functionally identical to cgiFormSelectSingle(), discussed earlier in this chapter. The radio button function is called cgiFormRadio().

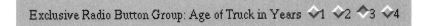

FIGURE 11–8 Radio buttons, as shown by Netscape

Checkbox Groups: Another Approach to Multiple Selections

The <SELECT MULTIPLE> tag approach is most useful for large numbers of items. When the number of items from which to choose is relatively small, you can use a collection of <INPUT> tags with the TYPE attribute set to CHECKBOX. Again, the rule is simple: All checkbox buttons with the same NAME attribute are grouped together. Unlike with radio buttons, any number of checkboxes in a group can be selected at any one time. The CHECKED attribute can be set in advance for any or all of the buttons in the group.

Consider the following HTML:

```
<p>
Nonexclusive Checkbox Button Group: Vote for Zero to Four Candidates
<input type="checkbox" name="age" value="1"> 1
<input type="checkbox" name="age" value="2"> 2
<input type="checkbox" name="age" value="3"> 3
<input type="checkbox" name="age" value="4"> 4
```

When this collection of tags is encountered as part of an HTML form, it will be displayed as a set of checkbox buttons. The text following each input tag is used as a label. This is distinct from the value submitted when that button is checked, which is indicated by the VALUE attribute. If the user checks another button, the previously chosen button is automatically unchecked.

When the form is submitted, one name/value pair will be submitted for each selected checkbox. The name for each will be set to the NAME attribute shared by all of the buttons, and the value of each will be set to the VALUE attribute of each selected button.

Multiple-selection menus are submitted in exactly the same way. The same techniques can be used to retrieve the information, so the code examples are not repeated here (for code examples, see "Multiple Selections: 'onions and garlic, but no cucumbers, please,'" earlier in the chapter.)

cgic does provide a separate function for checkbox groups, but it is functionally identical to cgiFormSelectMultiple(), discussed earlier in the chapter. The multiple checkbox function is called cgiFormCheckboxMultiple().

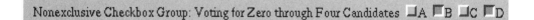

FIGURE 11–9 Multiple checkboxes in a group, as shown by Netscape

A Complete Example

The previous code exerpt are not complete CGI programs. Consider the following complete code example, which tests most of the form elements discussed. First, the HTML page that is intended to work with this test program:

```
<html>
<head>
<title>Test Form</title>
</head>
<body>
<h1>Test Form</h1>
<form method="POST" action="http://CHANGE_THIS_URL!">
<p>
Password Field
<p>
<input type="password" name="name">Your Secret Agent Name
<p>
Multiple-Line Text Field
<p>
<textarea NAME="address" ROWS=4 COLS=40>
Default contents go here.
</textarea>
<p>
Checkbox
<p>
<input type="checkbox" name="hungry" checked>Hungry
<p>
Text Field containing a Numeric Value
<p>
<input type="text" name="temperature" value="98.6">
Blood Temperature (80.0-120.0)
<p>
Text Field containing an Integer Value
<p>
<input type="text" name="frogs" value="1">
Frogs Eaten
<p>
Single-SELECT
<br>
<select name="colors">
<option value="Red">Red
<option value="Green">Green
<option value="Blue">Blue
</select>
<br>
Multiple-SELECT
<br>
<select name="flavors" multiple>
<option value="pistachio">Pistachio
<option value="walnut">Walnut
```

```
<option value="creme">Creme
</select>
<p>Exclusive Radio Button Group: Age of Truck in Years
<input type="radio" name="age" value="1">1
<input type="radio" name="age" value="2">2
<input type="radio" name="age" value="3" checked>3
<input type="radio" name="age" value="4">4
<p>Nonexclusive Checkbox Group: Voting for Zero through Four
Candidates
<input type="checkbox" name="vote" value="A">A
<input type="checkbox" name="vote" value="B">B
<input type="checkbox" name="vote" value="C">C
<input type="checkbox" name="vote" value="D">D
<p>
<input type="submit" name="submit1" value="Submit Request">
<input type="reset" value="Reset Request">
</form>
</body>
</html>
```

Now, consider the actual code presented next. A variant of the C version of this test program is also available in the cgic distribution.

Advanced Form Elements in C: Source Code of cgictest.c

The following is the C source code for the cgictest program.

```
#include <stdio.h>
#include "cgic.h"

void Name();
void Address();
void Hungry();
void Temperature();
void Frogs();
void Color();
void Flavors();
void NonExButtons();
void RadioButtons();

int cgiMain() {
    cgiHeaderContentType("text/html");
    fprintf(cgiOut, "<HTML><HEAD>\n");
```

```
        fprintf(cgiOut, "<TITLE>cgic test</TITLE></HEAD>\n");
        fprintf(cgiOut, "<BODY><H1>cgic test</H1>\n");
        Name();
        Address();
        Hungry();
        Temperature();
        Frogs();
        Color();
        Flavors();
        NonExButtons();
        RadioButtons();
        fprintf(cgiOut, "</BODY></HTML>\n");
        return 0;
}

void Name() {
        char name[81];
        cgiFormStringNoNewlines("name", name, 81);
        fprintf(cgiOut, "Name: %s<BR>\n", name);
}

void Address() {
        char address[241];
        cgiFormString("address", address, 241);
        fprintf(cgiOut, "Address: <PRE>\n%s</PRE>\n", address);
}

void Hungry() {
        if (cgiFormCheckboxSingle("hungry") == cgiFormSuccess) {
                fprintf(cgiOut, "I'm Hungry!<BR>\n");
        } else {
                fprintf(cgiOut, "I'm Not Hungry!<BR>\n");
        }
}

void Temperature() {
        double temperature;
        cgiFormDoubleBounded("temperature", &temperature, 80.0, 120.0, 98.6);
        fprintf(cgiOut, "My temperature is %f.<BR>\n", temperature);
}

void Frogs() {
        int frogsEaten;
        cgiFormInteger("frogs", &frogsEaten, 0);
        fprintf(cgiOut, "I have eaten %d frogs.<BR>\n", frogsEaten);
}
```

```c
char *colors[] = {
      "Red",
      "Green",
      "Blue"
} ;

void Color() {
      int colorChoice;
      cgiFormSelectSingle("colors", colors, 3, &colorChoice, 0);
      fprintf(cgiOut, "I am: %s<BR>\n", colors[colorChoice]);
}

char *flavors[] = {
      "pistachio",
      "walnut",
      "creme"
} ;

void Flavors() {
      int flavorChoices[3];
      int i;
      int result;
      int invalid;
      result = cgiFormSelectMultiple("flavors", flavors, 3,
            flavorChoices, &invalid);
      if (result == cgiFormNotFound) {
            fprintf(cgiOut, "I hate ice cream.<p>\n");
      } else {
            fprintf(cgiOut, "My favorite ice cream flavors are:\n");
            fprintf(cgiOut, "<ul>\n");
            for (i=0; (i < 3); i++) {
                  if (flavorChoices[i]) {
                        fprintf(cgiOut, "<li>%s\n", flavors[i]);
                  }
            }
            fprintf(cgiOut, "</ul>\n");
      }
}

char *ages[] = {
      "1",
      "2",
      "3",
      "4"
} ;
```

```c
void RadioButtons() {
      int ageChoice;
      char ageText[10];
      /* Approach #1: check for one of several valid responses.
           Good if there are a short list of possible button values and
           you wish to enumerate them. */
      cgiFormRadio("age", ages, 4, &ageChoice, 0);

      fprintf(cgiOut, "Age of Truck: %s (method #1)<BR>\n",
           ages[ageChoice]);

      /* Approach #2: just get the string. Good
           if the information is not critical or if you wish
           to verify it in some other way. Note that if
           the information is numeric, cgiFormInteger,
           cgiFormDouble, and related functions may be
           used instead of cgiFormString. */
      cgiFormString("age", ageText, 10);

      fprintf(cgiOut, "Age of Truck: %s (method #2)<BR>\n", ageText);
}

char *votes[] = {
      "A",
      "B",
      "C",
      "D"
} ;

void NonExButtons() {
      int voteChoices[4];
      int i;
      int result;
      int invalid;

      char **responses;

      /* Method #1: check for valid votes. This is a good idea,
           since votes for nonexistent candidates should probably
           be discounted... */
      fprintf(cgiOut, "Votes (method 1):<BR>\n");
      result = cgiFormCheckboxMultiple("vote", votes, 4,
           voteChoices, &invalid);
```

```
        if (result == cgiFormNotFound) {
            fprintf(cgiOut, "I hate them all!<p>\n");
        } else {
            fprintf(cgiOut, "My preferred candidates are:\n");
            fprintf(cgiOut, "<ul>\n");
            for (i=0; (i < 4); i++) {
                if (voteChoices[i]) {
                    fprintf(cgiOut, "<li>%s\n", votes[i]);
                }
            }
            fprintf(cgiOut, "</ul>\n");
        }

        /* Method #2: get all the names voted for and trust them.
            This is good if the form will change more often
            than the code and invented responses are not a danger
            or can be checked in some other way. */
        fprintf(cgiOut, "Votes (method 2):<BR>\n");
        result = cgiFormStringMultiple("vote", &responses);
        if (result == cgiFormNotFound) {
            fprintf(cgiOut, "I hate them all!<p>\n");
        } else {
            int i = 0;
            fprintf(cgiOut, "My preferred candidates are:\n");
            fprintf(cgiOut, "<ul>\n");
            while (responses[i]) {
                fprintf(cgiOut, "<li>%s\n", responses[i]);
                i++;
            }
            fprintf(cgiOut, "</ul>\n");
        }
        /* We must be sure to free the string array or a memory
            leak will occur. Simply calling free() would free
            the array but not the individual strings. The
            function cgiStringArrayFree() does the job completely. */
        cgiStringArrayFree(responses);
    }
```

Compiling cgictest.c

To build cgictest, you must compile cgictest.c and link it to the cgic library. See Appendix 5 and the CD for a suitable Unix Makefile for all the C programs in this book.

Advanced Form Elements in Perl: Source Code of cgictest

The following is the Perl source code for the cgictest proram.

```perl
#!/usr/local/bin/perl

require "cgi-lib.pl";

&ReadParse(*values);

print "Content-type: text/html\n\n";

print "<HTML><HEAD>\n";
print "<TITLE>cgic test</TITLE></HEAD>\n";
print "<BODY><H1>cgic test</H1>\n";
&Name;
&Address;
&Hungry;
&Temperature;
&Frogs;
&Color;
&Flavors;
&NonExButtons;
&RadioButtons;
print "</BODY></HTML>\n";
exit 0;

sub Name {
      print "Name: ", $values{'name'} , "<BR>\n";
}

sub Address {
      print "Address: <PRE>\n", $values{'address'} , "</PRE>\n";
}

sub Hungry {
      if (defined($values{'hungry'} )) {
            print "I'm Hungry!<BR>\n";
      } else {
            print "I'm Not Hungry!<BR>\n";
      }
}
```

```perl
sub Temperature {
      print "My temperature is ", $values{'temperature'} , ".<BR>\n";
}

sub Frogs {
      print "I have eaten ", $values{'frogs'} , " frogs.<BR>\n";
}

sub Color {
      print "I am: ", $values{'colors'} , "<BR>\n";
}

sub Flavors {
      print "My favorite ice cream flavors are:\n";
      print "<ul>\n";
      @flavors = split(/\0/, $values{'flavors'} );
      foreach $f (@flavors) {
            print "<li>", $f, "\n";
      }
      print "</ul>\n";
}

sub RadioButtons {
      print "Age of Truck: ", $values{'age'} , "<BR>\n";
}

sub NonExButtons {
      @votes = split(/\0/, $values{'vote'} );
      print "My preferred candidates are:\n";
      print "<ul>\n";
      foreach $v (@votes) {
            print "<li>", $v, "\n";
      }
      print "</ul>\n";
}
```

Testing the cgictest Program

cgictest can be tested by installing the Perl script or compiled binary like any other CGI program and then altering the ACTION attribute of the <FORM> tag in the HTML document provided previously.

Conclusion

HTML forms provide a respectable range of user interface controls. In this chapter I fully explored the set of standard and commonly used controls, along with the proper mechanisms to retrieve the data entered in the form. In the next chapter, I demonstrate several advanced CGI and HTML features not related to forms including client pull and server push animations. These features are often found in the flashiest CGI applications.

CHAPTER 12

Advanced CGI and HTML Features

The features of the CGI standard discussed in previous chapters are sufficient for most purposes. Perhaps 90 percent of all CGI applications will never use additional features. As is often the case, though, the remaining 10 percent are among the most impressive applications. These envelope-stretching capabilities, as well as advanced means of debugging and improving complicated CGI programs, are the subject of this chapter.

A Problem: Sending Updated Information to the User

 "The Web is great. Users can connect to the server when they want and get the information they want. But what if the information changes over time? How can I keep the user's display up to date?"

 Until the arrival of Netscape 1.1, the answer to this question was simply, "You can't." Since then, however, two solutions to the problem have been available: client pull and server push. Many other browsers have begun to implement these features, although support is by no means universal.

Client Pull: Web Pages That Update Themselves

Since the advent of Netscape 1.1 and Microsoft Internet Explorer 2.0, it has been possible to construct a Web page that contains a command to reload itself at a particular time. This feature is called *client pull*.

This handy trick is accomplished by sending a special `Refresh:` header as part of the HTTP response from the CGI program. Alternatively, interesting client pull "slide shows" can be constructed without reference to any CGI program. However, client pull is commonly used within CGI applications.

A Simple Client Pull Example

Consider the following HTML document:

```
<html>
<head>
<meta HTTP_EQUIV="Refresh" CONTENT="5">
<title>Self-Reloading Document</title>
</head>
<body>
<h1>Self-Reloading Document</h1>
</body>
</html>
```

Try opening this page with Netscape 1.1 or a later version, with Microsoft Internet Explorer 2.0 or later, or with any other Web browser that claims to support client pull. You will (I hope) note that the page reloads itself every five seconds.

> **NOTE:** This trick may not work if the page is not installed on an actual Web server! If you test it with a local file and nothing special happens, try it on an actual Web server. This behavior is somewhat browser-dependent.

Q　*"What's that meta tag all about?"*

A　The `<meta>` tag, which should appear between the `<head>` and `</head>` tags, can be used to ask the Web browser to pretend it received various HTTP headers from the server. In this case, the browser is instructed to pretend that the HTTP header specified by HTTP_EQUIV was received and with the content specified by CONTENT.

Aren't you sorry you asked? The important thing to remember is to use a <meta> tag like the one given here and with CONTENT set to the number of seconds before the page should be reloaded.

Q *"Great, but this isn't very useful. I always get the same page. How can I create a slide show of several pages?"*

A Actually, reloading the same page can be useful, if the page is generated anew every time by a CGI program. However, there is a way to instruct the browser to fetch a different page for each "slide" in the presentation.

Consider the following pair of short HTML documents:

page1.html:

```
<html>
<head>
<meta HTTP_EQUIV="Refresh" CONTENT="5; URL=page2.html">
<title>Slide Show Page #1</title>
</head>
<body>
<h1>Slide Show Page #1</h1>
</body>
</html>
```

page2.html:

```
<html>
<head>
<meta HTTP_EQUIV="Refresh" CONTENT="5; URL=page1.html">
<title>Slide Show Page #2</title>
</head>
<body>
<h1>Slide Show Page #2</h1>
</body>
</html>
```

Once `page1.html` is opened, the two pages will appear in a loop, switching from one to the other every five seconds. Additional pages can also be added to the slide show.

Q *"This is useful. But what if there is a form on the page, and the user is halfway done typing in information?"*

A Then the user is out of luck. This unhappy disadvantage has no complete solution in most Web browsers. Netscape version 2.0 supports a new mechanism, called frames, that can be used to present several distinct HTML documents as part of the same larger document. The effect is much like a newspaper with many distinct stories, and it is possible for one of several frames to be regularly updated via client pull while the remainder stay put. However, this feature is not yet a standard across numerous browsers.

Limitations of Client Pull

One would hope that outputting a `Refresh:` header for an individual inline image would result in that particular inline image's being reloaded and the rest of the page remaining undisturbed. Unfortunately, at least in Netscape 1.1, that is not what happens. The entire page is replaced by the new image, which appears by itself.

Fortunately, this trick can be accomplished successfully using the server push technique, which is discussed later in this chapter.

Client Pull in CGI: Retrieving a Series of Images

Client pull for a sequence of images is exactly like client pull for HTML pages themselves, except there is nowhere to insert a <meta> tag! Fortunately, the <meta> tag is just a substitute for the HTTP `Refresh:` header. The following CGI program, cgipull, takes advantage of `Refresh:` and the `PATH_INFO` environment variable to deliver a list of files in sequence.

> **NOTE:** As mentioned earlier, this technique cannot be used for inline images. However, the server push version of this program, presented later in this chapter, can be.

While the <meta> tag is handy when the documents to be pulled are all HTML pages, a CGI program can send Refresh: headers for images as well, thus allowing a slide show to be presented without the use of HTML. This CGI program delivers a series of images in the GIF format. It can be easily adapted for other formats; the only concern is that the correct Content-type: line must be generated.

Client Pull in C: cgipull.c

The following is the C source code for the cgipull program.

```c
#include <string.h>
#include "cgic.h"

/* This filename must be changed. The file it points to
     must contain a list of GIF files on your system,
     specified by complete paths. */

#define GIF_LIST_FILE "/CHANGE/THIS/PATH/giflist.txt"

int cgiMain()
{
    FILE *in;
    int choice = 0;
    int count = 0;
    in = fopen(GIF_LIST_FILE, "r");
    if (strlen(cgiPathInfo)) {
        /* Ignore the leading slash */
        choice = atoi(cgiPathInfo + 1);
    }
    while (1) {
        char s[256];
        char *filename;
        if (!fgets(s, 256, in)) {
            fclose(in);
            break;
        }
        /* The filename is everything up to the line break */
        filename = strtok(s, "\r\n\t ");
        if (count == choice) {
            /* If there will be another, output a Refresh */
            char s2[256];
            if (fgets(s2, 256, in)) {
                fprintf(cgiOut,
```

```
                              "Refresh: 10; URL=%d.gif\n",
                              choice + 1);
                  }
                  /* Now output the file */
                  cgiHeaderContentType("image/gif");
                  fclose(in);
                  in = fopen(filename, "rb");
                  while (1) {
                          int ch;
                          ch = getc(in);
                          if (ch == EOF) {
                                  break;
                          }
                          putc(ch, cgiOut);
                  }
                  fclose(in);
                  break;
          }
          count++;
      }
      return 0;
}
```

Client Pull in Perl: cgipull

The following is the Perl source code for the cgipull program.

```perl
#!/usr/local/bin/perl

# This filename must be changed. The file it points to
# must contain a list of GIF files on your system,
# specified by complete paths.

$gifListFile = "/CHANGE/THIS/PATH/giflist.txt";

$choice = 0;

$_ = $ENV{'PATH_INFO'} ;

if (/\/(\d+).gif/) {
    $choice = $1;
}

open(IN, $gifListFile);
@list = <IN>;
```

```
close(IN);

if ($choice != $#list) {
      print "Refresh: 10; URL=", $choice+1, ".gif\n";
}
# Now output the file
print "Content-type: image/gif\n\n";

$list[$choice] =~ s/\n//g;

open(IN, $list[$choice]);

while (read(IN, $buffer, 4096)) {
      print $buffer;
}

close(IN);

exit 0;
```

Installing and Using cgipull

The C version of cgipull takes advantage of the cgic library, so be sure to link it to cgic. A Makefile for the C examples in the book is included in Appendix 5 and on the CD.

The cgipull program must be referenced correctly if it is to work properly. Consider the following HTML document:

```
<html>
<head>
<title>Client Pull of an Inline Image</title>
</head>
<body>
<h1>Client Pull of an Inline Image</h1>
<img src="/cgi-bin/cgipull/0.gif">
<p>
```

and the following sample giflist.txt file. You must rewrite this file so that it lists the full paths (not URLs) of several GIF images present on your system:

```
/home/boutell/images/bixby.gif
/home/boutell/images/gooley.gif
/home/boutell/images/me.gif
```

The <img> tag in the HTML page does the magic by referencing the cgipull program. In this example, cgipull is assumed to be installed in the cgi-bin directory. Change the <img src> line if you install your CGI programs differently.

Note that after the first page is displayed, the HTML portion of the page disappears and only images are presented. The image frames change every 10 seconds.

This particular program does not create an infinite loop. However, it is straightforward to modify cgipull to output 0.gif as the Refresh: header for the last GIF, thus closing the loop.

Q *"Why does /0.gif follow the name of the program?"*

A When cgipull sees /0.gif in the PATH_INFO environment variable, it outputs the first GIF in the list and generates a Refresh: header pointing to the next image, /1.gif. This has nothing to do with the real names of the GIF images listed in the giflist.txt file. The .gif extension, as mentioned in Chapter 10, is important in order to placate badly implemented Web browsers.

Server Push: Pushing the Limitations

Client pull is relatively painless and fits into the standard Web model reasonably well. If a Web browser does not support client pull, it simply receives only the first document and does not move automatically to the second. It is not very difficult to add "next" links to each page to enable users of such browsers to get the benefit of a slide show. However, client pull has the drawback that it cannot be used to update individual inline images.

Server push is another matter entirely. Also introduced in Netscape 1.1, server push is currently supported only by Netscape. In the case of client pull, the browser retrieves the next document all by itself after a particular interval has expired; a new HTTP connection is made to fetch each document. In the case of server push, however, one of the oldest rules of the HTTP protocol is broken: More than one document is sent by the same CGI program.

This can consume a great deal of bandwidth, but this may be worth the price if continuous updates are desired.

Multipart Documents

When server push is used, the CGI program specifies a special content type used only for multiple-part documents. Then the CGI program transmits the various pages or images one after another and usually sleeps in between to pace the transmission. In a significant break from most CGI programs, a server push program stays around as long as the server push connection remains in existence.

The special multipart content type looks like this:

```
Content-type: multipart/x-mixed-replace;boundary=goober
```

followed by a blank line if there are no more HTTP headers to be sent.

Boundary is the string that will be used to separate distinct documents from one another.

Then, for each actual document, the following must be sent:

```
--goober
Content-type: image/gif
```

Note that the boundary string (goober in this example) must be preceded by a line break and two dashes. After the boundary line, a normal content type is sent for the individual document (in this case a GIF). Any number of documents can be sent.

When the server push is complete, the following line must be sent, preceded by a line break:

```
--goober--
```

This signifies that there are no more documents to follow.

Some server push programs, such as endless loop animations, have no obvious point of termination. In such cases, the connection is not closed until the browser terminates it and the server kills the CGI program.

We're almost ready to construct a server push program. But there is one more problem to overcome: server buffering.

Writing Directly to the Browser: nph- scripts

One difficulty that comes up immediately in server push programs is the tendency of Web servers to buffer the output of CGI programs. Thus under normal circumstances, a CGI program cannot ensure that its output is being delivered to the user immediately. Instead, many server push frames may appear in a short burst, followed by a long delay, followed by another burst, and so on.

Q *"Fine, I'll just call* `fflush()` *after every frame."*

A That should work, but it doesn't! The problem is, the server does not normally relay its output directly to the user. Instead, it typically accepts the complete document from the CGI program before relaying it, or, if the document is large, it relays large buffers of data at one time. The server performs convenient services in exchange for this performance price. Specifically, it outputs the HTTP status code and other header information.

To get around this, you need to specifically tell the server that this particular CGI program does not want the server to intervene between it and the browser. Fortunately, most Web servers support a standard mechanism for doing this.

By giving the CGI program a name beginning with the characters nph-, you signal the Web server that this CGI program will produce all of its own HTTP headers and is solely responsible for communicating with the browser. The server should not attempt to parse the output in any way. To make this work, the program must also output an HTTP status header, since the server will not output such a header for it. This differs from the Status: header sometimes generated by ordinary CGI programs.

Consider the following example of acceptable output from an nph- program:

```
HTTP/1.0 200 OK
Content-type: text/html

<h1>This is a short HTML page.</h1>
```

Note the first line of output. The status line contains the version of the HTTP protocol in use, followed by a status code, followed by a short text message corresponding to the status message. The status code 200 indicates successful transmission of a document.

Limitations of Server Push

A word of warning: While most current Netscape browsers support server push, there is no guarantee that an individual browser is configured to support more than one simultaneous download.

What this means for server push is simple: It is unwise to assume that several inline images on a page can be simultaneously refreshed by server push, particularly if the animation is critical to the user's comprehension of the page.

Server push is at its best when what is desired is continuous updating rather than a new download every so often. Server push is also indicated when only a single inline image should be updated, without modification of the rest of the page.

nph-push: Nonstop Image Animation

We are now ready to implement the image animation program once again, this time by using server push. This version pushes a continuous stream of GIF-format frames to the client and correctly closes the server push connection after the last one. Modifying the program to output images in a continuous loop is trivial.

Server Push in C: nph-push.c

The following is the C source code for the nph-push program.

```
#include <string.h>
#include "cgic.h"

/* This filename must be changed. The file it points to
    must contain a list of GIF files on your system,
    specified by complete paths. */

#define GIF_LIST_FILE "/CHANGE/THIS/PATH/giflist.txt"

int cgiMain()
{
    FILE *in, *gifIn;
    int choice = 0;
    int count = 0;
    fprintf(cgiOut, "HTTP/1.0 200 OK\n");
```

```
cgiHeaderContentType(
        "multipart/x-mixed-replace;boundary=goober\n\n");

in = fopen(GIF_LIST_FILE, "r");
while (1) {
        char s[256];
        char *filename;
        if (!fgets(s, 256, in)) {
                fclose(in);
                break;
        }
        /* The filename is everything up to the line break */
        filename = strtok(s, "\r\n\t ");
        fprintf(cgiOut, "\n--goober\n");
        /* Now output the file */
        gifIn = fopen(filename, "rb");
        if (!gifIn) {
                /* Missing frame, skip it */
                break;
        }
        cgiHeaderContentType("image/gif");
        while (1) {
                int ch;
                ch = getc(gifIn);
                if (ch == EOF) {
                        break;
                }
                putc(ch, cgiOut);
        }
        fclose(gifIn);
        /* A short delay to make sure each frame is appreciated
*/
        sleep(1);
        count++;
}
fclose(in);
/* Now terminate the server push sequence altogether */
fprintf(cgiOut, "\n--goober--\n");
return 0;
}
```

Server Push in Perl: nph-push

The following is the Perl source code for the nph-push program.

```perl
#!/usr/local/bin/perl

# This filename must be changed. The file it points to
# must contain a list of GIF files on your system,
# specified by complete paths.

$gifListFile = "/CHANGE/THIS/PATH/giflist.txt";

open(IN, $gifListFile);
@list = <IN>;
close(IN);

print "HTTP/1.0 200 Document follows\n";
print "Content-type: multipart/x-mixed-replace;boundary=goober\n\n";

foreach $name (@list) {
     $name =~ s/\n//g;
     # Now output the file
     print "\n--goober\n";
     print "Content-type: image/gif\n\n";

     open(IN, $name);

     while (read(IN, $buffer, 4096)) {
          print $buffer;
     }
     close($name);
     # A short delay to make sure each frame is appreciated
     sleep(1);
}

print "\n--goober--\n";

exit 0;
```

Installing and Testing nph-push

The C version of nph-push takes advantage of the cgic library, so be sure to link it to cgic. A Unix Makefile for all example programs in this book is included in Appendix 5 and on the CD.

You may be in the habit of renaming CGI programs to meet the conventions of your particular Web server. It is important that the name you actually install this program under begin with the characters nph-. Otherwise, your server probably will not recognize that this program produces its own HTTP headers and does not desire buffering. I suggest the name `nph-push` or `nph-push.cgi`.

Before compiling, change `GIF_LIST_FILE` (or `$gifListFile`) to point to the same list of GIF files you used for the client pull example and modify the Web page used to test the client pull example to point to the server push example instead. For nph-push, `/0.gif` is not required at the end of the `<img src>` URL, although its presence will do no harm.

The complete set of images will be pushed to the client, with a one-second delay between frames to ensure the animation does not end too quickly when accessed from a local server. Feel free to try removing the `sleep()` call in order to send frames as fast as possible. However, not all versions of Netscape on all platforms can be easily interrupted when a server push animation never pauses.

Server Push Resizes Inline Images

If your `giflist.txt` file contains images of many different sizes, you will quickly note the following: When server push is used to update an inline image, all images after the first are stretched to occupy the same amount of space as the first image. So, it is best to ensure that all images in a server push sequence are of the same size.

Making Decisions Based on Browser Type

Server push looks great in Netscape. In most browsers at the time of this writing, however, server push fails completely and a "broken image" icon is displayed instead. This is not an ideal state of affairs. Fortunately, there is a way to work around this problem.

Taking Advantage of HTTP_USER_AGENT

As mentioned in Chapter 5, the `HTTP_USER_AGENT` CGI environment variable usually contains a string identifying the Web browser accessing the CGI program. You can take advantage of this to identify browsers that are definitely capable of handling server push.

It is important to keep up to date on the latest Web browser versions; it is always possible that a new browser will have emerged that supports server push. For instance, as of this writing, the most recent beta version of Microsoft Internet Explorer supports client pull, while a month ago, only Netscape did. New versions of existing browsers can pose a problem as well if the code to check the HTTP_USER_AGENT string is written naively.

What follows is an amended version of nph-push that tests first to see if Netscape is in use. If it isn't, only the first image in the giflist.txt file is sent.

Testing HTTP_USER_AGENT in C: nph-p2.c

The following is the C source code for the nph-p2 program.

```c
#include "cgic.h"
#include <string.h>
#include <stdlib.h>

/* This filename must be changed. The file it points to
        must contain a list of GIF files on your system,
        specified by complete paths. */

#define GIF_LIST_FILE "/CHANGE/THIS/PATH/giflist.txt"

/* Returns true if the browser supports server push,
        false otherwise. */
int SupportsServerPush();

int SupportsServerPush() {
        char *versionString;
        float version = 0.0;
        sscanf(cgiUserAgent, "Mozilla/%f", &version);
        if (version >= 1.1) {
                return 1;
        } else {
                return 0;
        }
}

int cgiMain()
{
        FILE *in, *gifIn;
        int choice = 0;
```

```
int count = 0;
int pushFlag = 1;
fprintf(cgiOut, "HTTP/1.0 200 OK\n");
if (!SupportsServerPush()) {
      /* Uh-oh, no server push. */
      pushFlag = 0;
}

if (pushFlag) {
      cgiHeaderContentType(
            "multipart/x-mixed-replace;boundary=goober\n\n");
}

in = fopen(GIF_LIST_FILE, "r");
while (1) {
      char s[256];
      char *filename;
      if (!fgets(s, 256, in)) {
            fclose(in);
            break;
      }
      /* The filename is everything up to the line break */
      filename = strtok(s, "\r\n\t ");
      if (pushFlag) {
            fprintf(cgiOut, "\n--goober\n");
      }
      /* Now output the file */
      gifIn = fopen(filename, "rb");
      if (!gifIn) {
            /* Missing frame, skip it */
            continue;
      }
      cgiHeaderContentType("image/gif");
      while (1) {
            int ch;
            ch = getc(gifIn);
            if (ch == EOF) {
                  break;
            }
            putc(ch, cgiOut);
      }
      fclose(gifIn);
      if (!pushFlag) {
```

```
                          /* Just the first image if server push is not used
*/
                    break;
               }
               /* A short delay to make sure each frame is appreciated */
               sleep(1);
               count++;
          }
          fclose(in);
          if (pushFlag) {
               /* Now terminate the server push sequence altogether */
               fprintf(cgiOut, "\n--goober--\n");
          }
          return 0;
     }
```

Testing HTTP_USER_AGENT in Perl: nph-p2

The following is the Perl source code for the nph-p2 program.

```
#!/usr/local/bin/perl

# This filename must be changed. The file it points to
# must contain a list of GIF files on your system,
# specified by complete paths.

$gifListFile = "/CHANGE/THIS/FILE/giflist.txt";

sub SupportsServerPush
{
     local($userAgent) = $ENV{'HTTP_USER_AGENT'} ;
     $version = 0;
     $_ = $userAgent;
     if (/Mozilla\/(\d\.\d)/) {
          if ($1 >= 1.1) {
               return 1;
          }
     }
     return 0;
}

open(IN, $gifListFile);
@list = <IN>;
close(IN);
```

```
print "HTTP/1.0 200 OK\n";

$pushFlag = &SupportsServerPush;

if ($pushFlag) {
      print "Content-type: multipart/x-mixed-
replace;boundary=goober\n\n";
}

foreach $name (@list) {
      $name =~ s/\n//g;
      # Now output the file
      if ($pushFlag) {
            print "\n--goober\n";
      }
      print "Content-type: image/gif\n\n";

      open(IN, $name);

      while (read(IN, $buffer, 4096)) {
            print $buffer;
      }
      close($name);
      if (! $pushFlag) {
            last;
      }
      # A short delay to make sure each frame is appreciated
      sleep(1);
}

if ($pushFlag) {
      print "\n--goober--\n";
}

exit 0;
```

Installing and Testing nph-p2

Install nph-p2 exactly as you installed nph-push. Be sure to modify the Web page to refer to the new program. When you test it, be sure to try accessing the Web page from a browser that does not support server push. You should see the first frame, instead of a "broken image" icon. Note, some browsers may claim to be Netscape for compatibility reasons.

Implementing Imagemaps

Imagemaps are a very popular way to add interesting methods of navigation to a Web page. Imagemaps, unlike ordinary image buttons, direct the user to a different page depending on where the user clicks in the image.

By now, many users are familiar with the process of creating imagemaps. Most HTML authors use a WYSIWYG tool, such as my Mapedit software, which is available for Microsoft Windows and for the X Window System. Both versions of Mapedit are included on the CD; see Appendix 5 for more information. Tools for the Macintosh, such as WebMap and MapMaker, are also available on the Web. See the World Wide Web FAQ[1] for more information.

WYSIWYG tools ease the pain of creating imagemaps in the standard formats expected by most Web servers. The NCSA format is the most common, followed by the CERN format.

But how is the imagemap actually implemented? What piece of software on the server end actually decides which page should be loaded in response to a click on an image with the `ISMAP` attribute? A CGI program does the work, of course.

The most recent browsers also allow client-side imagemaps. These imagemaps reside entirely in the HTML page, and the client does the work of delivering the appropriate page. This feature should be widespread by the time you read this. The various WYSIWYG imagemap editing tools will undoubtedly support it as well.

When CGI Isn't the Best Way

Client-side imagemaps are superior to server-side imagemaps for most applications. When all Web browsers support them, it will be a great convenience not to have to create a map file separate from the HTML page for every imagemap. Installing map files on Web servers is a source of much user confusion.

When CGI Is the Best Way

Sometimes it is not only desirable but essential that the server decide what happens in response to the imagemap. The best examples of this are applications in which the programmer wants to dynamically magnify or otherwise interact with the portion of the image that is clicked, perhaps using more information than the client possesses. In such applications, generating a grid of little rectangles to place in an imagemap file would be wasted effort. The CGI program should respond to the imagemap click by itself, rather than use the generic imagemap program or a client-side imagemap.

Parsing Imagemap Clicks in CGI Programs

Consider the following HTML excerpt:

```
<a href="/cgi-bin/imagemap.cgi/mapname">
<img src="image.gif" ISMAP>
</a>
```

Note the ISMAP attribute of the <img> tag. This attribute informs the browser that this image should be treated as a map and not as an ordinary image.

When the user clicks the image, the CGI program pointed to by the surrounding link is invoked with the following value for the QUERY_STRING environment variable:

```
x,y
```

where *x* and *y* will be the coordinates of the click on the image. The example program that follows takes advantage of this information to create a CGI "magnifying glass."

Dynamically Magnifying Images: A CGI Imagemap Example

The following program demonstrates something that ordinary imagemaps cannot do well: magnify an image and in the process center the new view on the position of the click.

This program takes advantage of the gd library, introduced in Chapter 10. The C version also uses the cgic library.

Magnifying Images in C: mag.c

The following is the source code for the mag program.

```c
#include "gd.h"
#include "cgic.h"

#define IMAGE_FILE "/CHANGE/THIS/FILE/name.gif"

void Magnify(int x, int y, gdImagePtr im);

int cgiMain() {
        int x = -1, y = -1;
        gdImagePtr im = 0;
        if (strstr(cgiPathInfo, ".gif")) {
                /* This is a request for an image */
                FILE *in;
                in = fopen(IMAGE_FILE, "rb");
                im = gdImageCreateFromGif(in);
                fclose(in);
        }
        sscanf(cgiQueryString, "%d,%d", &x, &y);
        if ((x != -1) && (y != -1)) {
                /* This is a request for a magnified portion
                        of the image, or the page it will appear in */
                Magnify(x, y, im);
                return 0;
        }
        if (im) {
                /* Top view: no magnification */
                cgiHeaderContentType("image/gif");
                gdImageGif(im, cgiOut);
        } else {
                /* Top page, with an <img src> tag pointing to
                        an unmagnified gif */
                cgiHeaderContentType("text/html");
                fprintf(cgiOut, "<html>\n");
                fprintf(cgiOut, "<head>\n");
                fprintf(cgiOut, "<title>CGI Magnifying Glass</title>\n");
                fprintf(cgiOut, "</head>\n");
                fprintf(cgiOut, "<body>\n");
                fprintf(cgiOut, "<h1>CGI Magnifying Glass</h1>\n");
                fprintf(cgiOut, "Click anywhere in the image for a\n");
                fprintf(cgiOut, "magnified view.\n");
                fprintf(cgiOut, "<p>\n");
                fprintf(cgiOut, "<a href=index.html>\n");
```

```
                fprintf(cgiOut, "<img src=\"image.gif\" ISMAP>\n");
                fprintf(cgiOut, "</a>\n");
                fprintf(cgiOut, "</body>\n");
                fprintf(cgiOut, "</html>\n");
        }
        /* Free the memory associated with the image */
        if (im) {
                gdImageDestroy(im);
        }
        return 0;
}


void Magnify(int x, int y, gdImagePtr im)
{
        if (im) {
                /* Generate a 4x magnified image */
                gdImagePtr mag;
                mag = gdImageCreate(200, 200);
                /* Copies and stretches the desired portion of the image */
                gdImageCopyResized(mag, im,
                        0, 0,
                        x - 25, y - 25,
                        200, 200,
                        50, 50);
                cgiHeaderContentType("image/gif");
                gdImageGif(mag, cgiOut);
                gdImageDestroy(mag);
        } else {
                /* A page with an <img src> tag pointing to
                        the magnified GIF and a link to return
                        to the normal top-down view */

                cgiHeaderContentType("text/html");
                fprintf(cgiOut, "<html>\n");
                fprintf(cgiOut, "<head>\n");
                fprintf(cgiOut, "<title>Magnified View</title>\n");
                fprintf(cgiOut, "</head>\n");
                fprintf(cgiOut, "<body>\n");
                fprintf(cgiOut, "<h1>Magnified View</h1>\n");
                fprintf(cgiOut, "<a href=\"index.html\">\n");
                fprintf(cgiOut, "Up to the complete image</a>\n");

                /* A trick to remember: we generate a src attribute
                        which will appear to the program just like the original
                        imagemap click did, but with "/image.gif" in
                        the PATH_INFO variable. This will invoke the
```

```
                          other branch of this function to generate the image. */

                  fprintf(cgiOut, "<p><img src=\"image.gif?%d,%d\">\n", x, y);

                  fprintf(cgiOut, "</body>\n");
                  fprintf(cgiOut, "</html>\n");
          }
          if (im) {
                  gdImageDestroy(im);
          }
  }
```

Magnifying Images in Perl: mag

The following is the Perl source code for the mag program.

```perl
#!/usr/local/bin/perl
require 5.001;
use GD;

$imageFile = "/CHANGE/THIS/FILE/name.gif";
$x = -1;
$y = -1;

if ($ENV{"PATH_INFO"}  eq "/image.gif") {
    # This is a request for an image
    open(IN, $imageFile);
    $im = newFromGif GD::Image(IN);
    close(IN);
    $image = 1;
}

$_ = $ENV{"QUERY_STRING"} ;

if (/(\d+), (\d+)/) {
    # This is a request for a magnified portion
    # of the image, or the page it will appear in
    &Magnify($1, $2, $im, $image);
    exit 0;
}

if ($image) {
    # Top view: no magnification
    print "Content-type: image/gif"\n\n";
    print $im->gif;
```

```perl
    } else {
          # Top page, with an <img src> tag pointing to
          # an unmagnified GIF image
          print "Content-type: text/html\n\n";
          print "<html>\n";
          print "<head>\n";
          print "<title>CGI Magnifying Glass</title>\n";
          print "</head>\n";
          print "<body>\n";
          print "<h1>CGI Magnifying Glass</h1>\n";
          print "Click anywhere in the image for a\n";
          print "magnified view.\n";
          print "<p>\n";
          print "<a href=\"index.html\">\n";
          print "<img src=\"image.gif\" ISMAP>\n";
          print "</a>\n";
          print "</body>\n";
          print "</html>\n";
    }

    exit 0;

    sub Magnify
    {
          local($x, $y, $im, $image) = @_;
          if ($image) {
                # Generate a 4x magnified image
                $mag = new GD::Image(200, 200);
                # Copies and stretches the desired portion of the image
                $mag->copyResized($im,
                      0, 0,
                      $x - 25, $y - 25,
                      200, 200,
                      50, 50);
                print "Content-type: image/gif\n\n";
                print $mag->gif;
          } else {
                # A page with an <img src> tag pointing to
                # the magnified GIF and a link to return
                # to the normal top-down view

                print "Content-type: text/html\n\n";
                print "<html>\n";
                print "<head>\n";
                print "<title>Magnified View</title>\n";
```

```
print "</head>\n";
print "<body>\n";
print "<h1>Magnified View</h1>\n";
print "<a href=\"index.html\">\n";
print "Up to the complete image</a>\n";

# A trick to remember: we generate a src attribute
# which will appear to the program just like the original
# imagemap click did, but with "/image.gif" in
# the PATH_INFO variable. This will invoke the
# other branch of this function to generate the image.

print "<p><img src=\"image.gif?", $x, ",", $y, "\">\n";
print "</body>\n";
print "</html>\n";
    }
  }
```

Installing the CGI Magnifying Glass

Before installing mag, be sure to set GIF_FILE_PATH or $gifFilePath to the location of a GIF file in your file system. To ensure interesting results, be sure to point to a fairly large GIF.

The C version of mag must be linked with both the gd library and the cgic library. See the CD and Appendix 5 for a single Makefile suitable to build all of the example C programs in the book.

The Perl version of mag requires that the GD.pm Perl module be properly installed on your system. See Chapter 10 for additional details.

Accessing the Magnifying Glass

Assuming you have installed the compiled program or Perl script at the URL http://mysite/cgi-bin/mag, open the following URL with your Web browser:

```
http://mysite/cgi-bin/mag/
```

Note the final slash. This is important. The relative URLs output by the magnifying glass program will not be interpreted correctly if this trailing slash is not present, and the program will not behave as expected.

Figures 12–1 and 12–2 provide examples of the magnifying glass program in use.

FIGURE 12–1 An overhead view generated by the CGI magnifying glass

Redirection: Forwarding Requests to Another URL

It is quite common for documents to move from one place to another. Usually, the forwarding address problem is solved by establishing a Web page at the old address that simply states the new URL, strongly encourages

FIGURE 12–2 A magnified view displayed by the CGI magnifying glass

the user to update the link that led to the page, and provides a link to the new location.

Sometimes, however, you may prefer to automatically forward the user to another page. This may be because you have given up all hope of eradicating old references to your old URL or because you prefer to provide the user with a smooth transition.

There are other applications for URL forwarding. For instance, you might want to redirect the user to a different URL in response to a particular imagemap click. This is how the standard server imagemap programs work.

To instruct the browser to load a different URL, simply output the following, and only the following, from a CGI program:

```
Location: URL
URI:URL
```

followed by two line breaks.

cgic provides a convenient call to implement this:

```
cgiHeaderLocation(url);
```

Then return from `cgiMain()`. Of course, outputting the `Location:` line "by hand" in a C or Perl program is not very difficult either.

> **NOTE:** Relative URLs are acceptable on the Location: line. However, keep in mind that if a relative URL is seen by the server, the server will attempt to resolve it internally without actually instructing the browser to load a new URL. Doing this produces a performance gain, with the disadvantage that the Web browser will still display the old URL at the top of the page. If this is undesirable, be sure to output a complete URL beginning with `http://host/...` at all times. Of course, other protocol specifiers besides `http:` are also acceptable.

Using capture: Debugging CGI Programs in Real Debuggers

Although CGI programs are often simple, even the simplest program can contain bugs. Most CGI programmers debug their code the old-fashioned way by inserting code to print the values of variables, studying the output, staring at the code in dismay for a few minutes or days, and making a fix.

While this technique is sometimes the best way to go, there are less painful ways to debug most programs. Perl programmers don't have to wait as long for the compiler to process a new version of their code. They typically find that using a few well-placed print commands to track down problems is sufficient. But C programmers who are familiar with good debugging tools are often used to being able to set breakpoints that cause the program to stop in mid-execution. Such debugging tools can then be used to check the values of variables, to step through the program line by line, and so on. The program's behavior can be examined in detail without the need to modify and recompile the code. Access to such tools from CGI programs is desirable.

The cgic capture Program

The cgic CGI library for C programmers includes two function calls that can be used to save and restore the CGI environment: cgiWriteEnvironment() and cgiReadEnvironment(). The cgiWriteEnvironment() function saves the values of environment variables as well as the information submitted to the CGI program through a form and so allows the state of a real CGI situation to be captured.

cgic includes a simple program, capture, that takes advantage of cgiWriteEnvironment() to write the entire CGI environment to a file.

Taking Advantage of capture

To use the capture program, first enter the cgic source directory and modify the first line of the main() function of capture.c. Change the filename to point to a file that is readable and writable by the Web server.

To install the capture program, simply install it in your CGI area and change the link or <form> tag action that currently points to the cgic program you wish to debug. Next, select the link (or submit the form) using your Web browser. Instead of seeing the normal output of your cgic program, you should see a message from the capture program acknowledging that the state of the CGI request was recorded.

Running Your cgic Program in the Debugger

Now that you have captured a CGI request with the capture program, all you have to do is make a small change to the program you are debugging in order to read the recorded state from the captured file.

First, make sure your program is compiled for debugging. Under Unix, this is typically done by specifying the -g option to the C compiler; otherwise, the debugger will not produce much useful output.

At the beginning of your cgiMain() function, add the following call:

```
cgiReadEnvironment("/file/where/capture/saved/data");
```

replacing the filename with the filename to which the capture program wrote its output.

Finally, launch your program in your debugger of choice. Under Unix, the gdb and dbx debuggers are most common. If you have gcc, you very likely have gdb installed as well.

Using gdb, for example, start your program with the following commands:

```
gdb myprogram
run
```

If your program crashes and you compiled it with the -g option, you will be informed of the line in your program that was responsible for the crash. Type the command

```
where
```

To see the stack of functions above the function where the program actually crashed. To see a few lines of source code above and below the location where the program crashed, type

```
list
```

Breakpoints in gdb

If your program is not crashing but is producing incorrect output, try setting a breakpoint so that you can investigate the values of variables. First type

```
list myfunction
```

to display the function that contains the location at which you want to examine variables. Then set a breakpoint at the relevant line by typing

```
break linenumber
```

Finally, type

```
run
```

The program will stop and return to the debugger temporarily when and if it reaches the line of code you specified. Use the command

```
print variablename
```

to see the value of a variable.

For more information about gdb and other debuggers, see the online documentation and manuals of your development tools. Under Unix, the command man gdb is bound to be informative. gdb also has a help command.

Don't forget to remove or comment out the cgiReadEnvironment() call once your program is working correctly!

Conclusion

In this chapter I have introduced numerous advanced features of CGI and examined debugging issues. I now have explored all of the commonly used CGI features and quite a few of its more difficult and impressive techniques. The set of features discussed so far is sufficient for most of what can reasonably be done with CGI.

Reasonable things, however, are not necessarily the most fun or the most impressive. In the next chapter, I put together many of these pieces in an application that pushes the limits of CGI. The result: an interactive, continuous-motion, graphical simulation of our solar system with user input.

References

1. Thomas Boutell, "World Wide Web Frequently Asked Questions." [URL:http://www.boutell.com/faq]

## CHAPTER 13

The Solar System Simulator: Pushing the Limitations of CGI

A s you know, CGI stands for Common Gateway Interface. When the standard was created, it was envisioned that it would primarily be used to provide simple gateways between the Web and various databases and information search facilities. As it turns out, however, CGI can be used for purposes the inventors doubtless did not have in mind. The Solar System Simulator (SSS) is such an application. The SSS presents an animated overview of our solar system.

In Chapter 12 the subject of server push animation was introduced, along with stern warnings that it currently works only with Netscape, that it uses a great deal of bandwidth, and so on. The SSS blithely ignores these warnings and implements a continuously animated application with a point-and-click user interface This is something that is not normally done via the Web.

Is CGI the Right Way to Do This?

Doubtless there are better ways to create continuous animation, given the technology to implement them. If you don't mind offering your software only to Windows users, you can write a Windows application to simulate the planets more quickly and convincingly than the SSS can. If you don't mind hiring many, many engineers or spending large sums of money for a cross-platform development system, you can write the same program for Windows, the Macintosh, and the X Window System.

If, on the other hand, you would rather have the application work automatically on any machine that offers Netscape 1.1 or later, CGI starts to look like a good choice. What CGI lacks in elegance and efficiency, it makes up for in market share and ease of access. Users can simply follow a link to the SSS and go. No need to install software.

Java Versus CGI

Needless to say, Sun's Java technology will change this picture considerably, especially for animation-intensive applications like the SSS. Java provides the capability to install client-side applets in Web browsers. Java applets can be downloaded automatically as part of Web pages. A version of the SSS written in Java would be able to execute entirely within the browser without downloading animation frames through the Internet.

However, there will probably always be sites that forbid Java for security reasons, despite the extensive and impressive security provisions in the Java system.

More information on this is provided in Chapter 15.

Designing the SSS: Overcoming CGI Limitations

The SSS functions much like any normal point-and-click software application installed on a Windows or Macintosh PC. This is remarkable, considering the Web is a stateless and largely static system. In most cases, nothing happens "in" a Web page until the user clicks a link, and most pages give no indication of awareness that they are carrying out an ongoing "conversation" with a particular user. The SSS overcomes these limitations by storing a complete copy of the status of each active session with a user, as explained next.

Recording State Information in the SSS

Normally, CGI programs accomplish one task, exit, and are content. Even programs such as the WBW discussed earlier in this book do not record information about the status of a session with a particular user. Instead, they generate links to themselves that completely describe the next thing that should happen. For instance, the WBW generates links to the list of birthdays for a particular month by setting PATH_INFO to /january or another appropriate value. There is not enough information about the session to require a more powerful solution.

The SSS, however, needs to store a large amount of information, too much to be stored in a URL. So, the information is kept in files on the server's end. This approach allows the SSS to keep a great deal of information about the current user's preferences and the state of the solar system.

The PATH_INFO technique discussed in earlier chapters is used to identify the current session of the SSS. Every link generated by the SSS contains the following:

```
http://site/path/to/nph-sss.cgi/ID:n/
```

followed by the action to be taken in response to that particular link.

Note the ID:n portion of the URL. In practice, n is replaced by an integer associated with a particular interactive session of the SSS.

 "Fine, but where is the actual information about the session stored?"

 A directory on the server is used to keep a set of files, one for each session. These files contain a complete description of the "state" of that session. For instance, the state files contain the position, velocity, and mass of each of the objects in the solar system, as well as the magnification setting chosen by the user.

 "Since there is no way to know for sure that the user is completely done with the program, won't the session files accumulate forever?"

 Theoretically they would. In practice, a simple cron job can be used to remove all of the .sav files at some hour of the night. However, because other time zones may be using the program at 2 A.M. local time, a better approach might be to write a short script that checks for .sav files that have not been modified for more than 24 hours and removes them.

Here is the crontab entry which removes my session files nightly:

```
0 2 * * * rm /home/boutell/sss/*.sav
```

For more information about the scheduling of cron jobs, see the manpages for the crontab program and the format of crontab files. On most Unix systems, these manpages are accessible by the commands man crontab and man 5 crontab, respectively.

Flow of Control in the SSS

The Page() Function

When the SSS is first accessed, it invokes the function Page() with the firstTime argument set to true. This function invokes SelectSessionId() to generate a new, never-before-used session ID number. Next, the ObjectsSetup() function is invoked to obtain the initial positions, names, velocities, and other parameters of the sun and planets.

The Page() function then goes on to generate an HTML page that provides several links to control the SSS. It also generates an imagemap anchor and an <img src> tag, followed by a form providing a way to quickly change many settings in the program. All of these links point right back to the SSS CGI program, with the session ID at the beginning of the PATH_INFO portion of the URL.

After the session ID, each link output by Page() contains a keyword indicating what the program should do when it is executed to retrieve that link. The most important keywords are /select, which is used for the imagemap anchor, and /canvas.gif, which is used for the inline image itself.

Once Page() has executed, the program exits. It counts on the Web browser to open a new connection to it in order to retrieve the inline image.

The Canvas() Function

The Canvas() function is invoked when the program receives a request for a URL ending in the string /canvas.gif. This function reads the current state of the session using the function ReadSessionState() and then enters a continuous loop.

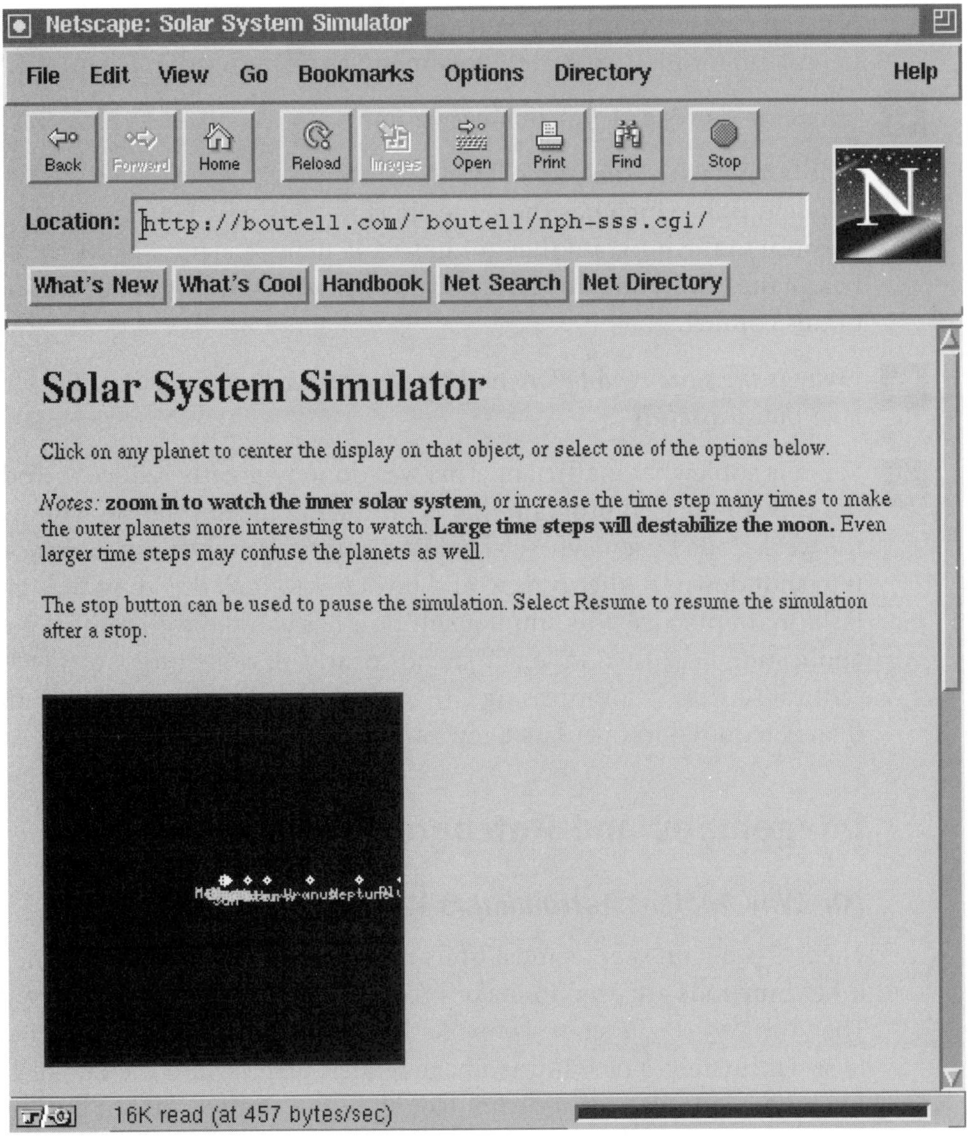

FIGURE 13–1 Initial appearance of the solar system

Within the loop, individual frames of animation are calculated and drawn. Each planet's velocity and position must be updated in accordance with Newton's laws of universal gravitation. Of course, this is just an approximate simulation and the orbits of the planets are not precisely correct (see Figure 13–1). Nor do they correspond to the real positions of the planets at some point in history.

Netscape's server push mechanism is used to send the individual frames as part of a multiple-part MIME document, as introduced in Chapter 12.

Q *"Does the* **Canvas()** *function ever exit?"*

A It does only when the user clicks the browser's Stop button or selects a different link, which has the same effect in Netscape. Unfortunately, the instance of the program that animates the planets is not always shut down before the new request arrives. See the next question for the consequences of this conflict.

Q *"Why is the state read before and saved after each movement of the planets? Isn't that wasteful?"*

A Yes, it is somewhat inefficient. This was done to greatly reduce the odds that the copy of the CGI program that is producing the animation will overwrite the work done by a newly selected link before the server has a chance to tell it to shut down. In theory, it would be better to lock the .sav files in some fashion. In practice, this simpler solution has worked well for this particular application because Canvas() spends nearly all of its time outside that "critical section." Compressing GIF images takes much more CPU effort than is required to calculate a few orbital positions.

Imagemaps and Retrograde Motion

(Or, Why Ancient Astronomers Were So Confused)

The SSS program spends most of its time in the Canvas() function. The other functions are used to make small changes to the state of the system. Then the Page() function is invoked with the firstTime argument set to false. Ultimately, a new inline image request arrives, and the Canvas() function begins executing again. Not all of the shorter "action button" functions are discussed here.

The Select() function, in particular, is interesting because it takes care of imagemap clicks in order to determine the nearest planet to the position clicked. Once this is determined, the Select() function changes the state of the session to indicate that the display should be centered on that particular object. To see what confused the ancient astronomers so terribly, select the Zoom In link several times to bring the inner solar system into clear view and then click Earth to center the display on that object.

The sun appears to orbit Earth. This is not the strangest thing that happens! Click the Time Step x 2 link several times to speed up the simulation. Soon, one or more of the inner planets will appear to change direction and move backwards for a period of time. See Figure 13–2.

This strange behavior, known as retrograde motion, is the clue that eventually permitted astronomers to prove that Earth orbits the Sun, rather than the other way around.

Losing the Moon

If the time step is increased to one day per step or more, the simulation will not be accurate enough to simulate the moon's orbit, the smallest orbit in the system. The moon will gradually separate from Earth and orbit the sun by itself. This isn't a bug; it's a (mis-)feature.

The Nemesis Encounter

Astronomers will note that the program would run much faster if it simply implemented Kepler's laws instead of making laborious calculations of gravitation. However, this would preclude a highly entertaining feature: the

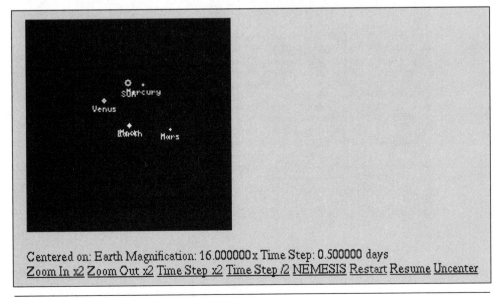

Centered on: Earth Magnification: 16.000000 x Time Step: 0.500000 days
Zoom In x2 Zoom Out x2 Time Step x2 Time Step /2 NEMESIS Restart Resume Uncenter

FIGURE 13–2 An ancient astronomer's viewpoint

NEMESIS encounter. Select the NEMESIS link to see what happens when a massive object crosses through our solar system.

When a request for a URL with /nemesis at the end is received, the SSS program invokes the Nemesis() function. This function, like most of the "action button" links, makes a few judicious changes to the state of the session and invokes Page(0) to resume the session. In this case, the change is rather malicious. The Nemesis() function searches the list of objects and finds the most massive object. Unless Nemesis() has previously been invoked, this will be the sun. An object of double that mass is then added to the system and given a velocity sufficient to cross the solar system in one year.

If you use the magnification option to watch the inner solar system in the aftermath of Nemesis' passage, it is not difficult to see the orbital havoc wreaked by a visit from such a large object! Even the sun itself begins to jitter significantly. See Figure 13–3.

Subsequent clicks on the NEMESIS button will introduce additional nemeses, each twice as massive as its predecessor. Before long, planets are being

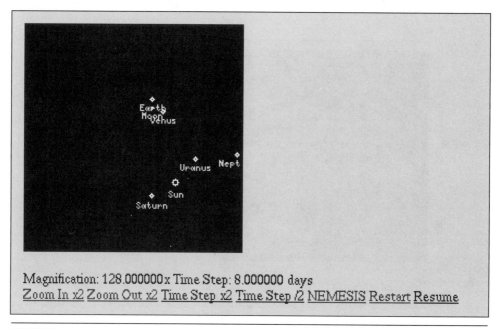

Magnification: 128.000000 x Time Step: 8.000000 days
Zoom In x2 Zoom Out x2 Time Step x2 Time Step /2 NEMESIS Restart Resume

FIGURE 13–3 The aftermath of nemesis

expelled violently from the solar system by gravitational slingshots. Or the outer planets may collapse inwards toward the sun. Many outcomes are possible, depending on exactly where the planets are positioned when the nemesis object makes its visit.

A Reminder Regarding nph- and Server Push

For server push programs to work as expected, they must be permitted to generate their own HTTP headers and their output must not be buffered by the server. So it is important that the name under which the SSS is installed begin with the characters nph- when installed on an NCSA, Apache, Netscape, or similar Web server.

When Caching Is a Bad Thing: The nocache Pragma

Web browsers regularly cache Web pages. If the same URL is accessed twice in a session or even over a longer period of time, most Web browsers will attempt to satisfy the request by displaying a copy of the page that has been kept in a cache. This is great, as it speeds up Web access considerably. However, for dynamic pages like those produced by the SSS program, it is usually incorrect to display old copies.

Fortunately, most Web browsers support a way of overriding this behavior. The following line can be output by the CGI program to prevent caching of the page:

```
Pragma: nocache
```

The SSS takes advantage of this feature to ensure that new data is always sent to the user.

The objects.dat File

The following are the contents of the objects.dat file, which describes the initial position of each object. Distance is measured in kilometers; velocity is measured in kilometers per day. The first line in the file specifies the universal constant of gravitation, a key constant in Newton's laws. For convenience in our trying out changes to the system, blank lines and lines beginning with a # character are ignored.

```
6.67e-10
Sun 0 0 0 0 1.99e30 13.92e6
Mercury 57.9e6 0 0 47.9e5 0.3289e24 4880
Venus 108.2e6 0 0 35e5 4.8737e24 12104
Moon 149.6e6 3.8e5 .8089e5 29.8e5 7.36e22 1738
Earth 149.6e6 0 0 29.8e5 5.98e24 12756
Mars 227.9e6 0 0 24.1e5 0.64584e24 6787
Jupiter 778.3e6 0 0 13.1e5 1901.042e24 142800
Saturn 1427e6 0 0 9.6e5 569.296e24 120000
Uranus 2869.6e6 0 0 6.8e5 87.308e24 51800
Neptune 4496.6e6 0 0 5.4e5 102.856e24 49500
Pluto 5900e6 0 0 4.7e5 .598e24 6000
```

Perl Notes

The Perl version of this program requires Perl5 and the GD.pm module, as well as cgi-lib.pl. For more information on GD.pm, see Chapter 10.

The SSS in C: nph-sss.c

The following is the C source code for the nph-sss program.

```c
/* The Solar System, simulated on the Web. */

#include <stdio.h>
#include <math.h>
#include <stdlib.h>
#include <unistd.h>
#include <signal.h>
#include <string.h>
#include "cgic.h"
#include "gd.h"
#include "gdfontt.h"

#define OBJECTS_FILE "/CHANGE/THIS/FILE/sss/objects.dat"
#define PROGRAM_URL "/CHANGE/THIS/URL/cgi-bin/nph-sss"
#define PROGRAM_DATA_PATH "/CHANGE/THIS/PATH/sss/"

int windowSize = 200;

typedef struct {
```

```c
  double x,y;
  double vx,vy;
  double mass;
  double radius;
  char name[20];
} object;

int objectsTotal = 0;

double gConstant;

double maxX;
double maxY;
double minX;
double minY;
double width;
double magnification = 1.0;

#define OBJECTS_MAX 100

object objects[OBJECTS_MAX];


#define SCALEX(x) (((x-minX)/(maxX-minX))*windowSize)
#define UNSCALEX(x) ((x*(maxX-minX)/windowSize)+minX)
#define SCALEY(y) (((y-minY)/(maxY-minY))*windowSize)
#define UNSCALEY(y) ((y*(maxY-minY)/windowSize)+minY)

#ifndef PI
#define PI 3.141592653
#endif /* PI */

int Page(int firstTime);
int Canvas();
int Select();
int ZoomIn();
int ZoomOut();
int TimePlus();
int TimeMinus();
int Resume();
int Nemesis();
int UnCenter();
int SizePlus();
int SizeMinus();
int Form();
```

```
void AccountForCenter();
void ObjectsSetup();

int sessionId;

void SelectSessionId();

void WriteSessionState();
void ReadSessionState();

void ParseSessionId();

char *pathInfoP;

int cgiMain() {
     int i;
     pathInfoP = cgiPathInfo;
     ParseSessionId();
     if (!strcmp(pathInfoP, "/canvas.gif")) {
          return Canvas();
     } else if (!strcmp(pathInfoP, "/form")) {
          return Form();
     } else if (!strcmp(pathInfoP, "/zoomin")) {
          return ZoomIn();
     } else if (!strcmp(pathInfoP, "/zoomout")) {
          return ZoomOut();
     } else if (!strcmp(pathInfoP, "/timeplus")) {
          return TimePlus();
     } else if (!strcmp(pathInfoP, "/timeminus")) {
          return TimeMinus();
     } else if (!strcmp(pathInfoP, "/sizeplus")) {
          return SizePlus();
     } else if (!strcmp(pathInfoP, "/sizeminus")) {
          return SizeMinus();
     } else if (!strcmp(pathInfoP, "/uncenter")) {
          return UnCenter();
     } else if (!strcmp(pathInfoP, "/nemesis")) {
          return Nemesis();
     } else if (!strcmp(pathInfoP, "/select")) {
          return Select();
     } else if (!strcmp(pathInfoP, "/resume")) {
          return Resume();
     } else {
          return Page(1);
     }
}
```

```
int centerFloating = 0;
int centerFloatingObject;
double timeStep=0.5;

int Page(int firstTime) {
    int i;
    if (firstTime) {
        SelectSessionId();
        ObjectsSetup();
        WriteSessionState();
    }
    fprintf(cgiOut,
        "HTTP/1.0 200 OK\n");
    fprintf(cgiOut,
        "Pragma: nocache\n");
    cgiHeaderContentType("text/html");
    fprintf(cgiOut,
        "<html><head><title>Solar System Simulator</title></head>\n");
    fprintf(cgiOut,
        "<body><h1>Solar System Simulator</h1>\n");
    fprintf(cgiOut,
        "Click on any planet to center the display\n");
    fprintf(cgiOut,
        "on that object, or select one of the options below.\n<p>");
    fprintf(cgiOut,
        "<em>Notes:</em> <strong>zoom in to watch the inner solar
system</strong>,\n");
    fprintf(cgiOut,
        "or increase the time step many times to make the outer
planets\n");
    fprintf(cgiOut,
        "more interesting to watch.\n");
    fprintf(cgiOut, "<strong>Large time steps will destabilize the
moon.</strong>\n");
    fprintf(cgiOut,
        "Even larger time steps may confuse the planets as
well.<p>\n");
    fprintf(cgiOut,
        "The stop button can be used to pause the simulation.
Select\n");
    fprintf(cgiOut,
        "Resume to resume the simulation after a stop.<p>");

    /* Imagemap link */
    fprintf(cgiOut,
```

```
                    "<br><a href=\"%s/ID:%d/select\">\n",
                    PROGRAM_URL,
                    sessionId);

            /* Image */
            fprintf(cgiOut,
                    "<img src=\"%s/ID:%d/canvas.gif\" ISMAP></a>\n",
                    PROGRAM_URL,
                    sessionId);
            fprintf(cgiOut, "<p>\n");

            /* Status display */
            if (centerFloating) {
                    fprintf(cgiOut,
                            "Centered on: %s ",
                            objects[centerFloatingObject].name);
            }
            fprintf(cgiOut,
                    "Magnification: %fx ", magnification);
            fprintf(cgiOut,
                    "Time Step: %f days<br>", timeStep);

            /* Various controls */
            fprintf(cgiOut,
                    "<a href=\"%s/ID:%d/zoomin\">Zoom In x2</a> ",
                    PROGRAM_URL,
                    sessionId);
            fprintf(cgiOut,
                    "<a href=\"%s/ID:%d/zoomout\">Zoom Out x2</a> ",
                    PROGRAM_URL,
                    sessionId);
            fprintf(cgiOut,
                    "<a href=\"%s/ID:%d/timeplus\">Time Step x2</a> ",
                    PROGRAM_URL,
                    sessionId);
            fprintf(cgiOut,
                    "<a href=\"%s/ID:%d/timeminus\">Time Step /2</a> ",
                    PROGRAM_URL,
                    sessionId);
            /* This code works, but Netscape is very difficult to use
                    if the window is any larger than 200x200, at least on
                    my system. Feel free to remove the #if/#endif pair
                    and see what happens. */
#if 0
        if (windowSize < 1600) {
```

```
            fprintf(cgiOut,
                    "<a href=\"%s/ID:%d/sizeplus\">Window Size x2</a> ",
                    PROGRAM_URL,
                    sessionId);
        }
        if (windowSize > 25) {
            fprintf(cgiOut,
                    "<a href=\"%s/ID:%d/sizeminus\">Window Size /2</a> ",
                    PROGRAM_URL,
                    sessionId);
        }
#endif
        fprintf(cgiOut,
                "<a href=\"%s/ID:%d/nemesis\">NEMESIS</a> ",
                PROGRAM_URL,
                sessionId);
        fprintf(cgiOut,
                "<a href=\"%s/\">Restart</a> ",
                PROGRAM_URL);
        fprintf(cgiOut,
                "<a href=\"%s/ID:%d/resume\">Resume</a> ",
                PROGRAM_URL,
                sessionId);
        if (centerFloating) {
            fprintf(cgiOut,
                    "<a href=\"%s/ID:%d/uncenter\">Uncenter</a> ",
                    PROGRAM_URL,
                    sessionId);
        }
        fprintf(cgiOut, "<p>\n");

        /* A form, for skilled users */
        fprintf(cgiOut, "<hr>Use this form if you wish to make several
changes quickly.<p>\n");
        fprintf(cgiOut, "<form action=\"%s/ID:%d/form\">\n",
                PROGRAM_URL,
                sessionId);
        fprintf(cgiOut, "<input type=submit value=\"Submit Changes\">
<input type=reset value=\"Clear Form\"><br>\n");
        fprintf(cgiOut, "<input type=text name=magnification
value=\"%f\"> Magnification<br>\n", magnification);
        fprintf(cgiOut, "<input type=text name=timestep value\"=%f\">
Time Step (days)<br>\n", timeStep);
        fprintf(cgiOut, "Center Display On:<br>");
        fprintf(cgiOut, "<select name=center>\n");
```

```
            if (centerFloating) {
                  fprintf(cgiOut, "<option value=\"-1\"> Nothing<br\n>");
            } else {
                  fprintf(cgiOut, "<option value=\"-1\" selected>
Nothing<br>\n");
            }
            for (i=0; (i < objectsTotal); i++) {
                  fprintf(cgiOut, "<option value=\"%d\" ", i);
                  if (centerFloating && (centerFloatingObject == i)) {
                        fprintf(cgiOut, "selected");
                  }
                  fprintf(cgiOut, "> %s<br>\n", objects[i].name);
            }
            fprintf(cgiOut, "</select>\n<br>");
            fprintf(cgiOut, "</form>\n");
            fprintf(cgiOut, "</body></html>\n");
            return 0;
      }

      int Canvas() {
            int i, j;
            int x,y;
            int done = 0;
            int labels = 0;
            int trails = 0;
            gdImagePtr im;
            int black;
            int white;
            int blue;
            fprintf(cgiOut,
                  "HTTP/1.0 200 OK\n");

            cgiHeaderContentType(
                  "multipart/x-mixed-replace;boundary=goober");
            while (!done) {
                  /* Re-read the session state, do the computations
                        as quickly as possible, and write the state
                        again. */
                  ReadSessionState();
                  for (i=0; (i < objectsTotal); i++) {
                        double x,y;
                        for (j=0; (j < objectsTotal); j++) {
                              if (i != j) {
                                    double dist;
                                    double pull;
```

```
                            dist = hypot(
                                    objects[i].x - objects[j].x,
                                    objects[i].y - objects[j].y);
                            if (dist != 0.0) {
                                    pull=(gConstant *
                                            objects[j].mass /
                                            (dist * dist));
                                    objects[i].vx +=
                                            (objects[j].x -
                                                    objects[i].x) /
                                            dist * pull * timeStep;
                                    objects[i].vy +=
                                            (objects[j].y -
                                                    objects[i].y) /
                                            dist * pull * timeStep;
                            }
                    }
            }
    }
    for (i=0; (i < objectsTotal); i++) {
            objects[i].x += (objects[i].vx * timeStep);
            objects[i].y += (objects[i].vy * timeStep);
    }
    WriteSessionState();
    AccountForCenter();
    /* Now build a GIF */
    im = gdImageCreate(windowSize, windowSize);
    black = gdImageColorAllocate(im, 0, 0, 0);
    white = gdImageColorAllocate(im, 255, 255, 255);
    blue = gdImageColorAllocate(im, 192, 192, 255);
    for (i=0; (i<objectsTotal); i++) {
            object *o = &objects[i];
            double val = log10(o->radius);
            int x = SCALEX(o->x);
            int y = SCALEY(o->y);
            gdImageArc(im, x, y,
                    val, val, 0, 360, white);
            gdImageString(im, gdFontTiny,
                    x - (gdFontTiny->w *
                    strlen(o->name) / 2),
                    y + val,
                    o->name, blue);
    }
    sleep(1);
    fprintf(cgiOut, "\n--goober\n");
```

```c
                fprintf(cgiOut, "Content-type: image/gif\n\n");
                gdImageGif(im, cgiOut);
                gdImageDestroy(im);
                fflush(cgiOut);
        }
        fprintf(cgiOut, "\n--goober--\n");
        return 0;
}

void CenterClosest(int x, int y);

int Select() {
        int x, y;
        ReadSessionState();
        if (sscanf(cgiQueryString, "%d,%d", &x, &y) != 2) {
                cgiHeaderContentType("text/html");
                fprintf(cgiOut,
                    "HTTP/1.0 200 Document follows\n");
                fprintf(cgiOut, "<h1>Bad Click: %s</h1\n>",
cgiQueryString);
                return 0;
        }
        CenterClosest(x, y);
        WriteSessionState();
        return Page(0);
}

int UnCenter() {
        ReadSessionState();
        centerFloating = 0;
        WriteSessionState();
        return Page(0);
}

int ZoomIn() {
        ReadSessionState();
        magnification *= 2.0;
        WriteSessionState();
        return Page(0);
}

int ZoomOut() {
        ReadSessionState();
        magnification /= 2.0;
        WriteSessionState();
```

```
        return Page(0);
}

int TimePlus() {
        ReadSessionState();
        timeStep *= 2.0;
        WriteSessionState();
        return Page(0);
}

int TimeMinus() {
        ReadSessionState();
        timeStep /= 2.0;
        WriteSessionState();
        return Page(0);
}

int SizePlus() {
        ReadSessionState();
        if (windowSize < 200) {
                windowSize *= 2;
        }
        WriteSessionState();
        return Page(0);
}

int SizeMinus() {
        ReadSessionState();
        if (windowSize) {
                windowSize /= 2;
        }
        WriteSessionState();
        return Page(0);
}

int Resume() {
        ReadSessionState();
        return Page(0);
}
int Nemesis() {
        double largestMass = 1.0, largestRadius = 1.0;
        int i;
        object *o;
        ReadSessionState();
        if (objectsTotal == OBJECTS_MAX) {
```

```
                    /* Don't break the simulation */
                    return 0;
            }
            /* Wreak havoc: introduce an object as
                    large as the largest object in the
                    system and send it whizzing through. */
            for (i=0; (i < objectsTotal); i++) {
                    if ((!i) || (objects[i].mass > largestMass)) {
                            largestMass = objects[i].mass;
                    }
                    if ((!i) || (objects[i].radius > largestRadius)) {
                            largestRadius = objects[i].radius;
                    }
            }
            o = &objects[objectsTotal];
            /* Start in the upper left corner of the simulation */
            o->x = minX;
            o->y = minY;
            /* Fast enough to cross in 365 days */
            o->vx = (maxX - minX) / 365.0;
            o->vy = (maxY - minY) / 365.0;
            /* Very big, very nasty */
            o->mass = largestMass * 2;
            o->radius = largestRadius * 2;
            strcpy(o->name, "NEMESIS");
            objectsTotal++;
            WriteSessionState();
            return Page(0);
    }

void SelectSessionId() {
        FILE *in;
        FILE *out;
        char s[256];
        /* Come up with a new, never-before-used session id. */
        sprintf(s, "%s/id", PROGRAM_DATA_PATH);

        in = fopen(s, "r");

        if (!fscanf(in, "%d\n", &sessionId)) {
                sessionId = 0;
        }
        fclose(in);
```

```
        out = fopen(s, "w");
        fprintf(out, "%d\n", sessionId+1);
        fclose(out);
}

void ParseSessionId() {
        if (!strncmp(pathInfoP, "/ID:", 4)) {
                char *next;
                sessionId = atoi(pathInfoP + 4);
                next = strchr(pathInfoP + 4, '/');
                if (next) {
                        pathInfoP = next;
                } else {
                        pathInfoP = "";
                }
        }
}

void CenterClosest(int x, int y) {
        double smallestDist;
        int i;
        double centerX, centerY;
        centerFloating = 1;
        AccountForCenter();
        centerX = UNSCALEX(x);
        centerY = UNSCALEY(y);
        for (i=0; (i<objectsTotal); i++) {
                double dist;
                dist = hypot(objects[i].x -
                        centerX,objects[i].y - centerY);
                if (dist < smallestDist || (!i)) {
                        smallestDist = dist;
                        centerFloatingObject = i;
                }
        }
}

void AccountForCenter() {
        if (centerFloating) {
                minX = objects[centerFloatingObject].x -
                        width / 2.0 / magnification;
                maxX = objects[centerFloatingObject].x +
                        width / 2.0 / magnification;
                minY = objects[centerFloatingObject].y -
                        width / 2.0 / magnification;
```

```
                maxY = objects[centerFloatingObject].y +
                       width / 2.0 / magnification;
        } else {
            double cX, cY;
            cX = (minX + maxX) / 2.0;
            cY = (minY + maxY) / 2.0;
            minX = cX - width / 2.0 / magnification;
            maxX = cX + width / 2.0 / magnification;
            minY = cY - width / 2.0 / magnification;
            maxY = cY + width / 2.0 / magnification;
        }
}

int Form() {
        int center;
        ReadSessionState();

        /* cgic makes this very easy. Use the current values
                as the defaults. */
        cgiFormDouble("magnification", &magnification, magnification);
        cgiFormDouble("timestep", &timeStep, timeStep);

        /* Find out which object was centered on, if any. */
        cgiFormInteger("center", &center, -1);
        if (center == -1) {
            centerFloating = 0;
        } else if ((center >= 0) && (center < objectsTotal)) {
            centerFloating = 1;
            centerFloatingObject = center;
        }
        WriteSessionState();
        return Page(0);
}

void ObjectsSetup(void) {
        FILE* in;
        object *o;
        char line[256];
        objectsTotal = 0;
        if (!(in = fopen(OBJECTS_FILE, "r"))) {
                exit(1);
        }
        do {
                if (!fgets(line, 256, in)) {
                        return;
                }
```

```
      }  while ((line[0] == '#') || (line[0] == '\n'));
      gConstant = atof(line);
      while (!feof(in)) {
            int ch;
            o = &objects[objectsTotal];
            if (!fgets(line, 256, in)) {
                  break;
            }
            if ((line[0] == '#') || (line[0] == '\n')) {
                  continue;
            }
            if (sscanf(line,"%20s %lf %lf %lf %lf %lf %lf",
                  o->name,
                  &(o->x), &(o->y),
                  &(o->vx), &(o->vy),
                  &(o->mass), &(o->radius)) < 7)
            {
                  continue;
            }
            objectsTotal++;
            if (objectsTotal == OBJECTS_MAX) {
                  break;
            }
      }
      fclose(in);
}

void WriteSessionState() {
      FILE *out;
      char sold[256], snew[256];
      int i;
      /* Write to a different filename initially, then
            delete the old and rename the new at the
            end. This reduces the probability that an
            untimely kill signal will cause problems. */
      sprintf(sold, "%s/%d.sav", PROGRAM_DATA_PATH, sessionId);
      sprintf(snew, "%s/%d.dtn", PROGRAM_DATA_PATH, sessionId);
      out = fopen(snew, "w");
      if (!out) {
            /* Can't access memo file */
            return;
      }
      fprintf(out, "%d\n", objectsTotal);
      fprintf(out, "%e\n", gConstant);
      fprintf(out, "%d\n", windowSize);
      fprintf(out, "%d\n", centerFloating);
```

```
        fprintf(out, "%d\n", centerFloatingObject);
        fprintf(out, "%e\n", timeStep);
        fprintf(out, "%e\n", magnification);
        for (i=0; (i < objectsTotal); i++) {
                object *o = &objects[i];
                fprintf(out, "%e %e %e %e %e %e %20s\n",
                        o->x, o->y, o->vx, o->vy,
                        o->mass, o->radius, o->name);
        }
        fclose(out);
        /* OK, swap the files quickly. */
        unlink(sold);
        rename(snew, sold);
}

void ReadSessionState() {
        FILE *in;
        char s[256];
        int i;
        maxX=0;
        minX=0;
        maxY=0;
        minY=0;
        sprintf(s, "%s/%d.sav", PROGRAM_DATA_PATH, sessionId);
        in = fopen(s, "r");
        if (!in) {
                /* Can't access memo file */
                return;
        }
        fscanf(in, "%d\n", &objectsTotal);
        fscanf(in, "%lf\n", &gConstant);
        fscanf(in, "%d\n", &windowSize);
        fscanf(in, "%d\n", &centerFloating);
        fscanf(in, "%d\n", &centerFloatingObject);
        fscanf(in, "%lf\n", &timeStep);
        fscanf(in, "%lf\n", &magnification);
        for (i=0; (i < objectsTotal); i++) {
                object *o = &objects[i];
                fscanf(in, "%lf %lf %lf %lf %lf %lf %s\n",
                        &o->x, &o->y, &o->vx, &o->vy,
                        &o->mass, &o->radius, &o->name);
                if (o->x < minX || !objectsTotal) {
                        minX = o->x;
                }
                if (o->x > maxX || !objectsTotal) {
```

```
                maxX = o->x;
            }
            if (o->y < minY || !objectsTotal) {
                minY = o->y;
            }
            if (o->y > maxY || !objectsTotal) {
                maxY = o->y;
            }
        }
        fclose(in);
        if ((-maxX) < minX) {
            minX = -maxX;
        } else {
            maxX = -minX;
        }
        if ((-maxY) < minY) {
            minY = - maxY;
        } else {
            maxY = - minY;
        }
        if (minX < minY) {
            minY = minX;
        } else {
            minX = minY;
        }
        if (maxX > maxY) {
            maxY = maxX;
        } else {
            maxX = maxY;
        }
        width = (maxX - minX);
    }
```

The SSS in Perl: nph-sss

The following is the Perl source code for the nph-sss program.

```
#!/usr/local/bin/perl

# The Solar System, simulated on the Web.

require "cgi-lib.pl";
require "flush.pl";
```

```
use GD;

$objectsFile = "/CHANGE/THIS/FILE/objects.dat";
$programUrl = "/CHANGE/THIS/URL/nph-sss.cgi";
$programDataPath = "/CHANGE/THIS/PATH/sss/";

$windowSize = 200;

$objectsTotal = 0;

$magnification = 1.0;

sub SCALEX {
     local($x) = @_;
     return ((($x - $minX)/($maxX - $minX)) * $windowSize);
}

sub UNSCALEX {
     local($x) = @_;
     return (($x * ($maxX - $minX) / $windowSize) + $minX);
}

sub SCALEY {
     local($y) = @_;
     return ((($y - $minY)/($maxY - $minY)) * $windowSize);
}

sub UNSCALEY {
     local($y) = @_;
     return (($y * ($maxY - $minY) / $windowSize) + $minY);
}

$PI = 3.141592653;
$centerFloating = 0;
$timeStep = 0.5;

$pathInfo = $ENV{'PATH_INFO'} ;

&ParseSessionId();

if ($pathInfo eq "/canvas.gif") {
     &Canvas;
} elsif ($pathInfo eq "/form") {
     &Form;
} elsif ($pathInfo eq "/zoomin") {
```

```perl
        &ZoomIn;
    } elsif ($pathInfo eq "/zoomout") {
        &ZoomOut;
    } elsif ($pathInfo eq "/timeplus") {
        &TimePlus;
    } elsif ($pathInfo eq "/timeminus") {
        &TimeMinus;
    } elsif ($pathInfo eq "/sizeplus") {
        &SizePlus;
    } elsif ($pathInfo eq "/sizeminus") {
        &SizeMinus;
    } elsif ($pathInfo eq "/uncenter") {
        &UnCenter;
    } elsif ($pathInfo eq "/nemesis") {
        &Nemesis;
    } elsif ($pathInfo eq "/select") {
        &Select;
    } elsif ($pathInfo eq "/resume") {
        &Resume;
    } else {
        &Page(1);
    }


sub Page {
        local($firstTime) = @_;
        local($i);
        if ($firstTime) {
                &SelectSessionId;
                &ObjectsSetup;
                &WriteSessionState;
        }
        print "HTTP/1.0 200 OK\n";
        print "Pragma: nocache\n";
        print "Content-type: text/html\n\n";
        print "<html><head><title>Solar System Simulator</title></head>\n";
        print "<body><h1>Solar System Simulator</h1>\n";
        print "Click on any planet to center the display\n";
        print "on that object, or select one of the options below.\n<p>";
        print "<em>Notes:</em> <strong>zoom in to watch the inner solar
system</strong>,\n";
        print "or increase the time step many times to make the outer planets\n";
        print "more interesting to watch.\n";
        print "<strong>Large time steps will destabilize the moon.</strong>\n";
        print "Even larger time steps may confuse the planets as well.<p>\n";
```

```perl
print "The stop button can be used to pause the simulation. Select\n";
print "Resume to resume the simulation after a stop.<p>";

# Imagemap link
print "<br><a href=\"", $programUrl, "/ID:", $sessionId,
      "/select\">\n";
# Image
print "<img src=\"", $programUrl, "/ID:", $sessionId,
      "/canvas.gif\" ISMAP></a>\n";
print "<p>\n";

# Status display
if ($centerFloating) {
      print "Centered on: ",
            $objects[$centerFloatingObject]{'name'} , " ";
}

# Use printf for consistent numeric presentation
printf "Magnification: %f", $magnification;
printf " Time Step: %f days<br>", $timeStep;

# Various controls
print "<a href=\"", $programUrl, "/ID:", $sessionId,
      "/zoomin\">Zoom In x2</a> ";
print "<a href=\"", $programUrl, "/ID:", $sessionId,
      "/zoomout\">Zoom Out /2</a> ";
print "<a href=\"", $programUrl, "/ID:", $sessionId,
      "/timeplus\">Time Step x2</a> ";
print "<a href=\"", $programUrl, "/ID:", $sessionId,
      "/timeminus\">Time Step /2</a> ";

# This code works, but Netscape is very difficult to use
# if the window is any larger than 200x200, at least on
# my system. Feel free to remove the comment marks
# and see what happens.

#      if ($windowSize < 1600) {
#            print "<a href=\"", $programUrl, "/ID:", $sessionId,
#                  "/sizeplus\">Window Size x2</a> ";
#      }
#      if ($windowSize > 25) {
#            print "<a href=\"", $programUrl, "/ID:", $sessionId,
#                  "/sizeminus\">Window Size /2</a> ";
#      }
      print "<a href=\"", $programUrl, "/ID:", $sessionId,
```

```perl
                "/nemesis\">NEMESIS</a> ";

        print "<a href=\"", $programUrl, "/\">Restart</a> ";
        print "<a href=\"", $programUrl, "/ID:", $sessionId,
                "/resume\">Resume</a> ";
        if ($centerFloating) {
                print "<a href\"", $programUrl, "/ID:", $sessionId,
                        "/uncenter\">Uncenter</a>";
        }
        print "<p>\n";

        # A form, for skilled users
        print "<hr>Use this form if you wish to make several changes
quickly.<p>\n";
        print "<form action=\"", $programUrl, "/ID:", $sessionId, "/form\">\n";
        print "<input type=submit value=\"Submit Changes\">";
        print "<input type=reset value=\"Clear Form\"><br>\n";
        print "<input type=text name=magnification value=\"", $magnification,
                "\"> Magnification<br>\n";
        print "<input type=text name=timestep value=\"", $timeStep,
                "\"> Time Step (days)<br>\n";
        print "Center Display On:<br>";
        print "<select name=center>\n";
        if ($centerFloating) {
                print "<option value=\"-1\"> Nothing<br>\n";
        } else {
                print "<option value=\"-1\" selected> Nothing<br>\n";
        }
        for ($i=0; ($i < $objectsTotal); $i++) {
                print "<option value=\"", $i, "\" ";
                if ($centerFloating && ($centerFloatingObject == $i)) {
                        print "selected";
                }
                print "> ", $objects[$i]{'name'} , "<br>\n";
        }
        print "</select>\n<br>";
        print "</form>\n";
        print "</body></html>\n";
        return 0;
}


sub Canvas {
        local($i, $j, $x, $y, $done, $labels, $trails,
                $im, $black, $white, $blue);
        print "HTTP/1.0 200 OK\r\n";
```

```perl
print "Content-type: multipart/x-mixed-replace;boundary=goober\n\n";
&flush(STDOUT);
while (!$done) {
      # Re-read the session state, do the computations
      # as quickly as possible, and write the state
      # again.
      &ReadSessionState;
      for ($i=0; ($i < $objectsTotal); $i++) {
            local($x, $y);
            for ($j=0; ($j < $objectsTotal); $j++) {
                  if ($i != $j) {
                        local($dist, $pull);
                        $dist = &hypot(
                              $objects[$i]{'x'}  -
                              $objects[$j]{'x'} ,
                              $objects[$i]{'y'}  -
                              $objects[$j]{'y'} );
                        if ($dist != 0.0) {
                              $pull=($gConstant *
                                    $objects[$j]{'mass'}  /
                                    ($dist * $dist));
                              $objects[$i]{'vx'}  +=
                                    (($objects[$j]{'x'}  -
                                    $objects[$i]{'x'} ) /
                                    $dist) * $pull *
                                    $timeStep;
                              $objects[$i]{'vy'}  +=
                                    (($objects[$j]{'y'}  -
                                    $objects[$i]{'y'} ) /
                                    $dist) * $pull *
                                    $timeStep;
                        }
                  }
            }
      }
      for ($i=0; ($i < $objectsTotal); $i++) {
            $objects[$i]{'x'}  += ($objects[$i]{'vx'}  * $timeStep);
            $objects[$i]{'y'}  += ($objects[$i]{'vy'}  * $timeStep);
      }
      &WriteSessionState;
      &AccountForCenter;
      # Now build a GIF
      $im = new GD::Image($windowSize, $windowSize);
      $black = $im->colorAllocate(0, 0, 0);
      $white = $im->colorAllocate(255, 255, 255);
```

```perl
                    $blue = $im->colorAllocate(192, 192, 255);
                    for ($i=0; ($i < $objectsTotal); $i++) {
                        local($val, $x, $y);
                        $val = &log10($objects[$i]{'radius'} );
                        $x = &SCALEX($objects[$i]{'x'} );
                        $y = SCALEY($objects[$i]{'y'} );
                        $im->arc($x, $y, $val, $val, 0, 360, $white);
                        $im->string(gdTinyFont,
                            $x - (gdTinyFont->width *
                            length($objects[$i]{'name'} ) / 2),
                            $y + $val,
                            $objects[$i]{'name'} , $blue);
                    }
                    sleep(1);
                    print "\n--goober\n";
                    print "Content-type: image/gif\n\n";
                    &flush(STDOUT);
                    print $im->gif;
                    &flush(STDOUT);
                }
            print "\n--goober--\n";
            return 0;
}


sub Select {
        local($x, $y);
        &ReadSessionState;
        $_ = $ENV{'QUERY_STRING'} ;
        if (/(\d+),(\d+)/) {
                $x = $1;
                $y = $2;
                &CenterClosest($x, $y);
                &WriteSessionState;
                return &Page(0);
        } else {
                print "text/html\n\n";
                print "HTTP/1.0 200 Document follows\n";
                print "<h1>Bad Click: ", $cgiQueryString, "</h1>\n";
                return 0;
        }
}


sub UnCenter {
        &ReadSessionState;
        $centerFloating = 0;
```

```
        &WriteSessionState;
        return &Page(0);
}

sub ZoomIn {
        &ReadSessionState;
        $magnification *= 2.0;
        &WriteSessionState;
        return &Page(0);
}

sub ZoomOut {
        &ReadSessionState;
        $magnification /= 2.0;
        &WriteSessionState;
        return &Page(0);
}

sub TimePlus {
        &ReadSessionState;
        $timeStep *= 2.0;
        &WriteSessionState;
        return &Page(0);
}

sub TimeMinus {
        &ReadSessionState;
        $timeStep /= 2.0;
        &WriteSessionState;
        return &Page(0);
}

sub SizePlus {
        &ReadSessionState;
        if ($windowSize < 200) {
                $windowSize *= 2.0;
        }
        &WriteSessionState;
        return &Page(0);
}

sub SizeMinus {
        &ReadSessionState;
        if ($windowSize) {
                $windowSize /= 2.0;
```

```perl
    }
    &WriteSessionState;
    return &Page(0);
}


sub Resume {
    &ReadSessionState;
    return &Page(0);
}


sub Nemesis {
    local($largestMass, $largestRadius, $i, $t);
    $largestMass = 1.0;
    $largestRadius = 1.0;
    &ReadSessionState;
    # Wreak havoc: introduce an object as
    # large as the largest object in the
    # system and send it whizzing through.
    for ($i=0; ($i < $objectsTotal); $i++) {
        if ((!$i) || ($objects[i]{'mass'} > $largestMass)) {
            $largestMass = $objects[i]{'mass'} ;
        }
        if ((!$i) || ($objects[i]{'radius'} > $largestRadius)) {
            $largestRadius = $objects[i]{'radius'} ;
        }
    }
    $t = $objectsTotal;
    # Start in the upper left corner of the simulation
    $objects[$t]{'x'}  = $minX;
    $objects[$t]{'y'}  = $minY;
    # Fast enough to cross in 365 days
    $objects[$t]{'vx'}  = ($maxX - $minX) / 365.0;
    $objects[$t]{'vy'}  = ($maxY - $minY) / 365.0;
    # Very big, very nasty
    $objects[$t]{'mass'}  = $largestMass * 2;
    $objects[$t]{'radius'}  = $largestRadius * 2;
    $objects[$t]{'name'}  = "NEMESIS";
    $objectsTotal++;
    &WriteSessionState;
    return &Page(0);
}


sub SelectSessionId {
    # Come up with a new, never-before-used session id.
    $s = $programDataPath . "/id";
```

```perl
        open(IN, $s);
        $sessionId = <IN>;
        close(IN);
        # Clean it up by casting it
        $sessionId = int($sessionId);
        open(OUT, ">" . $s);
        print OUT $sessionId + 1, "\n";
        close(OUT);
}

sub ParseSessionId {
        $_ = $pathInfo;
        if (/\/ID:(\d+)\/(.*)/) {
                $sessionId = $1;
                $pathInfo = "/" . $2;
        }
}

sub CenterClosest {
        local($x, $y) = @_;
        local($smallestDist, $i, $centerX, $centerY);
        $centerFloating = 1;
        &AccountForCenter;
        $centerX = &UNSCALEX($x);
        $centerY = &UNSCALEY($y);
        for ($i = 0; ($i < $objectsTotal); $i++) {
                local($dist);
                $dist = &hypot($objects[i]{'x'}  -
                        $centerX, $objects[i]{'y'}  - $centerY);
                if ($dist < $smallestDist || (!$i)) {
                        $smallestDist = $dist;
                        $centerFloatingObject = $i;
                }
        }
}

sub AccountForCenter {
        if ($centerFloating) {
                $minX = $objects[$centerFloatingObject]{'x'}  -
                        $width / 2.0 / $magnification;
                $maxX = $objects[$centerFloatingObject]{'x'}  +
                        $width / 2.0 / $magnification;
                $minY = $objects[$centerFloatingObject]{'y'}  -
                        $width / 2.0 / $magnification;
                $maxY = $objects[$centerFloatingObject]{'y'}  +
```

```
                   $width / 2.0 / $magnification;
       } else {
             local($cX, $cY);
             $cX = ($minX + $maxX) / 2.0;
             $cY = ($minY + $maxY) / 2.0;
             $minX = $cX - $width / 2.0 / $magnification;
             $maxX = $cX + $width / 2.0 / $magnification;
             $minY = $cY - $width / 2.0 / $magnification;
             $maxY = $cY + $width / 2.0 / $magnification;
       }
}

sub Form {
       local($center, $mag, $t);
       &ReadSessionState;
       &ReadParse(*input);

       $mag = $input{'magnification'} ;

       # Don't forbid negative numbers; they can actually be a lot of fun here
       if ($mag != 0) {
             $magnification = $mag;
       }
       $t = $input{'timestep'} ;
       if ($t != 0) {
             $timeStep = $t;
       }

       # Find out which object was centered on, if any.
       $center = $input{'center'} ;
       if ($center == -1) {
             $centerFloating = 0;
       } elsif (($center >= 0) && ($center < $objectsTotal)) {
             $centerFloating = 1;
             $centerFloatingObject = $center;
       }
       &WriteSessionState;
       return &Page(0);
}

sub hypot {
       local($s1, $s2) = @_;
       return sqrt(($s1 * $s1) + ($s2 * $s2));
}
```

```perl
sub log10 {
     local($n) = @_;
     return log($n) / log(10);
}

sub ObjectsSetup {
     local($f, $i);
     $objectsTotal = 0;
     open(IN, $objectsFile) || exit 1;

     do {
          $line = <IN>;
          $f = substr($line, 0, 1);
     } while (($f eq "#") || ($f eq "\n"));

     $gConstant = $line;

     while($line = <IN>) {
          $f = substr($line, 0, 1);
          if (($f eq "#") || ($f eq "\n")) {
               next;
          }
          $i = $objectsTotal;
          ($objects[$i]{'name'} ,
               $objects[$i]{'x'} ,
               $objects[$i]{'y'} ,
               $objects[$i]{'vx'} ,
               $objects[$i]{'vy'} ,
               $objects[$i]{'mass'} ,
               $objects[$i]{'radius'} ) = split(/\s+/, $line);
          $objectsTotal++;
     }
     close(IN);
}

sub WriteSessionState {
     local($sold, $snew, $i);

     # Write to a different filename initially, then
     # delete the old and rename the new at the
     # end. This reduces the probability that an
     # untimely kill signal will cause problems.
     $sold = $programDataPath . "/" . $sessionId . ".sav";
     $snew = $programDataPath . "/" . $sessionId . ".dtn";
     open(OUT, ">" . $snew) || return;
```

```perl
        # Because of the need for careful control of the
        # output format, particularly exponential notation,
        # printf is a good choice to use here.
        printf OUT "%d\n", $objectsTotal;
        printf OUT "%e\n", $gConstant;
        printf OUT "%d\n", $windowSize;
        printf OUT "%d\n", $centerFloating;
        printf OUT "%d\n", $centerFloatingObject;
        printf OUT "%e\n", $timeStep;
        printf OUT "%e\n", $magnification;
        for ($i=0; ($i < $objectsTotal); $i++) {
                printf OUT "%e %e %e %e %e %e %s\n",
                        $objects[$i]{'x'} ,
                        $objects[$i]{'y'} ,
                        $objects[$i]{'vx'} ,
                        $objects[$i]{'vy'} ,
                        $objects[$i]{'mass'} ,
                        $objects[$i]{'radius'} ,
                        $objects[$i]{'name'} ;
        }
        close(OUT);
        # OK, swap the files quickly.
        unlink($sold);
        rename($snew, $sold);
}

sub ReadSessionState {
        local($i);
        $maxX = 0;
        $minX = 0;
        $maxY = 0;
        $minY = 0;
        $s = $programDataPath . "/" . $sessionId . ".sav";
        open(IN, $s) || return;

        $objectsTotal = <IN>;
        $gConstant = <IN>;
        $windowSize = <IN>;
        $centerFloating = <IN>;
        $centerFloatingObject = <IN>;
        $timeStep = <IN>;
        $magnification = <IN>;
        for ($i = 0; ($i < $objectsTotal); $i++) {
                $line = <IN>;
                ($objects[$i]{'x'} ,
```

```perl
                        $objects[$i]{'y'} ,
                        $objects[$i]{'vx'} ,
                        $objects[$i]{'vy'} ,
                        $objects[$i]{'mass'} ,
                        $objects[$i]{'radius'} ,
                        $objects[$i]{'name'} ) = split(/\s+/, $line);
            if ($objects[$i]{'x'}  < $minX || (!$objectsTotal)) {
                $minX = $objects[$i]{'x'} ;
            }
            if ($objects[$i]{'x'}  > $maxX || (!$objectsTotal)) {
                $maxX = $objects[$i]{'x'} ;
            }
            if ($objects[$i]{'y'}  < $minY || (!$objectsTotal)) {
                $minY = $objects[$i]{'y'} ;
            }
            if ($objects[$i]{'y'}  > $maxY || (!$objectsTotal)) {
                $maxY = $objects[$i]{'y'} ;
            }
        }
        close(IN);
        if ((- $maxX) < $minX) {
            $minX = - $maxX;
        } else {
            $maxX = - $minX;
        }
        if ((- $maxY) < $minY) {
            $minY = - $maxY;
        } else {
            $maxY = - $minY;
        }
        if ($minX < $minY) {
            $minY = $minX;
        } else {
            $minX = $minY;
        }
        if ($maxX > $maxY) {
            $maxY = $maxX;
        } else {
            $maxX = $maxY;
        }
        $width = ($maxX - $minX);
    }
```

Installing and Using the Solar System Simulator

To use the SSS program, first create a data directory for it and place objects.dat in that directory. Second, under Unix and other systems with multiple users, make sure that directory is readable, executable, *and* writable by the user under whose identity the Web server runs. Third, correct the path variables at the beginning of the program to point to the correct locations for your system. Finally, correct the URL at the beginning of the program to the URL at which you will install the program.

To try it out, simply access the URL of the program. The controls are self-explanatory, and most of them are discussed in detail earlier in this chapter.

Conclusion

This chapter presented a complex CGI application, which took advantage of many of CGI's features to effectively subvert certain limitations of the Web.

The SSS program serves to demonstrate both the capabilities and the limitations of CGI. While the SSS succeeds in displaying an animated graphic and allowing the user to interact with it, this is in large part due to the fact that each frame is purposely kept small. The Solar System Simulator and applications like it probably represent the outer limits of the CGI interface as an environment for interactive applications.

Beyond this point (some would say before it), the time arrives to consider "browser-side programming languages" such as Java, PGPSafePerl, and SafeTCL. These languages extend Web browsers with enough programmability to provide rich, complex user interfaces on the client side, and promise adequate security to prevent software viruses from being implemented within them. Such languages have the potential to make server push, inline images as "buttons" and similar bandwidth-intensive trickery unnecessary for most applications.

This concludes our brief visit to the realm of unreasonable applications of CGI. Chapter 14 returns to the reasonable and highly practical, presenting a complete interface to a fictional financial trading system: World Wide Web Wall Street.

Say that five times fast.

World Wide Web Wall Street: An Advanced CGI Application

World Wide Web Wall Street (WWWWS) is one of two complete, large-scale CGI applications presented in this book. Chapter 13 described the Solar System Simulator, an application that deliberately pushes CGI somewhat beyond its design specification.

This chapter turns to a useful, practical application to which CGI is eminently suited: implementing a stock market trading system that allows customers to examine their portfolio, buy and sell stocks, and track the performance of stocks over time. The code presented in this chapter simulates such a system. A real trading system could be readily constructed by interfacing the program with a real database of stock market data, making provisions for faster price updates and, most important, using a proper security mechanism.

The Security Problem

Obviously, a real stock market trading system implemented over the Web would absolutely require adequate security. It is not safe to make large financial transactions through unprotected HTTP transactions.

The WWWWS program expects and requires that an authentication system be in place. Virtually all Web servers feature HTTP 1.0 basic authentication. This is a simple mechanism to password-protect directories. It requires each user to enter a valid account name and password to access any page in that directory and those beneath it (see Figure 14–1). It is essential that you activate this mechanism and set up a handful of accounts with which to test the program. Under the NCSA and Apache servers for Unix, this is done using the htpasswd program and an .htaccess file for the directory in which WWWWS is installed.

The .htaccess file I used to test the program is shown next:

```
AuthUserFile /home/boutell/wwwws/passwords
AuthName World Wide Web Wall Street
AuthType Basic
<Limit GET POST>
require valid-user
</Limit>
```

The presence of this file ensures that the NCSA Web server will not allow access to any URL in or beneath the directory unless the user submits a valid name and password found in the file /home/boutell/wwwws/passwords. Note that the directory containing the password file is not part of a directory visible to the Web server. This is obviously significant for security reasons. The password file itself contains encrypted passwords created using the htpasswd program. Consider the following sequence of commands as an example:

```
cd /home/boutell/wwwws/passwds
htpasswd -c passwords
htpasswd passwords tboutell
```

Most Web servers correctly pass the authenticated user name to CGI programs as the environment variable REMOTE_USER. The WWWWS program checks this environment variable and will not proceed if it does not contain the name of a user found in the customer database.

Basic Authentication Is Not Enough

While this form of authentication is sufficient to verify that the program works as designed, it is not adequate for a real financial trading system. This is because the user name and password travel across the Internet in plain

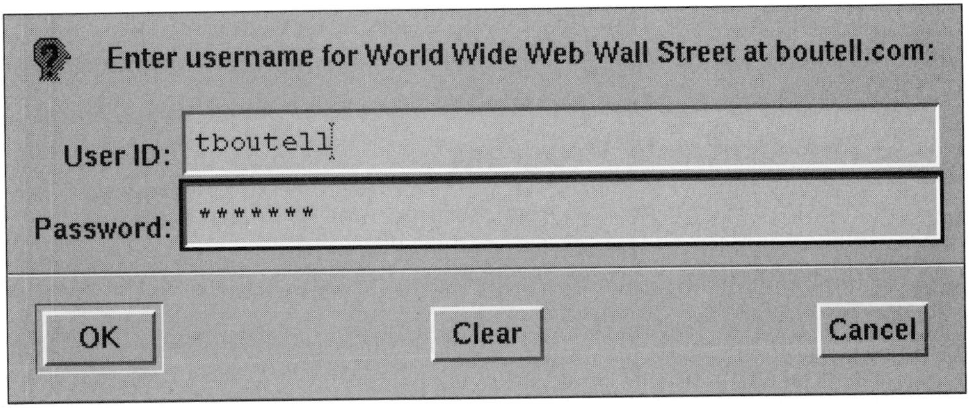

FIGURE 14–1 Basic authentication in use

text form, as do the Web pages themselves. It is not difficult for a determined hacker to hack access to an account, and money is a very strong motivation to learn how.

Fortunately, there are better security methods. Netscape's SSL system is one such mechanism that is difficult to crack, although there are unfortunate limitations on its security imposed by United States cryptography export laws. Still, a determined effort involving very large amounts of computer time is necessary to break it. The SHTTP is another strong security mechanism, subject to the same limiting legal constraints, as are all encryption systems produced in the United States. The design details of secure Internet protocols are beyond the scope of this book. However, the USENET news-groups sci.crypt and talk.politics.crypto are good places to find more information about the latest developments in this area.

Happily, when true secure authentication protocols are used, the environment variable HTTP_REMOTE_USER is set just as it is for basic authentication. If you have access to a server offering SSL or SHTTP, refer to your server's documentation regarding the necessary configuration details.

The Design of WWWWS

The WWWWS system consists of two programs: simtrade and trade. The simtrade program is used to update the database of stock prices and so simulates a day's price fluctuations. The trade program is the CGI program that

responds to user input, accepts or rejects stock trades, and presents information about the user's portfolio and the performance of various stocks.

The simtrade Program

The simtrade program generates random price fluctuations to simulate a
day of activity on the market. Depending on your past experiences with the
stock market, you may find this method of simulation entirely realistic.

In a commercial system, the simtrade program would be replaced with an
interface to a source of actual stock prices. Such feeds are readily available
by modem and through the Internet itself. Of course, in a commercial
system, price updates more often than once per day would also be desirable.

The database is implemented as a simple text file that is kept in a subdirectory that contains all data files for the simulation. It is important that this
directory be both readable and writable by the Web server.

Each line of the file database consists of a stock ticker symbol followed by
up to 30 days of stock prices, with the current price at the far right. To
initially set up the system, you must enter a list of stock ticker symbols. I
used the following list to initialize the system during my tests:

```
ECR
JA
MT
NT
BPA
X
ALFV
KA
MGLY
MLG
```

If no prices are present, the simtrade program will randomly generate a
plausible price for each stock the first time it is run.

The Parse Module: Accessing Text-based Databases in C

Both the simtrade and trade programs access databases kept in text files. As
a long-time C language enthusiast, I was somewhat humbled to discover

how much more straightforward it is to parse text files of information in Perl. This is largely because Perl has a built-in string type and many facilities designed to manipulate strings in elegant ways.

To alleviate the tedium of processing C strings and allow simple databases in text files to be less awkwardly manipulated, I have written a simple C module that provides straightforward access to such files.

The function `SetFieldSeparator()` is invoked to set the character that will separate fields in the database. The function `GetField()` is used to retrieve one field from the file and store its contents in a null-terminated C string; when it returns false, there are no more fields in that record. The function `NextRecord()` is used to advance to the next record in the file, whether or not all fields in the current record have been read. When it returns false, there are no more records in the file. Records are always separated by line feeds, which may require modification under MSDOS, Windows, and Windows NT.

The amount of space available to store the field is always passed as an argument to `GetField()`. If there is insufficient space, the parsing module will still correctly advance to the next field and will retrieve a valid, shortened, null-terminated C string occupying the available space.

Declarations for the Database Parsing Module: parse.h

The following is the `#include` file for the parsing module.

```
#ifndef PARSE_H
#define PARSE_H 1

#include <stdio.h>

void SetFieldSeparator(char separator);
int GetField(FILE *in, char *field, int space);
int NextRecord(FILE *in);

#endif /* PARSE_H */
```

Source Code for the Database Parsing Module: parse.c

The following is the C source code for the parsing module.

```
#include <stdio.h>
#include <strings.h>
#include <stdlib.h>
```

```
static char fieldSeparator = '^';

int GetField(FILE *in, char *field, int space)
{
     int ch;
     int begun = 0;
     int len = 0;
     while(1) {
          ch = getc(in);
          if ((ch == fieldSeparator) || (ch == '\n') || (ch == EOF)) {
               if (len < space) {
                    field[len] = '\0';
               } else {
                    field[space-1] = '\0';
               }
               if (ch == '\n') {
                    ungetc(ch, in);
                    if (!begun) {
                         return 0;
                    }
               }
               return 1;
          }
          if (!begun) {
               if (!isspace(ch)) {
                    begun = 1;
               }
          }
          if (begun) {
               if (len < space) {
                    field[len] = ch;
               }
               len++;
          }
     }
}

int NextRecord(FILE *in)
{
     int ch;
     while(1) {
          ch = getc(in);
          if (ch == EOF) {
               return 0;
          }
```

```
                    if (ch == '\n') {
                        while(1) {
                            ch = getc(in);
                            if (ch == EOF) {
                                return 0;
                            }
                            if (!isspace(ch)) {
                                ungetc(ch, in);
                                return 1;
                            }
                        }
                    }
                }
            }
        }

        void SetFieldSeparator(char sep) {
            fieldSeparator = sep;
        }
```

With the parsing module in place, it is now straightforward to write the stock trade simulator itself.

Simulating Stock Prices in C: simtrade.c

The following is the C source code of the stock activity simulator.

```
/* simtrade.c. This program simulates fluctuating
   stock prices for the WWWS system. */

#include <stdlib.h>
#include <time.h>

#include "parse.h"

#define PATH_SPACE 256
#define SYMBOL_SPACE 64
#define HISTORY_SIZE 30

#define DATA_PATH "/CHANGE/THIS/PATH/wwws"

int main(int argc, char *argv[]) {
    FILE *in, *out;
```

```c
        char s[PATH_SPACE], snew[PATH_SPACE];
        int iterations = 1;
        time_t now;
        int i;
        /* Now we should have a different random seed */
        time(&now);
        srand((int) now);
        if (argc == 2) {
            iterations = atoi(argv[1]);
        } else if (argc == 1) {
            /* OK, assume 1 iteration */
        } else {
            fprintf(stderr, "Usage: simtrade [# of iterations]\n");
            return 1;
        }
        for (i=0; (i < iterations); i++) {
            int stocks = 0;
            sprintf(s, "%s/database", DATA_PATH);
            sprintf(snew, "%s/database.new", DATA_PATH);
            in = fopen(s, "r");
            if (!in) {
                fprintf(stderr, "Can't open database file %s for
reading.\n",
                        s);
                exit(1);
            }
            out = fopen(snew, "w");
            if (!out) {
                fprintf(stderr, "Can't open temporary file %s for
writing.\n",
                        snew);
                fclose(in);
                exit(1);
            }
            SetFieldSeparator(' ');
            do {
                char symbol[SYMBOL_SPACE];
                char priceString[SYMBOL_SPACE];
                double history[HISTORY_SIZE];
                int historyPos = 0;
                int i;
                if (!GetField(in, symbol, SYMBOL_SPACE)) {
                    break;
                }
                while (GetField(in, priceString, SYMBOL_SPACE)) {
```

```
                        /* Discard the oldest price. */
                        history[historyPos++] = atof(priceString);
                }
                /* If the history is full, discard the oldest price. */
                if (historyPos == HISTORY_SIZE) {
                        for (i = 0; (i < (HISTORY_SIZE - 1)); i++) {
                                history[i] = history[i+1];
                        }
                        historyPos--;
                }
                /* Generate a price fluctuation at random. Some would say
this
                        method is quite realistic. */
                if (historyPos) {
                        history[historyPos] =
                                history[historyPos-1] +
                                ((double)(abs(rand() >> 8) % 40) - 19.5) *
.125;
                        if (history[historyPos] < 0.0) {
                                history[historyPos] = 0.125;
                        }
                } else {
                        history[historyPos] = (double)(abs(rand() >> 8) % 80
+ 80)
                                / 2.0;
                }
                historyPos++;
                /* Write the updated record. */
                fprintf(out, "%s ", symbol);
                for (i=0; (i < historyPos); i++) {
                        fprintf(out, "%f ", history[i]);
                }
                fprintf(out, "\n");
                stocks++;
        }  while (NextRecord(in));
        printf("%d stocks updated.\n", stocks);
        fclose(in);
        fclose(out);
        unlink(s);
        rename(snew, s);
    }
    return 0;
}
```

Simulating Stock Prices in Perl: simtrade

The following is the Perl source code of the stock activity simulator.

```perl
#!/usr/local/bin/perl

# simtrade. This program simulates fluctuating
# stock prices for the WWWWS system.

$historySize = 30;

$dataPath = "/home/boutell/wwwws";

$iterations = 1;

srand();

if (int(@ARGV) == 1) {
    $iterations = $ARGV[0];
} elsif (int(@ARGV) == 0) {
    # OK, assume 1 iteration
} else {
    die "Usage: simtrade [# of iterations]\n";
}
for ($iter = 0; ($iter < $iterations); $iter++) {
    $stocks = 0;
    $s = $dataPath . "/database";
    $snew = $dataPath . "/database.new";
    open(IN, $s) || die "Can't open database file " . $s . "for
reading.\n";
    open(OUT, ">" . $snew) ||
        die "Can't open temporary file " . $s . " for
writing.\n";
    while(<IN>) {
        #Remove any trailing space
        s/\s+$//g;
        @fields = split(/ /);
        $symbol = $fields[0];
        if ($symbol eq "") {
            break;
        }
        $historyTotal = int(@fields) - 1;
        if ($historyTotal == $historySize) {
            for ($i = 0; ($i < ($historySize - 1)); $i++) {
```

```
                            $fields[$i + 1] = $fields[$i + 2];
                    }
                    $#fields -= 1;
                    $historyTotal--;
            }
            # Generate a price fluctuation at random. Some would say
 this
            # method is quite realistic.
            if ($historyTotal) {
                    $fields[$historyTotal + 1] =
                            $fields[$historyTotal] +
                            (int(rand(40)) - 19.5) * .125;
                    if ($fields[$historyTotal + 1] < 0.0) {
                            $fields[$historyTotal + 1] = 0.125;
                    }
            } else {
                    $fields[$historyTotal + 1] =
                            (int(rand(80)) + 80) / 2.0;
            }
            $historyTotal++;
            # Write the updated record.
            print OUT join(' ', @fields), "\n";
            $stocks++;
        }
        print $stocks, " stocks updated.\n";
        close(IN);
        close(OUT);
        rename($snew, $s);
    }
    exit 0;
```

Installing and Using simtrade

At the beginning of the simtrade program, a path to the wwws data directory is specified. This directory setting must be changed to a subdirectory
created by you for this purpose. Under Unix, that directory must also be
made readable, executable, and writable by the Web server, which probably
does not run with your own user ID. If your Web server runs CGI programs
under the user IDs of the authors of the programs, you may be able to avoid
this requirement.

Under Unix, the command

```
chmod -R 777 wwwws
```

executed from the parent directory will make the wwwws directory readable, executable, and writable by all users. Needless to say, for a commercial system, it would be better to use a directory belonging to the Web server's own user ID rather than a directory accessible by everyone.

If you have not yet created the file database and entered an initial list of stock ticker symbols, you must do so before executing simtrade. See the example database presented earlier in this chapter.

Simulating Many Days of Trading

To make the system as interesting as possible, execute the command simtrade 30 to simulate 30 days of trading. This will ensure that the information displayed by the CGI application will be interesting. Graphs with only one data point tend to be uninspiring.

The trade Program: Interacting with the User

The trade program carries out all CGI interactions with the user. It generates several different pages: a portfolio page, a newspaper page, a transaction history page, and a stock price history page for each stock.

Accessing the Customer's Assets

In Chapter 13, the Solar System Simulator program solved the problem of identifying the user with which it was interacting by creating a file for each session. The program stored an ID number corresponding to the session as part of every URL in its output to the user, thus ensuring that every action taken would be applied to the correct session.

Since the WWWWS system takes advantage of user authentication, a simpler mechanism can be employed. Instead of generating an ID number to be incorporated into every URL, the system simply uses the REMOTE_USER environment variable to determine to which customer it is talking.

The customer.dat Files

Information about each customer is kept in a separate file in the wwwws data directory. Each file is named `customer.dat`, where `customer` is replaced by the actual name under which the user authenticated. Note these names cannot contain spaces.

Consider the following example, which contains my hard-won assets from my tests of the system:

```
1952.5
X 250
NT 200
MLG 20
ECR 20
```

A Warning: Money, Powers of Two, and Misery

The first record of the database contains the amount of money currently available in the customer's investment account. This field must be set up in advance by the system administrator. It is trivial to add a function to the trade program that updates this field by adding to it when the user submits a correct credit card number. Of course, such a function would be a very poor idea unless proper security measures were in place.

The trade program represents all monetary amounts as floating point numbers. This is fine for a simulation, but it must be emphasized that small errors will gradually accumulate, since binary floating point numbers are represented by powers of two and do not precisely represent decimal values containing a decimal point.

In a commercial system, this can be corrected by representing all monetary values in terms of cents. Integers can then be used to represent amounts. Even then, however, very large values can prove to be a problem. Libraries are available in most languages to deal with very large integer values with precise accuracy. For commercial applications dealing with very large sums, such methods are recommended despite the added complexity. Fortunately, if monetary values above approximately 40 million dollars are not involved, ordinary C `long` variables are adequate to represent these amounts in terms of cents.

The WWWWS and 16-Bit DOS/ Windows 3.1 Compilers

It should be noted that the WWWWS system uses ordinary integers to represent the number of shares owned by the customer. Holdings of more than 32,767 shares will "wrap around" to negative values. If you are programming for the 16-bit DOS environment, you should consider using long integers instead. You should also strongly consider developing a 32-bit CGI application under Windows 95 or Windows NT to avoid unnecessary suffering.

Flow of Control in the trade Program: the Dispatcher

Much like the SSS program, the trade program takes advantage of the PATH_INFO environment variable to determine which page has been requested by the customer. Once the correct page is identified, the proper function is invoked to produce it. If additional information such as the name of the stock in question is present in PATH_INFO, that information is also extracted and passed to the function.

The Portfolio Page

The most important page generated by the trade program is the portfolio page. This page presents an HTML table that contains information about the customer's current holdings. The table also contains a convenient interface to buy or sell shares of each currently held stock. An additional interface beneath the table provides a way the user can purchase a new stock the user has not invested in previously. See Figure 14–2.

A Brief Overview of Tables

While this is not a book about HTML, the subject of tables is often passed over in discussions of HTML. The portfolio page makes extensive use of them, so a brief overview is provided here.

HTML tables provide a simple, elegant way to describe a spreadsheet-like table of values in a Web page. The <table> tag encloses a table. All tags

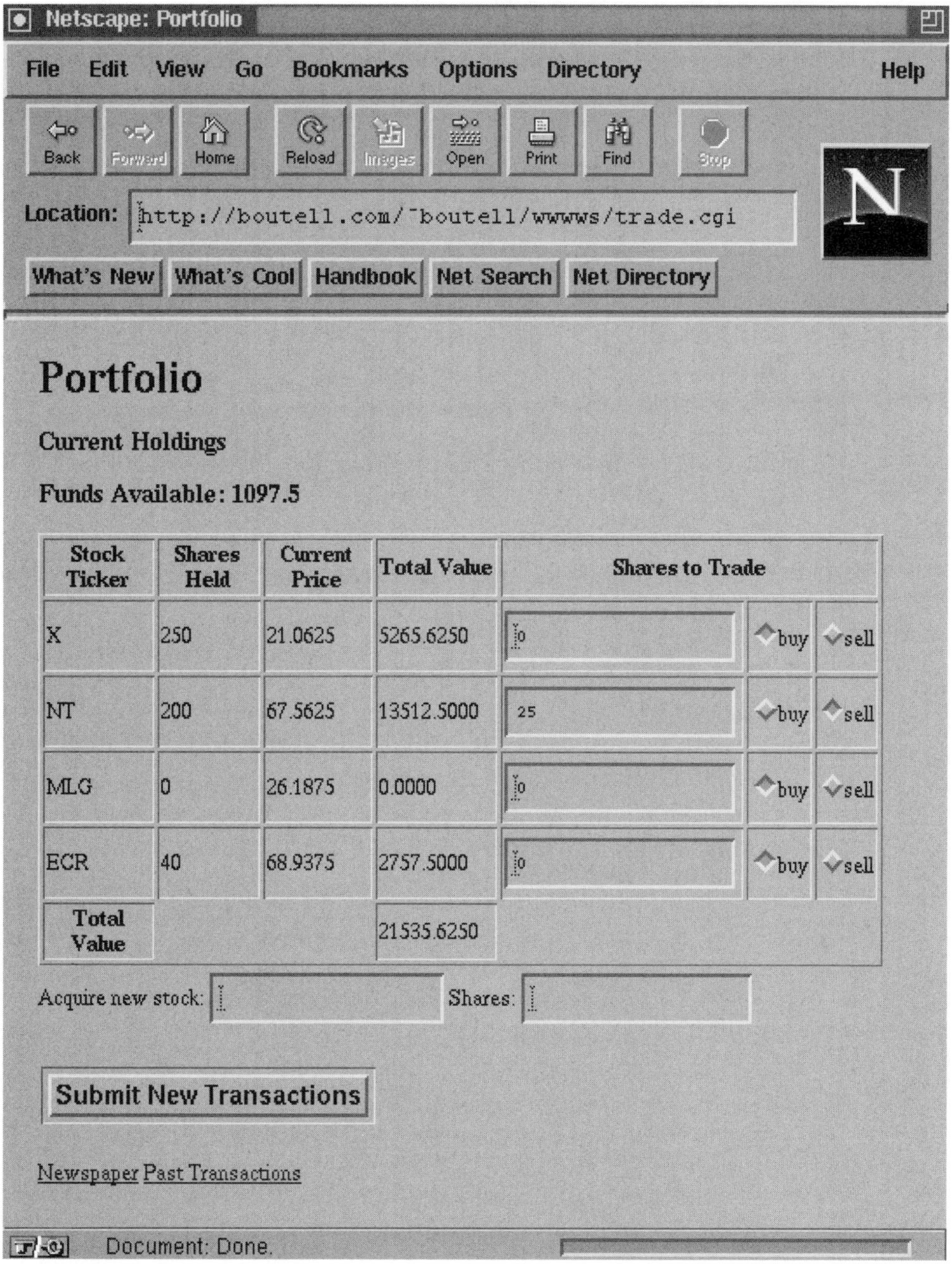
Netscape: Portfolio
File Edit View Go Bookmarks Options Directory Help
Back Forward Home Reload Images Open Print Find Stop
Location: http://boutell.com/~boutell/wwwws/trade.cgi
What's New What's Cool Handbook Net Search Net Directory
Portfolio
Current Holdings
Funds Available: 1097.5
Stock Ticker | Shares Held | Current Price | Total Value | Shares to Trade
X | 250 | 21.0625 | 5265.6250 | 0 | buy | sell
NT | 200 | 67.5625 | 13512.5000 | 25 | buy | sell
MLG | 0 | 26.1875 | 0.0000 | 0 | buy | sell
ECR | 40 | 68.9375 | 2757.5000 | 0 | buy | sell
Total Value | 21535.6250
Acquire new stock:
Shares:
Submit New Transactions
Newspaper Past Transactions
Document: Done.

FIGURE 14–2 The portfolio page

making up the table must appear between `<table>` and `</table>`. The `border` attribute is used to determine the appearance of the table borders. A value of 0 indicates the row and column lines making up the table's outline should be invisible. A value of 1 indicates table outlines should be visible. Since a spreadsheet-like table is a very natural appearance for financial data, the `border` attribute output by the `Portfolio()` function is set to 1.

Each row of the table is enclosed in a `<tr>` tag; the closing `</tr>` tag is optional. The text of each cell of the table is enclosed by a `<th>` or `<td>` tag. `<th>` is intended to be used for headings and is typically displayed in a bold font. Otherwise, `<th>` and `<td>` are identical.

The `<th>` and `<td>` tags may have `colspan-` and `rowspan-` attributes. `colspan`, used by the trade program, indicates the cell should span the space normally occupied by several cells. `rowspan` does the same for the space occupied by several rows. `<th>` and `<td>` may also have an align attribute, which will align the contents of the cell to the left (the default), in the middle of the cell, or to the right.

Tables are now supported by a fairly wide range of Web browsers, including Microsoft's Internet Explorer and Netscape's Navigator. Used properly, they give a professional and well-formatted appearance to a Web page, especially in a financial application such as this one.

Tables and Forms Together

Form entry blanks have a particularly elegant look and feel when presented inside an HTML form. However, enclosing tables inside forms is a little tricky.

The important thing to remember is that `<table>` tags and their contents should be placed inside the `<form>` tag, not the other way around. The HTML specification requires this order, and Web browser behavior will vary rather widely if it is not followed.

Table cells can contain any form element. The WWWWS system takes advantage of this to present an interface to buy and sell stocks as part of the portfolio.

Consider the following HTML page, generated by the WWWWS system. For clarity's sake, only one stock's table row is shown.

```
<html>
<head>
<title>Portfolio</title>
</head>
<body><h1>Portfolio</h1>
<body><h3>Current Holdings</h3>
<body><h3>Funds Available: 1952.5</h3>
<form method=POST action="/~boutell/wwwws/trade.cgi/trade">
<table border=1>
<tr><th>Stock Ticker</th>
<th>Shares Held</th>
<th>Current Price</th>
<th>Total Value</th>
<th colspan=3>Shares to Trade</th></tr>
<tr><td>X</td><td>250</td><td>21.0625</td><td>5265.6250</td>
<td>
<input type=text name="X shares" value="0">
</td>
<td><input type=radio value=buy name="X direction" checked>buy</td>
<td><input type="radio" value="sell" name="X direction">sell</td>
</td></tr>
<tr><th>Total Value</th><td colspan=2></td>
<td>20680.6250</td><td colspan=3></td></tr>
</table>
Acquire new stock:
<input type=text name="newbuy symbol">
Shares: <input type=text name="newbuy shares"><p>
<input type=submit value="Submit New Transactions">
</form><p>
<a href="/~boutell/wwwws/trade.cgi/newspaper">Newspaper</a>
<a href="/~boutell/wwwws/trade.cgi/transactions">Past
Transactions</a>
</body></html>
```

Note that the `colspan` attribute of the `<td>` tag is used to pad cells in cases where several consecutive cells are not relevant to a row. This is used for both the heading row at the top of the table and for the "totals" row at the bottom.

Handling Trades

The action of this example form contains the string /trade at the end. This ensures that the Trade() function will be invoked by the WWWWS system when the form is submitted to the server.

The Trade() function retrieves data from the form, using cgic in the case of the C version and cgi-lib.pl in the case of the Perl version. In both cases, the program retrieves a list of acceptable stock tickers from the database, one by one, and checks to see if a form field was submitted with the appropriate name.

The names of these fields are constructed like this:

```
tickersymbol shares
tickersymbol direction
```

where the shares field refers to the number of shares to be traded and the direction field is set by the Buy and Sell buttons. The C version uses the cgiFormRadio() function of cgic to determine which of these was set.

The Trade() function also checks for the purchase of a new, previously unowned stock. The relevant form field names are

```
newbuy tickersymbol
newbuy shares
```

Note, spaces are acceptable in form field names.

Transaction Logging

It is important to communicate the outcome of the customer's trades. This is done by the StartTransaction(), LogTransaction(), and EndTransaction() functions. At the beginning of the Trade() function, StartTransaction() is invoked to open two logging files: one of current transactions associated with this form submission and a separate, permanent log of the customer's activities since the dawn of time. LogTransaction() is used to log each individual transaction, and EndTransaction() is used to close both log files.

Responding to the Customer

After any new trades have been processed or rejected, the Trade() function invokes the Portfolio() function and exits. The Portfolio() function contains code that checks for a log file of recent transactions and displays the contents of that log file to the customer at the beginning of its output. It then removes the temporary log file.

The Newspaper Page

The newspaper page displays information about the current prices of all the stocks in the system, as opposed to the customer's current holdings (see Figure 14–3). Each stock is presented along with the change in price, if any,

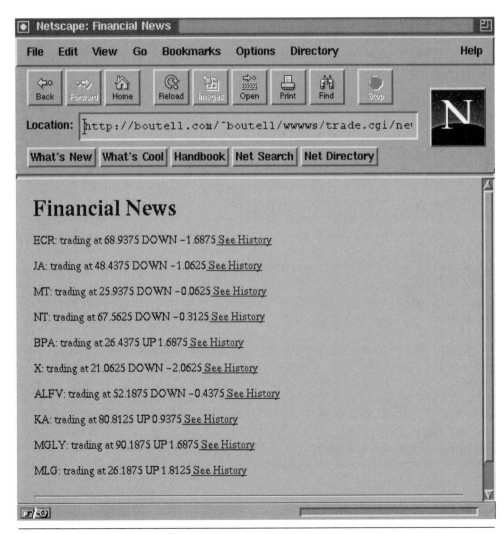

FIGURE 14–3 The newspaper page

from the previous day. Links to the history of each stock are provided. These links end with `/history/tickersymbol`, thus ensuring the `History()` function will be invoked with the correct ticker symbol when that link is selected.

The Stock Price History Pages

The stock price history pages display information about the recent activity of particular stocks (see Figure 14–4). The `History()` function itself is

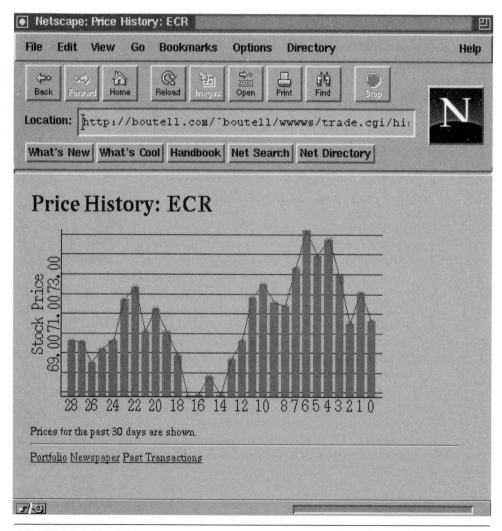

FIGURE 14–4 The history page

quite simple, as it merely generates a reference to an inline image. That inline image is generated by the `HistoryChart()` function.

Inline Images, Caching Problems, and the History Chart

In Chapter 13, I mentioned that it is possible to prevent a Web browser from caching a document, thereby ensuring the document will always be reloaded. This is done by outputting the string `Pragma: nocache` before the MIME type header. However, in the case of inline images, this simply does not work, at least not in Netscape versions up to 2.0 beta 3. Even though the `Pragma: nocache` line is output for both the page and the inline image itself, the browser persists in displaying the old image.

The `History()` function solves this problem by generating a random number as part of the URL of the inline image. The Web browser cannot tell that this is the same image it has seen before and so dutifully loads the new image. The dispatching code at the beginning of the program then strips out and ignores the random number in `PATH_INFO`.

Of course, this approach is not adequate if the Web browser does not respect `Pragma: nocache` for the HTML page itself. To prevent unwanted caching by such browsers, you must include a random component in every link generated by the program. It is possible to do this consistently and so strip out the random component early in your program.

While caching is often desirable for performance reasons, occasionally it must be prevented. These tactics should prove helpful in doing this.

Generating the History Chart

The stock price history chart is generated very easily, thanks to the charting function first presented in Chapter 10. The data is retrieved using the `getStockHistory()` function, which simply retrieves the available stock prices for the desired stock from the database.

It is perhaps a disadvantage that the charting function always stretches the display of stock price differences over the entire *y*-axis, especially if the actual change over the time period is very small. You may wish to experiment with modifications to the charting module to ensure the *y*-axis always begins from zero.

The Transaction History Page

The final function I will examine is the `Transaction()` function. This function accesses the permanent log of customer transactions and outputs it for the customer's review (see Figure 14–5).

A possible improvement to this function would be to have the log presented in reverse order, that is, to display the most recent trades first. Some customers would find such a reversed presentation confusing, so it would

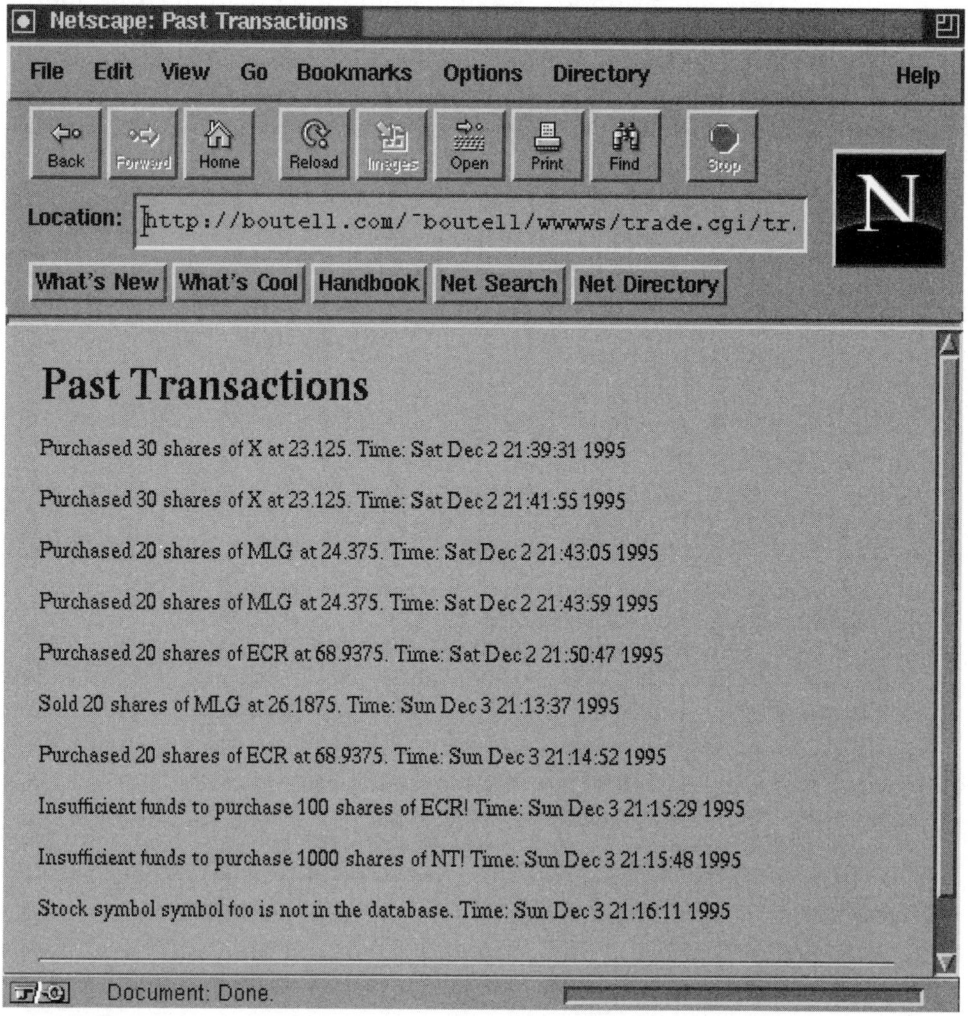

FIGURE 14–5 The transaction history page

be best to make this an option under the control of the customer and to record the current setting of the option in the customer's .dat file.

The Stock Market Trading Program, in C: trade.c

The following is the C source code of the WWWWS CGI program.

```c
/* trade.c. This program allows users to interact
        with the WWWWS system. Set these #defines
        appropriately before compiling. */

#define DATA_PATH "/CHANGE/THIS/PATH/wwwws"
#define PROGRAM_URL "/CHANGE/THIS/URL/cgi-bin/trade"

#include <stdlib.h>
#include <string.h>
#include <time.h>
#include <stdlib.h>
#include "parse.h"
#include "cgic.h"
#include "gd.h"
#include "chart.h"

#define PATH_SPACE 256
#define STRING_SPACE 256
#define HISTORY_SIZE 30

int getFunds(float *fundsP);

int setFunds(float funds);

int getStockPrice(char *sym, float *price);

int getStockHistory(char *sym, float *history, int *historySizeP);

int getStockShares(char *sym, int *sharesP);

int setStockShares(char *sym, int shares);

int Trade();
int History(char *symbol);
int HistoryChart(char *symbol);
int Transactions();
int Portfolio();
```

```
int Newspaper();
char *accountName;

int cgiMain() {
      time_t now;
      time(&now);
      srand((int) now);
      accountName = cgiRemoteUser;
      if (!strcmp(accountName, "")) {
            /* This shouldn't happen! But it will happen
                  if the program is not installed according
                  to the instructions, or if the server
                  has bugs regarding user authentication. */
            fprintf(cgiOut, "Pragma: nocache\n");
            cgiHeaderContentType("text/html");
            fprintf(cgiOut, "<html>\n");
            fprintf(cgiOut,
                  "<head><title>User Not Authenticated</title></head>\n");
            fprintf(cgiOut, "<body><h1>User Not Authenticated</h1>\n");
            fprintf(cgiOut, "The trade program was not installed in\n");
            fprintf(cgiOut, "a password-authenticated directory, or\n");
            fprintf(cgiOut, "there is a bug in the Web server.\n");
            fprintf(cgiOut, "Please report this problem to the\n");
            fprintf(cgiOut, "site administrator.\n");
            fprintf(cgiOut, "</body></html>\n");
            return 1;
      }
      if (!strcmp(cgiPathInfo, "/trade")) {
            return Trade();
      } else if (!strncmp(cgiPathInfo, "/history/", 9)) {
            return History(cgiPathInfo + 9);
      } else if (!strncmp(cgiPathInfo, "/historychart/", 14)) {
            /* Sigh, remove the image.gif thing at the end */
            char *s = (char *) malloc(strlen(cgiPathInfo + 14) + 1);
            char *im;
            int result;
            strcpy(s, cgiPathInfo + 14);
            im = strstr(s, "/image");
            if (im) {
                  *im = '\0';
            }
            result = HistoryChart(s);
            free(s);
      } else if (!strcmp(cgiPathInfo, "/transactions")) {
            return Transactions();
```

```
            } else if (!strcmp(cgiPathInfo, "/newspaper")) {
                return Newspaper();
            } else {
                return Portfolio();
            }
}

void DatabaseMissing();

char *directions[] = {
        "buy",
        "sell"
};

void StartTransaction();

void EndTransaction();

void TransactionLog(char *text);

void stockBuy(char *symbol, int shares);

void stockSell(char *symbol, int shares);

int Trade() {
        FILE *in;
        char symbol[STRING_SPACE], priceString[STRING_SPACE],
attr[STRING_SPACE];
        char s[PATH_SPACE];
        int shares;
        float funds;
        SetFieldSeparator(' ');
        sprintf(s, "%s/database", DATA_PATH);
        in = fopen(s, "r");
        if (!in) {
                DatabaseMissing();
                return 0;
        }
        StartTransaction();
        if (cgiFormString("newbuy symbol", symbol, STRING_SPACE)
                != cgiFormNotFound) {
                cgiFormInteger("newbuy shares", &shares, 0);
                if (shares) {
                        stockBuy(symbol, shares);
                }
```

```
      }
      do {
            if (!GetField(in, symbol, STRING_SPACE)) {
                  break;
            }
            sprintf(attr, "%s shares", symbol);
            cgiFormInteger(attr, &shares, 0);
            if (shares > 0) {
                  int direction;
                  sprintf(attr, "%s direction", symbol);
                  cgiFormRadio(attr, directions, 2, &direction, -1);
                  if (direction == -1) {
                        /* Not a complete submission.
                              Don't guess! There's serious
                              play money at stake here. */
                        char s[STRING_SPACE];
                        sprintf(s,
                              "Please specify buy or sell for %s. No transac-
tion performed.", symbol);
                        TransactionLog(s);
                        EndTransaction();
                        return 0;
                  }
                  if (direction == 0) {
                        stockBuy(symbol, shares);
                  } else {
                        stockSell(symbol, shares);
                  }
            } else if (shares == 0) {
                  /* OK, do nothing */
            } else if (shares < 0) {
                  char s[STRING_SPACE];
                  sprintf(s, "%s: negative numbers of shares are not accepted
for trades. Enter a positive number and select buy or sell.", symbol);
                  TransactionLog(s);
            }
      } while (NextRecord(in));
      fclose(in);
      EndTransaction();
      return Portfolio();
}

void stockBuy(char *symbol, int shares) {
      /* A purchase. Can we afford it? */
      float purchasePrice;
```

```c
        float price;
        float funds;
        if (!getFunds(&funds)) {
                char s[STRING_SPACE];
                sprintf(s,
                    "Unable to access your account. Please contact the site
administrator.");
                TransactionLog(s);
                return;
        }
        if (!getStockPrice(symbol, &price)) {
                char s[STRING_SPACE];
                sprintf(s,
                    "Stock symbol %s is not in the database.",
                    symbol);
                TransactionLog(s);
                return;
        }
        purchasePrice = shares * price;
        if (purchasePrice > funds) {
                /* No */
                char s[STRING_SPACE];
                sprintf(s,
                    "Insufficient funds to purchase %d shares of %s!",
                    shares, symbol);
                TransactionLog(s);
        } else {
                int currentShares;
                char s[STRING_SPACE];
                getStockShares(symbol, &currentShares);
                /* An ideal universe with no commissions! */
                currentShares += shares;
                funds -= purchasePrice;
                setStockShares(symbol, currentShares);

                sprintf(s,
                    "Purchased %d shares of %s at %.3f.", shares,
                    symbol, price);
                TransactionLog(s);
        }
        setFunds(funds);
}

void stockSell(char *symbol, int shares) {
        /* A sale. Do we have that many shares? */
```

```
        float salePrice;
        int currentShares;
        float price;
        float funds;
        if (!getFunds(&funds)) {
                char s[STRING_SPACE];
                sprintf(s,
                    "Unable to access your account. Please contact the site
administrator.");
                TransactionLog(s);
                return;
        }
        if (!getStockPrice(symbol, &price)) {
                char s[STRING_SPACE];
                sprintf(s,
                    "Stock symbol %s is not in the database.",
                    symbol);
                TransactionLog(s);
                return;
        }
        salePrice = shares * price;
        getStockShares(symbol, &currentShares);
        if (currentShares < shares) {
                /* No */
                char s[STRING_SPACE];
                sprintf(s,
                    "Can't sell %d shares of %s: you only have %d shares!",
                    shares, symbol, currentShares);
                TransactionLog(s);
        } else {
                char s[STRING_SPACE];
                /* An ideal universe with no commissions! */
                currentShares -= shares;
                funds += salePrice;
                setStockShares(symbol, currentShares);
                sprintf(s,
                    "Sold %d shares of %s at %.3f.", shares, symbol, price);
                TransactionLog(s);
        }
        setFunds(funds);
}

void DatabaseMissing() {
        fprintf(cgiOut, "Pragma: nocache\n");
        cgiHeaderContentType("text/html");
```

```
            fprintf(cgiOut, "<html><head><title>Database Missing</title></head>\n");
            fprintf(cgiOut, "<body><h1>Database Missing</h1>\n");
            fprintf(cgiOut, "Please contact the site administrator.\n");
            fprintf(cgiOut, "</body></html>\n");
}

FILE *currentOut;
FILE *permanentOut;

void StartTransaction() {
        char s[PATH_SPACE];
        sprintf(s, "%s/%s.cur", DATA_PATH, accountName);
        currentOut = fopen(s, "w");
        sprintf(s, "%s/%s.log", DATA_PATH, accountName);
        permanentOut = fopen(s, "a");
}

void EndTransaction() {
        fprintf(currentOut, "End of transaction.<p>\n");
        fclose(currentOut);
        fclose(permanentOut);
}

void TransactionLog(char *text) {
        time_t now;
        time(&now);
        fprintf(currentOut, "%s<p>\n", text);
        fprintf(permanentOut, "%s Time: %s<p>", text, ctime(&now));
}

int History(char *symbol)
{
        float history[HISTORY_SIZE];
        int size;
        fprintf(cgiOut, "Pragma: nocache\n");
        cgiHeaderContentType("text/html");
        fprintf(cgiOut, "<html>\n");
        fprintf(cgiOut, "<head><title>Price History: %s</title></head>\n",
                symbol);
        fprintf(cgiOut, "<body><h1>Price History: %s</h1>\n", symbol);
        if (!getStockHistory(symbol, history, &size)) {
                fprintf(cgiOut,
                        "<h2>There is no stock with that ticker symbol.</h2>\n");
        } else {
                /* Add a random component to the URL in order to
```

```
                            prevent Web browsers from caching the chart
                            when it is out of date. */
                fprintf(cgiOut,
                    "<img src=%s/historychart/%s/image%d.gif><p>\n",
                    PROGRAM_URL, symbol, abs((rand() >> 8) % 1000));
            }
            fprintf(cgiOut,
                "Prices for the past 30 days are shown.\n");
            fprintf(cgiOut,
                "<hr><a href=\"%s/portfolio\">Portfolio</a> \n",
                PROGRAM_URL);
            fprintf(cgiOut,
                "<a href=\"%s/newspaper\">Newspaper</a>\n ",
                PROGRAM_URL);
            fprintf(cgiOut,
                "<a href=\"%s/transactions\">Past Transactions</a> \n",
                PROGRAM_URL);
            fprintf(cgiOut, "</body></html>\n");
            return 0;
        }


int HistoryChart(char *symbol)
{
        float history[HISTORY_SIZE];
        char *labels[HISTORY_SIZE];
        int size;
        int i;
        gdImagePtr im;
        im = gdImageCreate(400, 200);
        getStockHistory(symbol, history, &size);
        for (i = 0; (i < size); i++) {
                labels[i] = (char *) malloc(20);
                sprintf(labels[i], "%d", size - i - 1);
        }
        chartDraw(im, chartBar | chartCross | chartLine,
                labels, "Stock Price", history, size);
        fprintf(cgiOut, "Pragma: nocache\n");
        cgiHeaderContentType("image/gif");
        gdImageGif(im, cgiOut);
        gdImageDestroy(im);
}
int Transactions() {
        int ch;
        FILE *in;
        char s[PATH_SPACE];
```

```c
        sprintf(s, "%s/%s.log", DATA_PATH, accountName);
        in = fopen(s, "r");
        fprintf(cgiOut, "Pragma: nocache\n");
        cgiHeaderContentType("text/html");
        fprintf(cgiOut, "<html>\n");
        fprintf(cgiOut, "<head><title>Past Transactions</title></head>\n");
        fprintf(cgiOut, "<body><h1>Past Transactions</h1>\n");
        if (!in) {
                fprintf(cgiOut, "<h2>No transactions to date.</h2>\n");
        } else {
                while(1) {
                        ch = getc(in);
                        if (ch == EOF) {
                                break;
                        }
                        putc(ch, cgiOut);
                }
                fclose(in);
        }
        fprintf(cgiOut,
                "<hr><a href=\"%s/portfolio\">Portfolio</a> \n",
                PROGRAM_URL);
        fprintf(cgiOut,
                "<a href=\"%s/newspaper\">Newspaper</a> \n",
                PROGRAM_URL);
        fprintf(cgiOut, "</body></html>\n");
        return 0;
}

int Newspaper() {
        FILE *in;
        int found = 0;
        char s[PATH_SPACE];
        float history[HISTORY_SIZE];
        fprintf(cgiOut, "Pragma: nocache\n");
        cgiHeaderContentType("text/html");
        fprintf(cgiOut, "<html>\n");
        fprintf(cgiOut, "<head><title>Financial News</title></head>\n");
        fprintf(cgiOut, "<body><h1>Financial News</h1>\n");
        sprintf(s, "%s/database", DATA_PATH);
        in = fopen(s, "r");
        if (!in) {
                return 0;
        }
        SetFieldSeparator(' ');
```

```
        do {
            char symbol[STRING_SPACE];
            char priceString[STRING_SPACE];
            int historyPos = 0;
            if (!GetField(in, symbol, STRING_SPACE)) {
                break;
            }
            while (GetField(in, priceString, STRING_SPACE)) {
                history[historyPos++] = atof(priceString);
            }
            if (historyPos) {
                fprintf(cgiOut, "%s: trading at %.3f",
                    symbol, history[historyPos-1]);
                if (historyPos >= 2) {
                    float move = history[historyPos-1] -
                        history[historyPos-2];
                    if (move == 0.0) {
                        fprintf(cgiOut, " unchanged");
                    } else if (move > 0.0) {
                        fprintf(cgiOut, " up %.3f", move);
                    } else {
                        fprintf(cgiOut, " down %.3f", move);
                    }
                }
                fprintf(cgiOut, "<a href=\"%s/history/%s\">\n",
                    PROGRAM_URL, symbol);
                fprintf(cgiOut, "See History</a><p>\n");
            }
        } while (NextRecord(in));
        fclose(in);
        fprintf(cgiOut,
            "<hr><a href=\"%s/portfolio\">Portfolio</a> \n",
            PROGRAM_URL);
        fprintf(cgiOut,
            "<a href=\"%s/transactions\">Past Transactions</a> \n",
            PROGRAM_URL);
        fprintf(cgiOut, "</body></html>\n");
        return 0;
}

int Portfolio() {
    float funds;
    float price;
    FILE *in;
    int shares;
```

```
float total = 0.0;
char s[PATH_SPACE];
char fundsString[STRING_SPACE];
fprintf(cgiOut, "Pragma: nocache\n");
cgiHeaderContentType("text/html");
fprintf(cgiOut, "<html>\n");
fprintf(cgiOut, "<head><title>Portfolio</title></head>\n");
fprintf(cgiOut, "<body><h1>Portfolio</h1>\n");
sprintf(s, "%s/%s.cur", DATA_PATH, accountName);
in = fopen(s, "r");
if (in) {
     int ch;
     fprintf(cgiOut, "<h2>Transaction Report</h2>\n");
     while(1) {
          ch = getc(in);
          if (ch == EOF) {
               break;
          }
          putc(ch, cgiOut);
     }
     fclose(in);
     unlink(s);
}

sprintf(s, "%s/%s.dat", DATA_PATH, accountName);
in = fopen(s, "r");
if (!in) {
     /* Bad, bad news */
     fprintf(cgiOut, "<h2>No database record available</h2>\n");
     fprintf(cgiOut, "Your database entry is not available.\n");
     fprintf(cgiOut, "Please contact the site administrator.\n");
     fprintf(cgiOut, "</body></html>\n");
     return 0;
}
SetFieldSeparator(' ');
GetField(in, fundsString, STRING_SPACE);
funds = atof(fundsString);
fprintf(cgiOut, "<body><h3>Current Holdings</h3>\n");
fprintf(cgiOut, "<body><h3>Funds Available: %.3f</h3>\n", funds);
fprintf(cgiOut, "<form method=POST action=\"%s/trade\">\n",
     PROGRAM_URL);
fprintf(cgiOut, "<table border=1>\n");
fprintf(cgiOut, "<tr><th>Stock Ticker</th>\n");
fprintf(cgiOut, "<th>Shares Held</th>\n");
fprintf(cgiOut, "<th>Current Price</th>\n");
```

```
        fprintf(cgiOut, "<th>Total Value</th>\n");
        fprintf(cgiOut, "<th colspan=3>Shares to Trade</th></tr>\n");
        if (!NextRecord(in)) {
                fprintf(cgiOut,
                        "<tr><th colspan=7>No current holdings.</th></tr>\n");
        } else {
                do {
                        char symbol[STRING_SPACE];
                        char sharesString[STRING_SPACE];
                        if (!GetField(in, symbol, STRING_SPACE)) {
                                break;
                        }
                        if (!GetField(in, sharesString, STRING_SPACE)) {
                                break;
                        }
                        shares = atoi(sharesString);
                        getStockPrice(symbol, &price);
                        fprintf(cgiOut, "<tr><td>%s</td><td>%d</td><td>%.3f</td>",
                                symbol, shares, price);
                        fprintf(cgiOut, "<td>%.3f</td>\n", shares * price);
                        total += shares * price;
                        fprintf(cgiOut, "<td>\n");
                        fprintf(cgiOut,
                                "<input type=text name=\"%s shares\" value=\"0\">\n",
                                symbol);
                        fprintf(cgiOut, "</td>\n");
                        fprintf(cgiOut,
                                "<td><input type=radio value=buy name=\"%s direction\"
checked>buy</td>\n",
                                symbol);
                        fprintf(cgiOut,
                                "<td><input type=radio value=sell name=\"%s
direction\">sell</td>\n",
                                symbol);
                        fprintf(cgiOut, "</td></tr>\n");
                } while (NextRecord(in));
        }
        fclose(in);
        fprintf(cgiOut, "<tr><th>Total Value</th><td colspan=2></td>\n");
        fprintf(cgiOut, "<td>%.3f</td><td colspan=3></td></tr>\n", total);
        fprintf(cgiOut, "</table>\n");
        fprintf(cgiOut, "Acquire new stock: \n");
        fprintf(cgiOut, "<input type=text name=\"newbuy symbol\">\n");
        fprintf(cgiOut,
                "Shares: <input type=text name=\"newbuy shares\"><p>\n");
```

```
        fprintf(cgiOut, "<input type=submit value=\"Submit New
Transactions\">\n");
        fprintf(cgiOut, "</form><p>\n");
        fprintf(cgiOut,
            "<a href=\"%s/newspaper\">Newspaper</a>\n ",
            PROGRAM_URL);
        fprintf(cgiOut,
            "<a href=\"%s/transactions\">Past Transactions</a> \n",
            PROGRAM_URL);
        fprintf(cgiOut, "</body></html>\n");
        return 0;
}

int getStockPrice(char *sym, float *priceP) {
        FILE *in;
        int found = 0;
        char s[PATH_SPACE];
        sprintf(s, "%s/database", DATA_PATH);
        in = fopen(s, "r");
        if (!in) {
            return 0;
        }
        SetFieldSeparator(' ');
        do {
            char symbol[STRING_SPACE];
            char priceString[STRING_SPACE];
            float price;
            if (!GetField(in, symbol, STRING_SPACE)) {
                break;
            }
            if (strcmp(symbol, sym)) {
                /* Not the right record */
                continue;
            }
            while (GetField(in, priceString, STRING_SPACE)) {
                price = atof(priceString);
                found = 1;
            }
            if (found) {
                *priceP = price;
                break;
            }
        } while (NextRecord(in));
        fclose(in);
        return found;
```

```c
        }

        int getStockHistory(char *sym, float *history, int *historySizeP) {
                FILE *in;
                int found = 0;
                int historyPos = 0;
                char s[PATH_SPACE];
                sprintf(s, "%s/database", DATA_PATH);
                in = fopen(s, "r");
                if (!in) {
                        return 0;
                }
                SetFieldSeparator(' ');
                do {
                        char symbol[STRING_SPACE];
                        char priceString[STRING_SPACE];
                        if (!GetField(in, symbol, STRING_SPACE)) {
                                break;
                        }
                        if (strcmp(symbol, sym)) {
                                /* Not the right record */
                                continue;
                        }
                        found = 1;
                        while (GetField(in, priceString, STRING_SPACE)) {
                                history[historyPos++] = atof(priceString);
                        }
                        break;
                } while (NextRecord(in));
                fclose(in);
                *historySizeP = historyPos;
                return found;
        }

        int getFunds(float *fundsP) {
                FILE *in;
                char s[PATH_SPACE];
                char fundsString[STRING_SPACE];
                sprintf(s, "%s/%s.dat", DATA_PATH, accountName);
                in = fopen(s, "r");
                if (!in) {
                        *fundsP = 0;
                        return 0;
                }
                SetFieldSeparator(' ');
```

```
        if (!GetField(in, fundsString, STRING_SPACE)) {
            fclose(in);
            *fundsP = 0;
            return 0;
        }
        *fundsP = atof(fundsString);
        fclose(in);
        return 1;
}

int setFunds(float newFunds) {
        FILE *in, *out;
        int found = 0;
        float funds;
        char s[PATH_SPACE], snew[PATH_SPACE];
        char fundsString[STRING_SPACE];
        sprintf(s, "%s/%s.dat", DATA_PATH, accountName);
        sprintf(snew, "%s/%s.new", DATA_PATH, accountName);
        in = fopen(s, "r");
        if (!in) {
            return 0;
        }
        out = fopen(snew, "w");
        if (!out) {
            fclose(in);
            return 0;
        }
        SetFieldSeparator(' ');
        if (!GetField(in, fundsString, STRING_SPACE)) {
            fclose(in);
            return 0;
        }
        funds = atof(fundsString);
        fprintf(out, "%.3f\n", newFunds);
        while (NextRecord(in)) {
            char symbol[STRING_SPACE];
            char sharesString[STRING_SPACE];
            if (!GetField(in, symbol, STRING_SPACE)) {
                break;
            }
            if (!GetField(in, sharesString, STRING_SPACE)) {
                break;
            }
            fprintf(out, "%s %s\n", symbol, sharesString);
        }
```

```c
        fclose(in);
        fclose(out);
        rename(snew, s);
        return 1;
}


int getStockShares(char *sym, int *sharesP) {
        FILE *in;
        int found = 0;
        int shares;
        char s[PATH_SPACE];
        sprintf(s, "%s/%s.dat", DATA_PATH, accountName);
        in = fopen(s, "r");
        if (!in) {
                *sharesP = 0;
                return 0;
        }
        SetFieldSeparator(' ');
        /* Skip over the first record, which contains this customer's funds */
        *sharesP = 0;
        while (NextRecord(in)) {
                char symbol[STRING_SPACE];
                char sharesString[STRING_SPACE];
                if (!GetField(in, symbol, STRING_SPACE)) {
                        break;
                }
                if (strcmp(symbol, sym)) {
                        /* Not the right record */
                        continue;
                }
                found = 1;
                if (!GetField(in, sharesString, STRING_SPACE)) {
                        break;
                }
                shares = atoi(sharesString);
                break;
        }
        fclose(in);
        if (!found) {
                *sharesP = 0;
        }
        *sharesP = shares;
        return found;
}
```

```
int setStockShares(char *sym, int shares) {
      FILE *in, *out;
      int found = 0;
      float funds;
      char s[PATH_SPACE], snew[PATH_SPACE];
      char fundsString[STRING_SPACE];
      sprintf(s, "%s/%s.dat", DATA_PATH, accountName);
      sprintf(snew, "%s/%s.new", DATA_PATH, accountName);
      in = fopen(s, "r");
      if (!in) {
            return 0;
      }
      out = fopen(snew, "w");
      if (!out) {
            fclose(in);
            return 0;
      }
      SetFieldSeparator(' ');
      /* Handle the first record, which contains this customer's funds */
      if (!GetField(in, fundsString, STRING_SPACE)) {
            fclose(in);
            return 0;
      }
      funds = atof(fundsString);
      fprintf(out, "%.3f\n", funds);
      while (NextRecord(in)) {
            char symbol[STRING_SPACE];
            char sharesString[STRING_SPACE];
            if (!GetField(in, symbol, STRING_SPACE)) {
                  break;
            }
            if (!GetField(in, sharesString, STRING_SPACE)) {
                  break;
            }
            if (strcmp(symbol, sym)) {
                  /* Not the right record */
                  fprintf(out, "%s %s\n", symbol, sharesString);
                  continue;
            } else {
                  fprintf(out, "%s %d\n", sym, shares);
                  found = 1;
            }
      }
      fclose(in);
      if (!found) {
```

```
                    fprintf(out, "%s %d\n", sym, shares);
        }
        fclose(out);
        rename(snew, s);
        return 1;
}
```

The Stock Market Trading Program in Perl: trade

The following is the Perl source code of the WWWWS CGI program.

```perl
#!/usr/local/bin/perl

# trade.c. This program allows users to interact
# with the WWWWS system. Set these #defines
# appropriately before compiling.

$dataPath = "/CHANGE/THIS/PATH/wwwws";
$programUrl = "/CHANGE/THIS/URL/cgi-bin/trade";

require "cgi-lib.pl";
require "chart.pl";
require "ctime.pl";
$historySize = 30;

srand();
$accountName = $ENV{'REMOTE_USER'} ;
if ($accountName eq "") {
        # This shouldn't happen! But it will happen
        # if the program is not installed according
        # to the instructions, or if the server
        # has bugs regarding user authentication.
        print "Pragma: nocache\n";
        print "Content-type: text/html\n\n";
        print "<html>\n";
        print "<head><title>User Not Authenticated</title></head>\n";
        print "<body><h1>User Not Authenticated</h1>\n";
        print "The trade program was not installed in\n";
        print "a password-authenticated directory, or\n";
        print "there is a bug in the Web server.\n";
        print "Please report this problem to the\n";
        print "site administrator.\n";
        print "</body></html>\n";
        exit 1;
}
```

```perl
$pathInfo = $ENV{'PATH_INFO'} ;
$_ = $pathInfo;
#Perl is very, very good at this sort of pattern matching
if (/\/trade/) {
      exit &Trade;
} elsif (/\/history\/(\w+)/) {
      exit &History($1);
} elsif (/\/historychart\/(\w+)\/image\d+\.gif/) {
      exit &HistoryChart($1);
} elsif (/\transactions/) {
      exit &Transactions;
} elsif (/\newspaper/) {
      exit &Newspaper;
} else {
      exit &Portfolio;
}

sub Trade {
      local($symbol, $shares, $attr, $funds, $s);
      $s = $dataPath . "/database";
      if (!open(TRADEIN, $s)) {
            &DatabaseMissing();
            return 0;
      }
      &StartTransaction;
      &ReadParse(*input);
      if ($input{'newbuy symbol'} ne "") {
            $symbol = $input{'newbuy symbol'} ;
            $shares = $input{'newbuy shares'} ;
            if ($shares) {
                  &stockBuy($symbol, $shares);
            }
      }
      while(<TRADEIN>) {
            @fields = split(/\s/, $_);
            $symbol = $fields[0];
            if ($symbol eq "") {
                  last;
            }
            $attr = $symbol . " shares";
            $shares = $input{$attr} ;
            if ($shares > 0) {
                  local($direction);
                  $attr = $symbol . " direction";
                  $direction = $input{$attr} ;
```

```perl
                      if ($direction eq "buy") {
                          stockBuy($symbol, $shares);
                      } elsif ($direction eq "sell") {
                          stockSell($symbol, $shares);
                      } else {
                          # Not a complete submission.
                          # Don't guess! There's serious
                          # play money at stake here.
                          &LogTransaction(
                              "Please specify buy or sell for "
                              . $symbol .
                              "No transaction performed.");
                          EndTransaction();
                          return 0;
                      }
              } elsif ($shares == 0) {
                  # OK, do nothing
              } elsif ($shares < 0) {
                      &LogTransaction($symbol . ": negative numbers of shares are
not accepted for trades. Enter a positive number and select buy or sell.");
                  }
          }
      close(TRADEIN);
      &EndTransaction;
      return &Portfolio;
}


sub stockBuy {
      local($symbol, $shares) = @_;
      local($purchasePrice, $price, $funds);
      # A purchase. Can we afford it?
      if (! &getFunds($funds)) {
              &LogTransaction(
                  "Unable to access your account. Please contact the site
administrator.");
              return;
      }
      if (! &getStockPrice($symbol, $price)) {
              &LogTransaction("Stock symbol " . symbol .
                  "is not in the database.");
              return;
      }
      $purchasePrice = $shares * $price;
      if ($purchasePrice > $funds) {
              # No
```

```perl
        &LogTransaction(
                "Insufficient funds to purchase " . $shares .
                " shares of " . $symbol . "!");
    } else {
            local($currentShares);
            &getStockShares($symbol, $currentShares);
            # An ideal universe with no commissions!
            $currentShares += $shares;
            $funds -= $purchasePrice;
            &setStockShares($symbol, $currentShares);

            &LogTransaction("Purchased " . $shares . " shares of " .
                    $symbol . " at " . $price . ".");
    }
    &setFunds($funds);
}

sub stockSell {
    local($symbol, $shares) = @_;
    # A sale. Do we have that many shares?
    local($salePrice, $currentShares, $price, $funds);
    if (! &getFunds($funds)) {
            &LogTransaction("Unable to access your account. Please contact the
site administrator.");
            return;
    }
    if (! &getStockPrice($symbol, $price)) {
            &LogTransaction("Stock symbol " . $symbol .
                    " is not in the database.");
            return;
    }
    $salePrice = $shares * $price;
    &getStockShares($symbol, $currentShares);
    if ($currentShares < $shares) {
            # No
            &LogTransaction("Can't sell " . $shares . " shares of " .
                    $symbol . ": you only have " .
                    $currentShares . "shares!");
    } else {
            # An ideal universe with no commissions!
            $currentShares -= $shares;
            $funds += $salePrice;
            &setStockShares($symbol, $currentShares);

            &LogTransaction("Sold " . $shares . " shares of " . $symbol .
```

```
                    " at " . $price . ".");
        }
        &setFunds($funds);
}

sub DatabaseMissing {
        print "Pragma: nocache\n";
        print "Content-type: text/html\n\n";
        print "<html><head><title>Database Missing</title></head>\n";
        print "<body><h1>Database Missing</h1>\n";
        print "Please contact the site administrator.\n";
        print "</body></html>\n";
}

sub StartTransaction {
        $path = $dataPath . "/" . $accountName . ".cur";
        open(CURRENT, ">" . $path);
        $path = $dataPath . "/" . $accountName . ".log";
        open(PERMANENT, ">>" . $path);
}

sub EndTransaction {
        print CURRENT "End of transaction.<p>\n";
        close(CURRENT);
        close(PERMANENT);
}

sub LogTransaction {
        local($text) = @_;
        print CURRENT $text, "<p>\n";
        print PERMANENT $text, " Time: ", &ctime(time), "<p>\n";
}

sub History
{
        local($symbol) = @_;
        local(@history);
        print "Pragma: nocache\n";
        print "Content-type: text/html\n\n";
        print "<html>\n";
        print "<head><title>Price History: ", $symbol, "</title></head>\n";
        print "<body><h1>Price History: ", $symbol, "</h1>\n";
        if (! &getStockHistory($symbol, *history)) {
                print "<h2>There is no stock with that ticker
symbol.</h2>\n";
```

```perl
    } else {
        # Add a random component to the URL in order to
        # prevent Web browsers from caching the chart
        # when it is out of date.
        print "<img src=\"", $programUrl, "/historychart/", $symbol,
            "/image", int(rand(1000)), ".gif\"><p>\n";
    }
    print "Prices for the past 30 days are shown.\n";
    print "<hr><a href=\"", $programUrl, "/portfolio\">Portfolio</a>\n ";
    print "<a href=\"", $programUrl, "/newspaper\">Newspaper</a> \n";
    print "<a href=\"", $programUrl,
        "/transactions\">Past Transactions</a> \n";
    print "</body></html>\n";
    return 0;
}

sub HistoryChart {
    local($symbol) = @_;
    local(@history, @labels, $i, $im);
    $im = new GD::Image(400, 200);
    &getStockHistory($symbol, *history);
    for ($i = 0; ($i < int(@history)); $i++) {
        $labels[$i] = int(@history) - $i - 1;
    }
    &chartDraw($im, $chartBar | $chartCross | $chartLine,
        *labels, "Stock Price", *history);
    print "Pragma: nocache\n";
    print "Content-type: image/gif\n\n";
    print $im->gif;
}

sub Transactions {
    $path = $dataPath . "/" . $accountName . ".log";
    print "Pragma: nocache\n";
    print "Content-type: text/html\n\n";
    print "<html>\n";
    print "<head><title>Past Transactions</title></head>\n";
    print "<body><h1>Past Transactions</h1>\n";
    if (!open(TRANSACTIONSIN, $path)) {
        print "<h2>No transactions to date.</h2>\n";
    } else {
        while(<TRANSACTIONSIN>) {
            print $_;
        }
        close(TRANSACTIONSIN);
```

```
        }
        print "<hr><a href=\"", $programUrl, "/portfolio\">Portfolio</a> \n";
        print "<a href=\"", $programUrl, "/newspaper\">Newspaper</a> \n";
        print "</body></html>\n";
        return 0;
}


sub Newspaper {
        print "Pragma: nocache\n";
        print "Content-type: text/html\n\n";
        print "<html>\n";
        print "<head><title>Financial News</title></head>\n";
        print "<body><h1>Financial News</h1>\n";
        $path = $dataPath . "/database";
        open(NEWSPAPERIN, $path) || return 0;
        while(<NEWSPAPERIN>) {
                local(@fields, $symbol, $price);
                s/\s+$//g;
                @fields = split(/\s/, $_);
                $symbol = $fields[0];
                if ($symbol eq "") {
                        last;
                }
                $price = $fields[$#fields];
                if ($price eq $symbol) {
                        print $symbol, ": no price set<p>\n";
                } else {
                        print $symbol, ": trading at ", $price;
                        if (int(@fields) > 2) {
                                $move = $fields[$#fields] -
                                        $fields[$#fields - 1];
                                $move = sprintf("%.4f", $move);
                                if ($move == 0.0) {
                                        print " unchanged";
                                } elsif ($move > 0.0) {
                                        print " UP ", $move;
                                } else {
                                        print " DOWN ", $move;
                                }
                        }
                        print "<a href=\"", $programUrl, "/history/",
                                $symbol, "\">\n";
                        print "See History</a><p>\n";
                }
        }
}
```

```
        close(NEWSPAPERIN);
        print "<hr><a href=\"", $programUrl, "/portfolio\">Portfolio</a> \n";
        print "<a href=\"", $programUrl,
               "/transactions\">Past Transactions</a> \n";
        print "</body></html>\n";
        return 0;
}

sub Portfolio {
        local($funds, $total, $path, $stocks);
        $total = 0;
        $stocks = 0;
        print "Pragma: nocache\n";
        print "Content-type: text/html\n\n";
        print "<html>\n";
        print "<head><title>Portfolio</title></head>\n";
        print "<body><h1>Portfolio</h1>\n";
        $path = $dataPath . "/" . $accountName . ".cur";
        if (open(PORTFOLIOIN, $path)) {
               print "<h2>Transaction Report</h2>\n";
               while (<PORTFOLIOIN>) {
                      print $_;
               }
               close(PORTFOLIOIN);
               unlink($path);
        }

        $path = $dataPath . "/" . $accountName . ".dat";
        if (!open(PORTFOLIOIN, $path)) {
               # Bad, bad news
               print "<h2>No database record available</h2>\n";
               print "Your database entry is not available.\n";
               print "Please contact the site administrator.\n";
               print "</body></html>\n";
               return 0;
        }
        $funds = <PORTFOLIOIN>;
        $funds =~ s/\s+$//;
        print "<body><h3>Current Holdings</h3>\n";
        print "<body><h3>Funds Available: ", $funds, "</h3>\n";
        print "<form method=POST action=\"", $programUrl, "/trade\">\n";
        print "<table border=1>\n";
        print "<tr><th>Stock Ticker</th>\n";
        print "<th>Shares Held</th>\n";
        print "<th>Current Price</th>\n";
```

```perl
        print "<th>Total Value</th>\n";
        print "<th colspan=3>Shares to Trade</th></tr>\n";
        while (<PORTFOLIOIN>) {
                local($symbol, $shares, $price, $net);
                s/\s+$//g;
                ($symbol, $shares) = split(/ /);
                &getStockPrice($symbol, $price);
                print "<tr><td>", $symbol, "</td><td>", $shares,
                        "</td><td>", $price, "</td>";
                $net = sprintf("%.4f", $shares * $price);
                print "<td>", $net, "</td>\n";
                $total += $net;
                print "<td>\n";
                print "<input type=text name=\"", $symbol,
                        " shares\" value=\"0\">\n";
                print "</td>\n";
                print "<td><input type=radio value=buy ",
                        "name=\"", $symbol, " direction\" checked>buy</td>\n";
                print "<td><input type=radio value=sell ",
                        "name=\"", $symbol, " direction\">sell</td>\n";
                print "</td></tr>\n";
                $stocks++;
        }
        if (!$stocks) {
                print "<tr><th colspan=7>No current holdings.</th></tr>\n";
        }
        close(PORTFOLIOIN);
        print "<tr><th>Total Value</th><td colspan=2></td>\n";
        $total = sprintf("%.4f", $total);
        print "<td>", $total, "</td><td colspan=3></td></tr>\n";
        print "</table>\n";
        print "Acquire new stock:\n ";
        print "<input type=text name=\"newbuy symbol\">\n";
        print "Shares: <input type=text name=\"newbuy shares\"><p>\n";
        print "<input type=submit value=\"Submit New Transactions\">\n;
        print "</form><p>\n";
        print "<a href=\"", $programUrl, "/newspaper\">Newspaper</a> \n";
        print "<a href=\"", $programUrl,
                "/transactions\">Past Transactions</a> \n";
        print "</body></html>\n";
        return 0;
}

sub getStockPrice {
        local($sym, $s) = @_;
```

```perl
        local(@fields, $s);
        $s = $dataPath . "/database";
        if (!open(PRICEIN, $s)) {
                return 0;
        }
        while(<PRICEIN>) {
                s/\s+$//;
                @fields = split(/ /);
                if ($fields[0] eq $sym) {
                        if ($#fields) {
                                $_[1] = $fields[$#fields];
                                return 1;
                        }
                }
        }
        close(PRICEIN);
        return 0;
}

sub getStockHistory {
        local($sym, *history) = @_;
        local($i, $s, @fields);
        $s = $dataPath . "/database";
        if (!open(HISTORYIN, $s)) {
                return 0;
        }
        while(<HISTORYIN>) {
                s/\s+$//;
                @fields = split(/ /);
                if ($fields[0] eq $sym) {
                        for ($i = 0; ($i < ($#fields - 1)); $i++) {
                                $history[$i] = $fields[$i + 1];
                        }
                        $#history = $#fields - 2;
                        return 1;
                }
        }
        close(HISTORYIN);
        return 0;
}

sub getFunds {
        local($s, $funds);
        $s = $dataPath . "/" . $accountName . ".dat";
        if (!open(FUNDSIN, $s)) {
```

```
                    return 0;
            }
            $funds = <FUNDSIN>;
            $funds =~ s/\s+$//;
            $_[0] = $funds;
            close(FUNDSIN);
            return 1;
    }
    sub setFunds {
            local($funds) = @_;
            local($sold, $snew, $oldFunds);
            $sold = $dataPath . "/" . $accountName . ".dat";
            if (!open(FUNDSIN, $sold)) {
                    return 0;
            }
            $snew = $dataPath . "/" . $accountName . ".new";
            if (!open(FUNDSOUT, ">" . $snew)) {
                    close(FUNDSIN);
                    return 0;
            }
            $oldFunds = <FUNDSIN>;
            print FUNDSOUT $funds, "\n";
            while (<FUNDSIN>) {
                    print FUNDSOUT $_;
            }
            close(FUNDSIN);
            close(FUNDSOUT);
            rename($snew, $sold);
            return 1;
    }

    sub getStockShares {
            local($sym) = @_;
            local(@fields);
            $s = $dataPath . "/" . $accountName . ".dat";
            if (!open(SHARESIN, $s)) {
                    return 0;
            }
            while(<SHARESIN>) {
                    local($symbol, $shares);
                    s/\s+$//;
                    ($symbol, $shares) = split(/ /, $_, 2);
                    if ($symbol eq $sym) {
```

```perl
                        $_[1] = $shares;
                        close(SHARESIN);
                        return 1;
                }
        }
        close(SHARESIN);
        return 0;
}


sub setStockShares {
        local($sym, $shares) = @_;
        local($sold, $snew, $funds, $found);
        $sold = $dataPath . "/" . $accountName . ".dat";
        if (!open(SHARESIN, $sold)) {
                return 0;
        }
        $snew = $dataPath . "/" . $accountName . ".new";
        if (!open(SHARESOUT, ">" . $snew)) {
                close(SHARESIN);
                return 0;
        }
        $funds = <SHARESIN>;
        $funds =~ s/\s+$//;
        print SHARESOUT $funds, "\n";
        $found = 0;
        while (<SHARESIN>) {
                local($symbol, $oldShares);
                s/\s+$//;
                ($symbol, $oldShares) = split(/ /, $_, 2);
                if ($symbol eq $sym) {
                        $found = 1;
                        $oldShares = $shares;
                }
                print SHARESOUT $symbol, " ", $oldShares, "\n";
        }
        if (!$found) {
                print SHARESOUT $sym, " ", $shares, "\n";
        }
        close(SHARESIN);
        close(SHARESOUT);
        rename($snew, $sold);
        return 1;
}
```

Installing and Using the trade Program

To install the trade program, first be sure to properly create a wwws data directory and an initial database, as discussed earlier in this chapter. Second, ensure the directory from which the trade program will be served is protected by basic authentication and then create an account or two (this is also discussed earlier in the chapter). Next, be sure to configure and run the simtrade program to generate 30 days of stock price data; otherwise, the output will not be very interesting! Finally, correctly set the data directory path and program URL at the beginning of the trade program, compile the program (if you are using the C version), and install it in an authenticated directory.

To access the program, simply access its URL. If you have configured your server correctly, you will be immediately prompted for a name and password; otherwise, the program will generate an error message. Check your Web server's documentation regarding the use of authentication with your Web pages. Also, double-check the examples presented earlier in this chapter that apply to the NCSA and Apache Web servers.

Once you log in, you will be presented with a portfolio page. If you are told that there is no database entry for you, be sure to create a .dat file for your customer name in the wwws data directory.

If the program informs you that it cannot access the database to perform trades, be sure the database file exists and the wwws data directory is readable, executable, and writable by the user ID under which the Web server runs.

Conclusion

This chapter concludes an exploration of CGI programming. The stock trading system presented here and the Solar System Simulator presented in Chapter 13, approach the practical limits of what can be done effectively in CGI.

Doubtless other applications of and approaches to CGI remain to be found and exploited by enterprising programmers. However, there are new approaches to dynamic Web document programming that deserve serious consideration. The final chapter examines the future of CGI programming, the limitations of CGI, and new and exciting alternatives to the CGI approach to Web programming.

CHAPTER 15

What's Next: CGI and Beyond

CGI is a great way to extend the usefulness of Web servers. CGI programs do a great job of providing Web access to other information storage systems, such as databases. They also do a fairly solid job of accepting and processing user input, such as comment forms.

After that, though, CGI begins to lose steam. While CGI can be used to provide interactive interfaces, and even to generate animation, it is time to be honest about its limitations as a means of delivering applications. "Plain" CGI is probably not the best way to implement animation nor is it the best way to make full-powered applications available to end users unless the application happens to be well-suited to an HTML forms interface.

These drawbacks point out the basic problem with CGI programming: CGI does not take advantage of the computer on the user's desk as much as the programmer would like.

However, before I examine this fundamental limitation of CGI, I want to consider more immediate weaknesses and the available means of solving them.

For Some Tasks, CGI Is Overkill

While CGI is very simple, there are tasks for which CGI programming can appear to be too much effort. It would be convenient to be able to handle common tasks, such as processing imagemaps and inserting the current date into a Web page, within the server itself.

Built-in Imagemaps

Configuring an external CGI program to handle imagemaps, while effective, is clumsy and slow. The administrator must make sure the URLs are constructed correctly to reference the imagemap program and then the imagemap itself. The server itself must launch a separate program every time an imagemap click arrives. This is not an elegant state of affairs.

Several available Web servers address this problem by moving the image-map program into the server itself. One is the Netscape Communications Server,[1] which recognizes imagemaps and processes them internally, thereby improving speed and making it straightforward to create a correct link to an imagemap file.

Built-in Server Scripting Languages

There are also servers that address these problems by providing additional capabilities that extend the server side include interface normally used to insert entire documents. There are many variations on this approach, from simple directives to insert the time of day to complete server-side scripting languages that attempt a natural feel as an "extension" to HTML. These directives are executed by the Web server program as it delivers the page. Because an external CGI program need not be executed, these approaches can improve server performance. Of course, the down side is that the added features may still not include the feature you need. One server that supports such features is the SIAC HTTPD[2] for the Windows NT operating system.

Built-in Database Access

The desire to make a Web site searchable is very common. Many people cobble together CGI programs for this based on the Unix `grep` command, and these approaches can work surprisingly well. Equally often, a particular existing database must be made accessible on the Web. CGI programmers usually address this problem by taking advantage of the programmer's inter-face offered by the database from a CGI program.

Built-in database support in the Web server can be a valuable feature by providing good performance for Web site searches without the need for new programming. America Online's Navisoft server[3] offers built-in database search capabilities.

Improved APIs: Faster Replacements for CGI

The CGI standard is very straightforward, but this simplicity comes at a price. Every time a CGI document is accessed, the operating system must create a new, distinct process in which to run the CGI program and so must set the various CGI environment variables appropriately.

The trouble is that creating new processes consumes time and resources within the server's operating system. This is a fixed cost associated with every new execution of a CGI program.

Several companies offer alternatives to CGI that take advantage of light-weight *threads* instead of processes. Threads, like processes, are distinct "flows of execution" in the system, proceeding from one line of code to the next seemingly without regard for the other programs that may be executing at the same time.

Unlike processes, however, threads do not automatically receive completely separate memory spaces within the operating system; all threads within a particular program share the same memory space. Also, threads do not receive the environment variables and other resources that are given to every full-fledged process.

Because threads do not receive as many resources from the operating system, they are considered more lightweight than processes are. Most higher-performance alternatives to CGI use a single thread for each connection to the server, rather than an entirely new process.

The Netscape Communications Server[1] provides such an alternative interface. NSAPI programmers register new functions before launching the Netscape server, instead of installing CGI programs. Those functions are loaded into memory and treated as part of the Netscape server itself. The server then invokes the programmer's NSAPI functions when handling URLs within particular portions of the Web server's URL space.

NSAPI programming is likely to be somewhat daunting for Perl CGI programmers largely because it must be done in C. NSAPI is best used for programs that must run as quickly as possible. Developing a CGI-based version first and then porting it to the NSAPI is a reasonable approach, especially if which parts of the system will require maximum performance are not initially obvious.

These techniques can improve or beat CGI's performance at the tasks it was intended to do. However, while they make it easier to accomplish tasks traditionally done by using CGI programs, they do not fundamentally add new capabilities on the other end of the connection. And therein lies the most significant weakness of CGI.

The Fundamental Limitation of CGI

Why is CGI not ideal for elaborate applications? The answer is simple: CGI doesn't take sufficient advantage of the computer on the user's desk. Nearly any PC is capable of tasks such as animating graphics, recalculating spread-sheets, and validating form fields to make sure they are within a reasonable range. The tremendous portability of CGI and HTML has led programmers to employ them for things that traditional programming techniques can do better. Of course, until very recently, programming tools to extend Web browsers have not been available, and it has been necessary to implement everything using CGI or using platform-specific "external viewers."

Addressing CGI Limitations: Web Browser Programming Tools

Existing languages, or more accurately the libraries that come with them, have one significant problem with regard to the Internet: They are not oriented toward Internet communications. While C, Visual BASIC, and others can certainly be used to develop Internet applications, they are not currently available as standard parts of Web browsers. Also, these languages are not explicitly designed to prevent the writing of dangerous programs. Finally, these languages are not usually provided with a common, cross-platform set of libraries to perform useful functions and provide a user interface. New languages such as JavaScript and Java are intended to address these problems.

Security and Program Safety

Traditionally, it has been a given that any language can be used to write a computer virus or other harmful program. The burden has always been on the user to determine whether the author of a particular program is trustworthy. Operating systems such as Unix and Windows NT also provide protection against harmful software, as long as the user specifically avoids running untrusted software under a trusted account containing valuable information. However, the user must still make a special effort to decide which programs are safe. This is reasonable when a user downloads only perhaps three new programs a week from the Internet.

The desire to extend Web pages with custom programs on the browser side, however, changes this equation. A skilled programmer can add completely unique and compelling features to a site, so the demand for such content in Web pages will be very high, and many Web pages will feature it. While the user could be asked politely whether to trust programs embedded in each page, this defeats the desire to create convenient, interesting Web pages without forcing the user to jump through hoops and make decisions about whether to trust each Web page author. Doubtless most users would simply turn off the custom-code feature altogether, thereby making the Web a less interesting place.

Java addresses these problems by executing programs in a simulated "virtual machine," the boundaries of which cannot be overwritten by a program executing within it. This prevents the program from accidentally or deliberately overwriting the code data of the Web browser program itself. In addition, the Java libraries refuse requests to tamper with local files or open connections to nontrusted sites on the Internet.

Cross-Platform Programming

Visual BASIC programmers have, in the past, been confined to operating within Microsoft Windows and Macintosh environments, with most of the available extensions for Visual BASIC being available only for Windows. C programmers have the benefit of a standardized language available on practically all platforms, but the disadvantage that the libraries that do the real work are very platform-specific. A C programmer can write a program to count the lines of a file in standard ANSI C and expect it to work, for the most part, on any computer. But a C programmer cannot write a program that displays a graphical, friendly user interface and expect it to work on many platforms, without the purchase of expensive cross-platform development tools designed to address these problems.

Java, on the other hand, provides a standard collection of classes that can be used to implement graphical user interfaces, audio, animation, and more. Java programs take advantage of the standard user interface look and feel on a particular operating system without the need to be restricted to run only on that operating system.

Java Applets

While Java is capable of implementing standalone programs, its most common use is as a language to create new features that are not a standard part of a Web browser. A Java-enhanced Web page can offer a spreadsheet interface that automatically totals columns and ensures user input is reasonable before it is ever submitted to a Web server. These small programs that accessorize the Web browser are called *applets*.

For instance, the WWWWS application discussed in Chapter 14 would benefit from Java code. That code could verify that the trade the user is about to submit is reasonable before the user has to wait for the server to consider the question.

Also, the stock performance graphs would gain in speed if the data were simply sent to a Java applet instead of being rendered, compressed, and transmitted by the server as a GIF.

The SSS program presented in Chapter 13 is an even stronger example of an application that would benefit from being largely rewritten in Java. The entire simulation could reside in a Java applet, thus completely avoiding the need to transmit images of the solar system through the Internet. Yet using Java would retain the ease of access and portability to many platforms offered by CGI.

Why CGI Isn't Going Away Any Time Soon

With server-side improvements like the NSAPI and client-side programming environments like Java becoming available, it might appear that CGI programming is not long for this world. However, there are several reasons why CGI programming is unlikely to go away in the near future.

First, CGI programs are relatively easy to write. CGI programming is usually a simple matter of writing HTML to standard output, and it is easily accomplished not only in C but also in easier, high-level programming languages like Perl. These tools are widely available.

Second, since Web browsers do not know or care that they are communicating with a CGI program, there is no reason to stop using CGI, even if another technique becomes popular. Also, even if an alternative to CGI becomes highly popular on a particular server operating system, there is still no reason not to use CGI under another operating system. The browser doesn't care whether the request was answered by a CGI program or the latest threaded server programming tool. As long as Web browsers support the HTTP protocol and the HTML language, existing CGI programming techniques will likely continue to be useful.

Finally, CGI programs will continue to be popular as back ends for applications written in Java and other browser-side extension languages. For Java applets to interact with other resources on the Internet, they will often be required to contact CGI programs on the Web server from which they were downloaded. While Java is capable of opening Internet connections of its own, many sites will continue to use firewalls that forbid connections except through an HTTP proxy server. As a result, applets will often use the existing document-retrieval features of the Web browser to access information kept on the Web server. These document requests will very likely be answered by CGI programs.

Conclusion

In this chapter I provided a brief overview of the many emerging tools that augment, complement, or replace CGI programming. While the role of CGI programming will change in the near future, CGI programming will continue to serve an important purpose in the Web for a long time.

This book has explored the many ways in which CGI programming can be used to perform useful tasks and dramatically enhance Web pages. I hope you have enjoyed this exploration of CGI programming and its potential to make the Web a more interactive and dynamic environment.

References

1. Netscape Communications Corporation, "Netscape Server Central."
   [URL:http://home.mcom.com/comprod/server_central/index.html]

2. Science Application International Corporation, "SAIC-HTTP Server Site."
   [URL:http://Webserver.itl.saic.com/]

3. America Online, "Welcome to NaviService."
   [URL:http://www.navisoft.com/index.htm]

4. Sun Microsystems, "Java: Programming For the Internet."
   [URL:http://java.sun.com/]

CGI Environment Variables

CGI programs have access to a large amount of information about the URL being requested, the Web browser being used, the site from which the request is being made, and so on. This information is made available in the form of environment variables. This appendix contains a detailed list of those environment variables, along with the equivalent cgic variable names.

Note that environment variables may not always be set and that the C getenv() function may return a null pointer. The cgic variables are never null pointers. If the environment variable is not set, the cgic variable will point to an empty string.

For more information about accessing environment variables from C and Perl programs, see Chapter 2. For more information about using cgic to gain easy access to CGI environment variables, see Chapter 8.

Environment Variable: AUTH_TYPE
cgic Equivalent: char *cgiAuthType

Indicates the type of authentication used for the request, if any. Normally, if a CGI program is installed in an authenticated directory, it will never be invoked if authentication has not already succeeded. This variable is useful when a script is used in multiple situations, that is, when some are authenticated, and some not.

Environment Variable: CONTENT_LENGTH
cgic Equivalent: char *cgiContentLength

Indicates the number of bytes of form or query data received. In most cases, the programmer can take advantage of the cgi-lib or cgic libraries rather than parsing form data directly.

Environment Variable: CONTENT_TYPE
cgic Equivalent: char *cgiContentType

Indicates the MIME content type of the information submitted by the user, if any. If this variable matches application/x-www-form-urlencoded, the cgic and cgi-lib libraries will automatically examine the form data submitted. If this string has any other nonempty value, a different type of data has been submitted. This is currently rare, as most browsers can only submit forms. However, if the submitted nonform data is of interest to a cgic application, the submitted data can be read from the cgiIn file pointer. Non-cgic applications can read input data, if any, from standard input.

Environment Variable: GATEWAY_INTERFACE
cgic Equivalent: char *cgiGatewayInterface

Indicates the name of the gateway interface (currently CGI/1.1).

Environment Variable: HTTP_ACCEPT
cgic Equivalent: char *cgiAccept

This variable contains a space-separated list of Internet media types (MIME content types) acceptable to the browser. Unfortunately, this variable is not supplied by most current browsers. Programmers wishing to make decisions based on the capabilities of the browser are advised to instead check the USER_AGENT variable against a list of browsers and capabilities.

Environment Variable: HTTP_USER_AGENT
cgic Equivalent: char *cgiUserAgent

Indicates the name of the browser in use, if provided. This information is useful to determine which advanced HTML features should be used.

Environment Variable: PATH_INFO
cgic Equivalent: char *cgiPathInfo

Most Web servers recognize any additional path information in the URL of the request beyond the name of the CGI program itself and pass that information on to the program. PATH_INFO contains this additional path information. If it is set, it should always begin with a / character. However, this may vary depending on the server in use.

Environment Variable: PATH_TRANSLATED
cgic Equivalent: char *cgiPathTranslated

Most Web servers recognize any additional path information in the URL of the request beyond the name of the CGI program itself and pass that information on to the program. PATH_TRANSLATED contains this additional path information, which is translated by the server into a complete filesystem path on the local server beginning at the document root of the server. This is useful when implementing an extension to a server, such as a new server side include mechanism or imagemap handler.

Environment Variable: QUERY_STRING
cgic Equivalent: char *cgiQueryString

Contains any query information submitted by the user as a result of a GET-method form, an imagemap click, or an <ISINDEX> tag. For GET-method forms, parsing this environment variable directly is usually not necessary. The cgic and cgi-lib libraries can do this more conveniently.

Environment Variable: REMOTE_ADDR
cgic Equivalent: char *cgiRemoteAddr

Points to the dotted-decimal IP address of the browser. This variable is almost always set. However, note that if a proxy server is used by a particular set of users, many machines may appear to have one hostname.

Environment Variable: REMOTE_HOST
cgic Equivalent: char *cgiRemoteHost

Indicates the fully resolved hostname of the browser, if known. This variable is often not set. Some servers never set this variable in order to save DNS lookup time. Also note that if a proxy server is used by a particular group of users, many machines may appear to have one hostname.

Environment Variable: REMOTE_IDENT
cgic Equivalent: char *cgiRemoteIdent

Indicates the user name volunteered by the user's machine via the user identification protocol. This information is far from secure. Identification demons can be installed by individual users on insecure systems such as Microsoft Windows 3.1 systems.

Environment Variable: REQUEST_METHOD
cgic Equivalent: char *cgiRequestMethod

Indicates the method used in the request (usually GET or POST).

Environment Variable: REMOTE_USER
cgic Equivalent: char *cgiRemoteUser

Points to the user name under which the user has authenticated. If no authentication has taken place, this variable will not be set. The certainty of this information depends on the type of authentication in use.

Environment Variable: SCRIPT_NAME
cgic Equivalent: char *cgiScriptName

Indicates the filename under which the program was invoked. When set by the server, this variable can be used to conveniently discover the path at which the program is installed.

Environment Variable: SERVER_NAME
cgic Equivalent: char *cgiServerName

Indicates the name of the server, e.g. www.boutell.com, as configured by the administrator.

Environment Variable: SERVER_PORT
cgic Equivalent: char *cgiServerPort

Indicates the port number on which the server is listening for HTTP connections (usually 80).

Environment Variable: SERVER_PROTOCOL
cgic Equivalent: char *cgiServerProtocol

Indicates the protocol in use (usually HTTP/1.0).

Environment Variable: SERVER_SOFTWARE
cgic Equivalent: char *cgiServerSoftware

Indicates the name and version of the server software.

APPENDIX 2

Internet Media Content Types

This appendix details many of the currently used Internet media content types, also known as MIME types or simply as content types. These content types are particularly important when a CGI program wishes to transmit something other than an HTML document to the user. See Chapter 2 for an introduction to this subject and Chapter 10 for examples of non-HTML documents sent from a CGI program.

> **NOTE:** New media types are coming into existence regularly. The official registry is often well behind actual practice. The following list is based on that included with NCSA's public domain Web server as of September 1995.

No attempt is made here to document the format of the data associated with these content types. This list is intended to make it easier for you to determine what `Content-type:` header should be emitted before a particular type of document is sent to the browser.

Content Type	Comments
`application/activemessage`	
`application/andrew-inset`	
`application/applefile`	
`application/atomicmail`	
`application/dca-rft`	
`application/dec-dx`	

Content Type	Comments
application/mac-binhex40	
application/macwriteii	MacWrite Document
application/msword	Microsoft Word Document
application/news-message-id	
application/news-transmission	
application/octet-stream	Use for binary file downloads
application/oda	
application/pdf	Adobe Acrobat Documents
application/postscript	PostScript
application/remote-printing	
application/rtf	Rich Text Format
application/slate	
application/x-mif	
application/wita	
application/wordperfect5.1	WordPerfect 5.1 Documents
application/wordperfect6.0	WordPerfect 6.0 Documents
application/x-csh	Potentially dangerous[1]
application/x-dvi	TeX/LaTeX Output (not TeX source)
application/x-hdf	
application/x-latex	LaTeX Source
application/x-netcdf	
application/x-sh	Potentially dangerous[1]
application/x-tcl	Potentially dangerous[1]
application/x-tex	TeX Source
application/x-texinfo	
application/x-troff	Troff Formatter Source
application/x-troff-man	Troff Source, -man argument assumed
application/x-troff-me	Troff Source, -me argument assumed
application/x-troff-ms	Troff Source, -ms argument assumed
application/x-wais-source	
application/zip	Many IBM compatible systems have ZIP helper apps
application/x-bcpio	
application/x-cpio	cpio tape format (Unix)
application/x-gtar	gnu tar tape format (Unix)
application/x-shar	Potentially dangerous[1]
application/x-sv4cpio	
application/x-sv4crc	
application/x-ustar	
audio/basic	Sun-style format .au audio
audio/x-aiff	Amiga-format .aiff audio
audio/x-wav	Microsoft Windows-format .wav audio
image/gif	CompuServe GIF 8-bit lossless images
image/ief	

Content Type	Comments
image/jpeg	JPEG lossy photographic images
image/png	w3 consortium PNG lossless images
image/tiff	TIFF format images
image/x-cmu-raster	
image/x-portable-anymap	netpbm/pbmplus images (any subtype)
image/x-portable-bitmap	netpbm/pbmplus black and white images
image/x-portable-graymap	netpbm/pbmplus grayscale images
image/x-portable-pixmap	netpbm/pbmplus truecolor images
image/x-rgb	
image/x-xbitmap	X Window System black and white images
image/x-xpixmap	X Window System color images
image/x-xwindowdump	X Window System screen dump format
message/external-body	
message/news	
message/partial	
message/rfc822	
multipart/alternative	
multipart/appledouble	
multipart/digest	
multipart/mixed	Server push
multipart/parallel	
text/html	HTML documents
text/x-sgml	SGML documents, not limited to HTML
text/plain	Plain ASCII text
text/richtext	Not RTF (see application/rtf)
text/tab-separated-values	Useful for spreadsheet interchange
text/x-setext	
video/mpeg	MPEG video format; common on PCs, Unix
video/quicktime	Apple video format
video/x-msvideo	Microsoft/Intel AVI video format
video/x-sgi-movie	

[1] Browsers should almost never be configured to execute shell scripts. This is a dangerous practice, as the script in question could simply consist of rm * or another harmful command. Those interested in sending code to the browser should consider safe scripting languages such as Java, JavaScript, Safe-TCL, and PGP-SafePerl.

cgic Reference Manual

gic is a library for convenient C-language CGI programming. It is introduced in Chapter 8. See Appendix 5 for information about retrieving cgic from the CD and from other sources. cgi-lib, a simple Perl library for form processing, is also covered in that chapter.

cgic Variable Reference

This section provides a reference guide to the various global variables cgic provides for the programmer, except for the cgic copies of the environment variables.

> **NOTE:** The cgic copies of the CGI environment variables are covered in Appendix I, "CGI Environment Variables." That information is not repeated here.

Variable: `FILE *cgiIn`

Pointer to CGI input that indicates end-of-file after cgic processes any form data submitted. In 99% of cases, you will not need this variable. However, in future applications, documents other than forms may be posted to the server, in which case this file pointer may be read from in order to retrieve the contents. `cgiIn` is normally equivalent to `stdin`. However, it is recommended that `cgiIn` be used to ensure compatibility with future versions of cgic for specialized environments such as the Netscape server API.

Variable: `FILE *cgiOut`

Pointer to CGI output. The `cgiHeader` functions, such as
`cgiHeaderContentType`, should be used first to output the HTTP headers.
The output HTML page, GIF image, or other Web document should then be
written to `cgiOut` by the programmer using standard C I/O functions such
as `fprintf()` and `fwrite()`. cgiOut is normally equivalent to `stdout`.
However, it is recommended that `cgiOut` be used to ensure compatibility
with future versions of cgic for specialized environments such as the
Netscape server API.

cgic Result Codes

In most cases, cgic functions are designed to produce reasonable results
even when browsers and users do unreasonable things. However, it is sometimes important to know precisely which unreasonable things took place,
especially when assigning a default value or bounding a value is an inade-
quate solution. The following Result Codes are useful in making this deter-
mination.

These Result Codes are defined by the enumeration `cgiFormResultType`
in the file `cgic.h`. The exception is the environment save-and-restore Result
Codes, which are defined by the enumeration `cgiEnvironmentResultType`
in the same file.

Result Code: `cgiEnvironmentIO`

Indicates that an attempt to read or write the CGI environment to or from a
capture file failed due to an I/O error.

Result Code: `cgiEnvironmentMemory`

Indicates that an attempt to read or write the CGI environment to or from a
capture file failed due to an out-of-memory error.

Result Code: `cgiEnvironmentSuccess`

Indicates that an attempt to read or write the CGI environment to or from a capture file was successful.

Result Code: `cgiFormBadType`

Indicates that a numeric value submitted by the user was in fact not a legal number.

Result Code: `cgiFormConstrained`

Indicates that a numeric value was beyond the specified bounds and was forced to the lower or upper bound as appropriate.

Result Code: `cgiFormEmpty`

Indicates that a field was retrieved but contained no data.

Result Code: `cgiFormNoSuchChoice`

Indicates that the value submitted for a single-choice field (such as a radio-button group) was not an acceptable value. This usually means there is a discrepancy between the form and the program.

Result Code: `cgiFormNotFound`

Indicates that no value was submitted for a particular field.

Result Code: `cgiFormSuccess`

Indicates that the function successfully performed at least one action (or retrieved at least one value, where applicable).

Result Code: `cgiFormTruncated`

Indicates that a string value retrieved from the user was cut short to avoid overwriting the end of a buffer.

cgic Function Reference

Function: `cgiFormResultType cgiFormCheckboxMultiple(`
`char *name,`
`char **valuesText,`
`int valuesTotal,`
`int *result,`
`int *invalid)`

`cgiFormCheckboxMultiple()` determines which checkboxes among a
group of checkboxes with the same name are checked. This is distinct from
radio buttons (see `cgiFormRadio()`). `valuesText` should point to an
array of strings identifying the VALUE attribute of each checkbox.
`valuesTotal` should indicate the total number of checkboxes. `result`
should point to an array of integers with as many elements as there are
strings in the `valuesText` array. For each choice in the `valuesText` array
that is selected, the corresponding integer in the `result` array will be set to
one; other entries in the `result` array will be set to zero.
`cgiFormCheckboxMultiple` returns `cgiFormSuccess` if at least one valid
checkbox was checked or `cgiFormNotFound` if no valid checkboxes were
checked. The integer pointed to by `invalid` is set to the number of invalid
selections that were submitted, which should be zero unless the form and
the `valuesText` array do not agree.

Function: `cgiFormResultType cgiFormCheckboxSingle(`
`char *name)`

`cgiFormCheckboxSingle()` determines whether the checkbox with the
specified name is checked. `cgiFormCheckboxSingle()` returns
`cgiFormSuccess` if the button is checked or `cgiFormNotFound` if the
checkbox is not checked. `cgiFormCheckboxSingle()` is intended for
single checkboxes with a unique name. See later in this appendix for functions to deal with multiple checkboxes with the same name and functions
to deal with radio buttons.

Function: cgiFormResultType cgiFormDouble(
                char *name,
                double *result,
                double defaultV)

cgiFormDouble() attempts to retrieve the floating-point value sent for the specified input field. The value pointed to by result will be set to the value submitted. cgiFormDouble() returns cgiFormSuccess if the value was successfully retrieved, cgiFormEmpty if the value submitted is an empty string, cgiFormBadType if the value submitted is not a number, and cgiFormNotFound if no such input field was submitted. In the last three cases, the value pointed to by result is set to the specified default.

Function: cgiFormResultType cgiFormDoubleBounded(
                char *name,
                double *result,
                double min,
                double max,
                double defaultV)

cgiFormDoubleBounded() attempts to retrieve the floating-point value sent for the specified input field and constrains the result to be within the specified bounds. The value pointed to by result will be set to the value submitted. cgiFormDoubleBounded() returns cgiFormSuccess if the value was successfully retrieved, cgiFormConstrained if the value was out of bounds and result was adjusted accordingly, cgiFormEmpty if the value submitted is an empty string, cgiFormBadType if the value submitted is not a number, and cgiFormNotFound if no such input field was submitted. In the last three cases, the value pointed to by result is set to the specified default.

Function: cgiFormResultType cgiFormInteger(
                char *name,
                int *result,
                int defaultV)

cgiFormInteger() attempts to retrieve the integer sent for the specified input field. The value pointed to by result will be set to the value submitted. cgiFormInteger() returns cgiFormSuccess if the value was successfully retrieved, cgiFormEmpty if the value submitted is an empty string,

cgiFormBadType if the value submitted is not an integer, and
cgiFormNotFound if no such input field was submitted. In the last three
cases, the value pointed to by result is set to the specified default.

Function: cgiFormResultType cgiFormIntegerBounded(
                    char *name,
                    int *result,
                    int min,
                    int max,
                    int defaultV)

cgiFormIntegerBounded() attempts to retrieve the integer sent for the
specified input field and constrains the result to be within the specified
bounds. The value pointed to by result will be set to the value submitted.
cgiFormIntegerBounded() returns cgiFormSuccess if the value was
successfully retrieved, cgiFormConstrained if the value was out of bounds
and result was adjusted accordingly, cgiFormEmpty if the value submitted
is an empty string, cgiFormBadType if the value submitted is not an integer, and cgiFormNotFound if no such input field was submitted. In the last
three cases, the value pointed to by result is set to the specified default.

Function: cgiFormResultType cgiFormRadio(
                    char *name,
                    char **valuesText,
                    int valuesTotal,
                    int *result,
                    int defaultV)

cgiFormRadio() determines which, if any, of a group of radio boxes with
the same name was selected. valuesText should point to an array of strings
identifying the VALUE attribute of each radio box; valuesTotal should
indicate the total number of radio boxes. The value pointed to by result
will be set to the position of the actual choice selected within the
valuesText array, if any, or to the value of default if no radio box was
checked or an invalid selection was made. cgiFormRadio() returns
cgiFormSuccess if a checked radio box was found in the group,
cgiFormNotFound if no box was checked, and cgiFormNoSuchChoice if
the radio box submitted does not match any of the possibilities in the
valuesText array.

Function: cgiFormResultType cgiFormSelectMultiple(char *name, char **choicesText, int choicesTotal, int *result, int *invalid)

cgiFormSelectMultiple() retrieves the selection numbers associated with a <SELECT> element that does allow multiple selections. name should identify the NAME attribute of the <SELECT> element. choicesText should point to an array of strings identifying each choice; choicesTotal should indicate the total number of choices. result should point to an array of integers with as many elements as there are strings in the choicesText array. For each choice in the choicesText array that is selected, the corresponding integer in the result array will be set to one; other entries in the result array will be set to zero. cgiFormSelectMultiple() returns cgiFormSuccess if at least one valid selection was successfully retrieved or cgiFormNotFound if no valid selection was submitted. The integer pointed to by invalid is set to the number of invalid selections that were submitted, which should be zero unless the form and the choicesText array do not agree.

Function: cgiFormResultType cgiFormSelectSingle(
        char *name,
        char **choicesText,
        int choicesTotal,
        int *result,
        int defaultV)

cgiFormSelectSingle() retrieves the selection number associated with a <SELECT> element that does not allow multiple selections. name should identify the NAME attribute of the <SELECT> element. choicesText should point to an array of strings identifying each choice; choicesTotal should indicate the total number of choices. The value pointed to by result will be set to the position of the actual choice selected within the choicesText array, if any, or to the value of default if no selection was submitted or an invalid selection was made. cgiFormSelectSingle() returns cgiFormSuccess if the value was successfully retrieved, cgiFormNotFound if no selection was submitted, and cgiFormNoSuchChoice if the selection does not match any of the possibilities in the choicesText array.

Function: cgiFormResultType cgiFormString(
                char *name,
                char *result,
                int max)

cgiFormString() attempts to retrieve the string sent for the specified input field. The text will be copied into the buffer specified by result up to but not exceeding max-1 bytes; a terminating null is then added to complete the string. Regardless of the newline format submitted by the browser, cgiFormString() always encodes each newline as a single line feed (ASCII decimal 10). As a result, the final string may be slightly shorter than indicated by a call to cgiFormStringSpaceNeeded() but will never be longer. cgiFormString() returns cgiFormSuccess if the string was successfully retrieved, cgiFormTruncated if the string was retrieved but was truncated to fit the buffer, cgiFormEmpty if the string was retrieved but was empty, and cgiFormNotFound if no such input field was submitted. In the last case, an empty string is copied to result.

Function: cgiFormResultType cgiFormStringMultiple(
                char *name,
                char ***ptrToStringArray)

cgiFormStringMultiple() is useful in the unusual case in which several input elements in the form have the same name and, for whatever reason, the programmer does not wish to use the checkbox, radio button, and/or selection menu functions. This is occasionally needed if the programmer cannot know in advance what values might appear in a multiple-selection list or group of checkboxes on a form. The value pointed to by result will be set to a pointer to an array of strings; the last entry in the array will be a null pointer.

This array is allocated by the CGI library. **Important:** When you are done working with the array, you must call cgiStringArrayFree() with the array pointer as the argument. cgiFormStringMultiple() returns cgiFormSuccess if at least one occurrence of the name is found, cgiFormNotFound if no occurrence is found, or cgiFormMemory if not enough memory is available to allocate the array to be returned. In all cases except the last, ptrToStringArray is set to point to a valid array of strings, with the last element in the array being a null pointer; in the out-of-memory case, ptrToStringArray is set to a null pointer.

Function: cgiFormResultType cgiFormStringNoNewlines(
                 char *name,
                 char *result,
                 int max)

cgiFormStringNoNewlines() is exactly equivalent to
cgiFormString(), except that any carriage returns or line feeds that occur
in the input will be stripped out. The use of this function is recommended
for single-line text input fields, as some browsers will submit carriage
returns and line feeds when they should not.

Function: cgiFormResultType cgiFormStringSpaceNeeded(
                 char *name,
                 int *length)

cgiFormStringSpaceNeeded() is used to determine the length of the
input text buffer needed to receive the contents of the specified input field.
This is useful if the programmer wishes to allocate sufficient memory for
input of arbitrary length. The actual length of the string retrieved by a subsequent call to cgiFormString() may be slightly shorter but will never be
longer than *length. On success, cgiFormStringSpaceNeeded() sets the
value pointed to by length to the number of bytes of data, including the
terminating null, and returns cgiFormSuccess. If no value was submitted
for the specified field, cgiFormStringSpaceNeeded() sets the value
pointed to by length to 1 and returns cgiFormNotFound. The value 1 is
set to ensure space for an empty string (a single null character) if
cgiFormString is called despite the return value.

Function: void cgiHeaderContentType(
               char *mimeType)

cgiHeaderContentType() should be called if the programmer wishes to
output a new document in response to the user's request. This is the normal
case. The single argument is the MIME document type of the response.
Typical values are text/html for HTML documents, text/plain for plain
ASCII without HTML tags, image/gif for a GIF image, and audio/basic
for .au-format audio. See Appendix 2 for more information about MIME
types. Only one of the cgiHeader functions (cgiHeaderLocation,
cgiHeaderStatus, or cgiHeaderContentType) should be invoked for
each CGI transaction.

Function: `void cgiHeaderLocation(`
                    `char *redirectUrl)`

`cgiHeaderLocation()` should be called if the programmer wishes to redirect the user to a different URL. No futher output is needed in this case. Only one of the `cgiHeader` functions (`cgiHeaderLocation()`, `cgiHeaderStatus()`, or `cgiHeaderContentType()`) should be invoked for each CGI transaction.

Function: `void cgiHeaderStatus(`
                    `int status,`
                    `char *statusMessage)`

`cgiHeaderStatus()` should be called if the programmer wishes to output an HTTP error status code instead of a document. The status code is the first argument; the second argument is the status message to be displayed to the user. Only one of the `cgiHeader` functions (`cgiHeaderLocation`, `cgiHeaderStatus`, or `cgiHeaderContentType`) should be invoked for each CGI transaction.

Function: `int cgiMain()`

The programmer must write this function, which performs the unique task of the program. It is invoked by the true `main()` function, which is found in the cgic library itself. The return value from `cgiMain` will be the return value of the program. The user is expected to make numerous calls to the `cgiForm` family of functions from within this function.

Function: `cgiEnvironmentResultType cgiReadEnvironment(`
                    `char *filename)`

`cgiReadEnvironment()` restores a CGI environment saved to the specified file by `cgiWriteEnvironment()`. Of course, these will work as expected only if the programmer uses the cgic copies of the CGI environment variables and `cgiIn` and `cgiOut` rather than `stdin` and `stdout`. These functions are useful for capturing real CGI situations while the Web server is running and then recreating them in a debugging environment. Both functions return `cgiEnvironmentSuccess` on success, `cgiEnvironmentIO` on an I/O error, and `cgiEnvironmentMemory` on an out-of-memory error.

Function: `int cgiSaferSystem(`
                              `char *command)`

`cgiSaferSystem()` is a convenience function used to invoke the
`system()` function less dangerously. That is, `cgiSaferSystem()` escapes
the shell metacharacters ; and |, which can otherwise cause other programs
to be invoked beyond the one intended by the programmer. However,
understanding the shell commands you invoke and ensuring you do not
invoke the shell in ways that permit the Web user to run arbitrary programs
is your responsibility.

Function: `void cgiStringArrayFree(`
                              `char **stringArray)`

`cgiStringArrayFree()` is used to free the memory associated with a
string array created by `cgiFormStringMultiple()`.

Function: `cgiEnvironmentResultType cgiWriteEnvironment(`
                              `char *filename)`

`cgiWriteEnvironment()` can be used to write the entire CGI environment, including form data, to the specified output file.
`cgiReadEnvironment()` can then be used to restore that environment
from the specified input file for debugging. Of course, these will work as
expected only if the programmer uses the cgic copies of the CGI environment variables and `cgiIn` and `cgiOut` rather than `stdin` and `stdout`.
These functions are useful for capturing real CGI situations while the Web
server is running and then recreating them in a debugging environment.
Both functions return `cgiEnvironmentSuccess` on success,
`cgiEnvironmentIO` on an I/O error, and `cgiEnvironmentMemory` on an
out-of-memory error.

gd Reference Manual

The gd library is used to create and modify GIF images on the fly, a common activity in CGI programs. The GIF drawing library is available on the CD as well as on the Web; see Appendix 5 for more information. For an introduction to gd, see Chapter 10. Also see the online documentation included in the file gd.html in the gd distribution itself.

Type Reference

Type: gdFont

DESCRIPTION

A font structure used to declare the characteristics of a font. Consider the files gdfont1.c and gdfont1.h in the gd distribution for an example of the proper declaration of this structure. You can provide your own font data by providing such a structure and the associated pixel array. You can determine the width and height of a single character in a font by examining the w and h members of the structure. If you will not be creating your own fonts, you need not concern yourself with the rest of the components of this structure.

DETAILS

```
typedef struct {
        /* # of characters in font */
        int nchars;
```

```
        /* First character is numbered... (usually 32 = space) */
        int offset;
        /* Character width and height */
        int w;
        int h;
        /* Font data; array of characters, one row after another.
                Easily included in code, also easily loaded from
                data files. */
        char *data;
    } gdFont;
```

Type: gdFontPtr

DESCRIPTION

A pointer to a font structure. Text-output functions expect such a pointer as the second argument, following the gdImagePtr argument.

Type: gdImage

DESCRIPTION

The data structure in which gd stores images. gdImageCreate() returns a pointer to this type, and the other functions expect to receive a pointer to this type as their first argument. Macros are provided to access the members of interest, so directly manipulating the structure is not necessary. Most especially, do not set the members directly from your code; use the functions and macros provided.

DETAILS

```
    typedef struct {
        unsigned char ** pixels;
        int sx;
        int sy;
        int colorsTotal;
        int red[gdMaxColors];
        int green[gdMaxColors];
        int blue[gdMaxColors];
        int open[gdMaxColors];
        int transparent;
    } gdImage;
```

Type: gdImagePtr

DESCRIPTION

A pointer to a gdImage structure. gdImageCreate() returns this type, and the other functions expect it as the first argument.

Type: gdPoint

DESCRIPTION

Represents a point in the coordinate space of the image. It is used by gdImagePolygon() and gdImageFilledPolygon().

DETAILS

```
typedef struct {
        int x, y;
}  gdPoint, *gdPointPtr;
```

Type: gdPointPtr

DESCRIPTION

A pointer to a gdPoint structure. It is passed as an argument to gdImagePolygon() and gdImageFilledPolygon().

Constant Reference

Constant: gdBrushed

DESCRIPTION

Used in place of a color when the programmer invokes a line-drawing function such as gdImageLine() or gdImageRectangle(). When gdBrushed is used as the color, the brush image set with gdImageSetBrush is drawn in place of each pixel of the line (the brush is usually larger than one pixel, thus creating the effect of a wide paintbrush). See also gdStyledBrushed for a way to draw broken lines with a series of distinct copies of an image.

Constant: gdDashSize

DESCRIPTION

The length of a dash in a dashed line. Defined to be 4 for backwards compatibility with programs that use gdImageDashedLine. New programs should use gdImageSetStyle and call the standard gdImageLine function with the special color gdStyled or gdStyledBrushed.

Constant: gdMaxColors

DESCRIPTION

The constant 256. This is the maximum number of colors in a GIF file according to the GIF standard. It also is the maximum number of colors in a gd image.

Constant: gdStyled

DESCRIPTION

Used in place of a color when invoking a line-drawing function such as gdImageLine() or gdImageRectangle(). When the programmer uses gdStyled as the color, the colors of the pixels are drawn successively from the style that has been set with gdImageSetStyle. If the color of a pixel is equal to gdTransparent, that pixel is not altered. (This mechanism is completely unrelated to the "transparent color" of the image itself; see gdImageColorTransparent for that mechanism.) See also gdStyledBrushed.

Constant: gdStyledBrushed

DESCRIPTION

Used in place of a color when invoking a line-drawing function such as gdImageLine or gdImageRectangle. When gdStyledBrushed is used as the color, the brush image set with gdImageSetBrush is drawn at each pixel of the line, providing the style set with gdImageSetStyle contains a nonzero value (OR gdTransparent, which does not equal zero but is supported for consistency) for the current pixel. (Pixels are drawn successively from the style as the line is drawn, returning to the beginning when the available pixels in the style are exhausted.) Note that this differs from the behavior of gdStyled, in which the values in the style are used as actual pixel colors, except for gdTransparent.

Constant: `gdTiled`

DESCRIPTION

Used in place of a normal color in `gdImageFilledRectangle`, `gdImageFilledPolygon`, `gdImageFill`, and `gdImageFillToBorder`. It selects a pixel from the tile image set with `gdImageSetTile` in such a way as to ensure that the filled area will be tiled with copies of the tile image. See the discussions of `gdImageFill` and `gdImageFillToBorder` for special restrictions regarding those functions.

Constant: `gdTransparent`

DESCRIPTION

Used in place of a normal color in a style to be set with `gdImageSetStyle`. It is not the transparent color index of the image. For that functionality, please see `gdImageColorTransparent`.

Function Reference

Function: `void gdImageArc(`
                    `gdImagePtr im,`
                    `int cx,`
                    `int cy,`
                    `int w,`
                    `int h,`
                    `int s,`
                    `int e,`
                    `int color)`

DESCRIPTION

`gdImageArc()` is used to draw a partial ellipse centered at the given point, with the specified width and height in pixels. The arc begins at the position in degrees specified by s and ends at the position specified by e. The arc is drawn in the color specified by the last argument. A circle can be drawn by beginning from 0 degrees and ending at 360 degrees, with `width` and `height` being equal. e must be greater than s. Degree values greater than 360 are interpreted modulo 360.

EXAMPLE

... inside a function ...

```
gdImagePtr im;
int black;
int white;
im = gdImageCreate(100, 50);
/* Background color (first allocated) */
black = gdImageColorAllocate(im, 0, 0, 0);
/* Allocate the color white (red, green and blue all maximum). */
white = gdImageColorAllocate(im, 255, 255, 255);
/* Inscribe an ellipse in the image. */
gdImageArc(im, 50, 25, 98, 48, 0, 360, white);
/* ... Do something with the image, such as saving it to a file... */
/* Destroy it */
gdImageDestroy(im);
```

Function: `int gdImageBlue(`
`gdImagePtr im,`
`int color)`

DESCRIPTION

`gdImageBlue()` is a macro that returns the blue component of the specified color index. Use this macro rather than accessing the structure members directly.

Function: `int gdImageBoundsSafe(`
`gdImagePtr im,`
`int x,`
`int y)`

DESCRIPTION

`gdImageBoundsSafe()` returns true (1) if the specified point is within the bounds of the image and false (0) if not. This function is intended primarily for use by those who wish to add functions to gd. All of the gd drawing functions already clip safely to the edges of the image.

EXAMPLE

... inside a function ...

```
gdImagePtr im;
int black;
int white;
im = gdImageCreate(100, 100);
if (gdImageBoundsSafe(im, 50, 50)) {
        printf("50, 50 is within the image bounds\n");
} else {
        printf("50, 50 is outside the image bounds\n");
}
gdImageDestroy(im);
```

Function: `void gdImageChar(`
`                gdImagePtr im,`
`                gdFontPtr font,`
`                int x,`
`                int y,`
`                int c,`
`                int color)`

DESCRIPTION

`gdImageChar()` is used to draw single characters on the image. (To draw multiple characters, use `gdImageString()`.) The second argument is a pointer to a font definition structure. Five fonts are provided with gd: `gdFontTiny`, `gdFontSmall`, `gdFontMediumBold`, `gdFontLarge`, and `gdFontGiant`. You must `#include` the files `gdfontt.h`, `gdfonts.h`, `gdfontmb.h`, `gdfontl.h`, and `gdfontg.h`, respectively. The character specified by the `c` argument is drawn from left to right in the specified color. See `gdImageCharUp()` for a way of drawing vertical text. Pixels not set by a particular character retain their previous color.

EXAMPLE

```
#include "gd.h"
#include "gdfontl.h"
... inside a function ...
gdImagePtr im;
int black;
int white;
im = gdImageCreate(100, 100);
```

```
/* Background color (first allocated) */
black = gdImageColorAllocate(im, 0, 0, 0);
/* Allocate the color white (red, green and blue all maximum). */
white = gdImageColorAllocate(im, 255, 255, 255);
/* Draw a character. */
gdImageChar(im, gdFontLarge, 0, 0, 'Q', white);
/* ... Do something with the image, such as saving it to a file... */
/* Destroy it */
gdImageDestroy(im);
```

Function: void gdImageCharUp(
                   gdImagePtr im,
                   gdFontPtr font,
                   int x,
                   int y,
                   int c,
                   int color)

DESCRIPTION

gdImageCharUp() is used to draw single characters on the image, rotated
90 degrees. (To draw multiple characters, use gdImageStringUp().) The
second argument is a pointer to a font definition structure. Five fonts are
provided with gd: gdFontTiny, gdFontSmall, gdFontMediumBold,
gdFontLarge, and gdFontGiant. You must #include the files
gdfontt.h, gdfonts.h, gdfontmb.h, gdfontl.h, and gdfontg.h,
respectively. The character specified by the fifth argument is drawn from
bottom to top, rotated at a 90-degree angle, in the specified color. (See
gdImageChar() for a way of drawing horizontal text.) Pixels not set by a
particular character retain their previous color.

EXAMPLE

```
#include "gd.h"
#include "gdfontl.h"
... inside a function ...
gdImagePtr im;
int black;
int white;
im = gdImageCreate(100, 100);
/* Background color (first allocated) */
black = gdImageColorAllocate(im, 0, 0, 0);
/* Allocate the color white (red, green and blue all maximum). */
```

```
white = gdImageColorAllocate(im, 255, 255, 255);
/* Draw a character upwards so it rests against the top of the image.
*/
gdImageCharUp(im, gdFontLarge,
        0, gdFontLarge->h, 'Q', white);
/* ... Do something with the image, such as saving it to a file... */
/* Destroy it */
gdImageDestroy(im);
```

Function: nt gdImageColorAllocate(
              gdImagePtr im,
              int r,
              int g,
              int b)

DESCRIPTION

gdImageColorAllocate() finds the first available color index in the image specified, sets its RGB values to those requested (255 is the maximum for each), and returns the index of the new color table entry. When creating a new image (the first time you invoke this function) you are setting the background color for that image.

If all available colors have been allocated, gdImageColorAllocate() will return -1 to indicate failure. (This is not uncommon when working with existing GIF files that already use 256 colors.) Note that gdImageColorAllocate() does not check for existing colors that match your request. See gdImageColorExact() and gdImageColorClosest() for ways to locate existing colors that approximate the color desired in situations where a new color is not available.

EXAMPLE

... inside a function ...

```
gdImagePtr im;
int black;
int red;
im = gdImageCreate(100, 100);
/* Background color (first allocated) */
black = gdImageColorAllocate(im, 0, 0, 0);
/* Allocate the color red. */
red = gdImageColorAllocate(im, 255, 0, 0);
```

```
/* Draw a dashed line from the upper left corner to the lower right
corner. */
gdImageDashedLine(im, 0, 0, 99, 99, red);
/* ... Do something with the image, such as saving it to a file... */
/* Destroy it */
gdImageDestroy(im);
```

Function: int gdImageColorClosest(
                        gdImagePtr im,
                        int r,
                        int g,
                        int b)

DESCRIPTION

gdImageColorClosest() searches the colors that have been defined thus
far in the image specified and returns the index of the color with RGB values
closest to those of the request. Closeness is determined by Euclidian
distance, which is used to determine the distance between colors in three-
dimensional color space.

If no colors have yet been allocated in the image, gdImageColorClosest()
returns -1.

This function is most useful as a backup method for choosing a drawing
color when an image already contains gdMaxColors (256) colors and no
more can be allocated. (This is not uncommon when you are working with
existing GIF files that already use many colors.) See gdImageColorExact()
for a method of locating exact matches only.

EXAMPLE

... inside a function ...

```
gdImagePtr im;
FILE *in;
int red;
/* Let's suppose that photo.gif is a scanned photograph with
        many colors. */
in = fopen("photo.gif", "rb");
im = gdImageCreateFromGif(in);
fclose(in);
/* Try to allocate red directly */
red = gdImageColorAllocate(im, 255, 0, 0);
```

```
/* If we fail to allocate red... */
if (red == (-1)) {
        /* Find the closest color instead. */
        red = gdImageColorClosest(im, 255, 0, 0);
}
/* Draw a dashed line from the upper left corner to the lower right
corner */
gdImageDashedLine(im, 0, 0, 99, 99, red);
/* ... Do something with the image, such as saving it to a file... */
/* Destroy it */
gdImageDestroy(im);
```

Function: void gdImageColorDeallocate(
                    gdImagePtr im,
                    int color)

DESCRIPTION

gdImageColorDeallocate() marks the specified color as being available
for reuse. It does not attempt to determine whether the color index is still in
use in the image. After a call to this function, the next call to
gdImageColorAllocate() for the same image will set new RGB values for
that color index, thereby changing the color of any pixels that have that
index. If multiple calls to gdImageColorDeallocate() are made consecu-
tively, the lowest-numbered index among them will be reused by the next
gdImageColorAllocate call.

EXAMPLE

... inside a function ...

```
gdImagePtr im;
int red, blue;
in = fopen("photo.gif", "rb");
im = gdImageCreateFromGif(in);
fclose(in);
/* Look for red in the color table. */
red = gdImageColorExact(im, 255, 0, 0);
/* If red is present... */
if (red != (-1)) {
        /* Deallocate it. */
        gdImageColorDeallocate(im, red);
        /* Allocate blue, reusing slot in table.
            Existing red pixels will change color. */
```

```
            blue = gdImageColorAllocate(im, 0, 0, 255);
    }
    /* ... Do something with the image, such as saving it to a file... */
    /* Destroy it */
    gdImageDestroy(im);
```

Function: `int gdImageColorExact(`
`                    gdImagePtr im,`
`                    int r,`
`                    int g,`
`                    int b)`

DESCRIPTION

gdImageColorExact() searches the colors that have been defined thus far in the image specified and returns the index of the first color with RGB values that exactly match those of the request. If no allocated color matches the request precisely, gdImageColorExact returns -1. See gdImageColorClosest() for a way to find the color closest to the color requested.

EXAMPLE

... inside a function ...

```
    gdImagePtr im;
    int red;
    in = fopen("photo.gif", "rb");
    im = gdImageCreateFromGif(in);
    fclose(in);
    /* The image may already contain red; if it does, we'll save a slot
            in the color table by using that color. */
    /* Try to allocate red directly */
    red = gdImageColorExact(im, 255, 0, 0);
    /* If red isn't already present... */
    if (red == (-1)) {
            /* Second best: try to allocate it directly. */
            red = gdImageColorAllocate(im, 255, 0, 0);
            /* Out of colors, so find the closest color instead. */
            red = gdImageColorClosest(im, 255, 0, 0);
    }
    /* Draw a dashed line from the upper left corner to the lower right
    corner */
    gdImageDashedLine(im, 0, 0, 99, 99, red);
```

```
/* ... Do something with the image, such as saving it to a file... */
/* Destroy it */
gdImageDestroy(im);
```

Function: `int gdImageColorsTotal(`
                         `gdImagePtr im)`

DESCRIPTION

`gdImageColorsTotal()` is a macro that returns the number of colors currently allocated in the image. Use this macro to obtain this information; do not access the structure directly.

Function: `void gdImageColorTransparent(`
                         `gdImagePtr im,`
                         `int color)`

DESCRIPTION

`gdImageColorTransparent()` sets the transparent color index for the specified image to the specified index. To indicate that there should be no transparent color, the programmer should invoke `gdImageColorTransparent()` with a color index of –1.

The color index used should be an index allocated by `gdImageColorAllocate()`, whether explicitly invoked by your code or implicitly invoked by loading an image. To ensure your image has a reasonable appearance when viewed by users who do not have transparent background capabilities, be sure to give reasonable RGB values to the color you allocate for use as a transparent color, even though it will be transparent on systems that support transparency.

EXAMPLE

... inside a function ...

```
gdImagePtr im;
int black;
FILE *in, *out;
in = fopen("photo.gif", "rb");
im = gdImageCreateFromGif(in);
fclose(in);
/* Look for black in the color table and make it transparent. */
black = gdImageColorExact(im, 0, 0, 0);
```

```
/* If black is present... */
if (black != (-1)) {
        /* Make it transparent */
        gdImageColorTransparent(im, black);
}
/* Save the newly-transparent image back to the file */
out = fopen("photo.gif", "wb");
gdImageGif(im, out);
fclose(out);
/* Destroy it */
gdImageDestroy(im);
```

Function: void gdImageCopy(
                        gdImagePtr dst,
                        gdImagePtr src,
                        int dstX,
                        int dstY,
                        int srcX,
                        int srcY,
                        int w,
                        int h)

DESCRIPTION

gdImageCopy() is used to copy a rectangular portion of one image to another image. (For a way of stretching or shrinking the image in the process, see gdImageCopyResized().)

The dst argument is the destination image to which the region will be copied. The src argument is the source image from which the region is copied. The dstX and dstY arguments specify the point in the destination image to which the region will be copied. The srcX and srcY arguments specify the upper left-hand corner of the region in the source image. The w and h arguments specify the width and height of the region.

When you copy a region from one location in an image to another location in the same image, gdImageCopy() will perform as expected unless the regions overlap, in which case the result is unpredictable.

Important note on copying between images: Different images do not necessarily have the same color tables, so pixels are not simply set to the same color index values to copy them. gdImageCopy() will invoke gdImageColorExact() in an attempt to find an identical RGB value in the destination image for each pixel in the copied portion of the source image. If such a value is not found, gdImageCopy() will attempt to allocate colors as needed using gdImageColorAllocate(). If both of these methods fail, gdImageCopy() will invoke gdImageColorClosest() to find the color in the destination image that most closely approximates the color of the pixel being copied.

EXAMPLE

... Inside a function ...

```
gdImagePtr im_in;
gdImagePtr im_out;
int x, y;
FILE *in;
FILE *out;
/* Load a small gif to tile the larger one with */
in = fopen("small.gif", "rb");
im_in = gdImageCreateFromGif(in);
fclose(in);
/* Make the output image four times as large on both axes */
im_out = gdImageCreate(im_in->sx * 4, im_in->sy * 4);
/* Now tile the larger image using the smaller one */
for (y = 0; (y sx, y * im_in->sy,
                    0, 0,
                    im_in->sx, im_in->sy);
        }
}
out = fopen("tiled.gif", "wb");
gdImageGif(im_out, out);
fclose(out);
gdImageDestroy(im_in);
gdImageDestroy(im_out);
```

Function: `void gdImageCopyResized(`
            `gdImagePtr dst,`
            `gdImagePtr src,`
            `int dstX,`
            `int dstY,`
            `int srcX,`
            `int srcY,`
            `int destW,`
            `int destH,`
            `int srcW,`
            `int srcH)`

DESCRIPTION

`gdImageCopyResized()` is used to copy a rectangular portion of one image to another image. The X and Y dimensions of the original region and the destination region can vary, resulting in stretching or shrinking of the region as appropriate. (For a simpler version of this function that does not deal with resizing, see `gdImageCopy()`.)

The `dst` argument is the destination image to which the region will be copied. The `src` argument is the source image from which the region is copied. The `dstX` and `dstY` arguments specify the point in the destination image to which the region will be copied. The `srcX` and `srcY` arguments specify the upper left-hand corner of the region in the source image. The `dstW` and `dstH` arguments specify the width and height of the destination region. The `srcW` and `srcH` arguments specify the width and height of the source region and can differ from the destination size, thus allowing a region to be scaled during the copying process.

When you copy a region from one location in an image to another location in the same image, `gdImageCopyResized()` will perform as expected unless the regions overlap, in which case the result is unpredictable. If this presents a problem, create a scratch image in which to keep intermediate results.

Important note on copying between images: Images do not necessarily have the same color tables, so pixels are not simply set to the same color index values to copy them. `gdImageCopyResized()` will invoke `gdImageColorExact()` in an attempt to find an identical RGB value in the destination image for each pixel in the copied portion of the source image.

If such a value is not found, gdImageCopy() will attempt to allocate colors as needed using gdImageColorAllocate(). If both of these methods fail, gdImageCopyResized() will invoke gdImageColorClosest() to find the color in the destination image that most closely approximates the color of the pixel being copied.

EXAMPLE

... Inside a function ...

```
gdImagePtr im_in;
gdImagePtr im_out;
int x, y;
FILE *in;
FILE *out;
/* Load a small gif to expand in the larger one */
in = fopen("small.gif", "rb");
im_in = gdImageCreateFromGif(in);
fclose(in);
/* Make the output image four times as large on both axes */
im_out = gdImageCreate(im_in->sx * 4, im_in->sy * 4);
/* Now copy the smaller image, but four times larger */
gdImageCopyResized(im_out, im_in, 0, 0, 0, 0,
        im_out->sx, im_out->sy,
        im_in->sx, im_in->sy);
out = fopen("large.gif", "wb");
gdImageGif(im_out, out);
fclose(out);
gdImageDestroy(im_in);
gdImageDestroy(im_out);
```

Function: gdImagePtr gdImageCreate(
                    int sx,
                    int sy)

DESCRIPTION

gdImageCreate() is called to create images. Invoke gdImageCreate() with the *x* and *y* dimensions of the desired image. gdImageCreate() returns a gdImagePtr to the new image or null if unable to allocate the image. The image must eventually be destroyed using gdImageDestroy().

EXAMPLE

... inside a function ...

```
gdImagePtr im;
im = gdImageCreate(64, 64);
/* ... Use the image ... */
gdImageDestroy(im);
```

Function: `gdImagePtr gdImageCreateFromGd(`
`FILE *in)`

DESCRIPTION

`gdImageCreateFromGd()` is called to load images from gd format files. Invoke `gdImageCreateFromGd()` with an already opened pointer to a file containing the desired image in the gd file format, which is specific to gd and intended for very fast loading. (It is not intended for compression or for use on the Web; for all external purposes, use GIF.) `gdImageCreateFromGd()` returns a `gdImagePtr` to the new image or null if unable to load the image (most often because the file is corrupt or does not contain a gd format image). `gdImageCreateFromGd()` does not close the file. Use `gdImageSX()` and `gdImageSY()` to determine the size of the image. The image must eventually be destroyed by using `gdImageDestroy()`.

EXAMPLE

... inside a function ...

```
gdImagePtr im;
FILE *in;
in = fopen("mygd.gd", "rb");
im = gdImageCreateFromGd(in);
fclose(in);
/* ... Use the image ... */
gdImageDestroy(im);
```

Function: `gdImagePtr gdImageCreateFromGif(`
`FILE *in);`

DESCRIPTION

`gdImageCreateFromGif()` is called to load images from GIF format files. Invoke `gdImageCreateFromGif()` with an already opened pointer to a file containing the desired image. gdImageCreateFromGif() returns a gdImagePtr to the new image or null if unable to load the image (most often because the file is corrupt or does not contain a GIF image). gdImageCreateFromGif() does not close the file.

You can use gdImageSX() and gdImageSY() to determine the size of the image. The image must eventually be destroyed by using gdImageDestroy().

EXAMPLE

... inside a function ...

```
gdImagePtr im;
FILE *in;
in = fopen("mygif.gif", "rb");
im = gdImageCreateFromGif(in);
fclose(in);
/* ... Use the image ... */
gdImageDestroy(im);
```

Function: gdImagePtr gdImageCreateFromXbm(
                        FILE *in);

DESCRIPTION

gdImageCreateFromXbm() is called to load images from X bitmap format files. Invoke gdImageCreateFromXbm() with an already opened pointer to a file containing the desired image. gdImageCreateFromXbm() returns a gdImagePtr to the new image or null if unable to load the image (most often because the file is corrupt or does not contain an X bitmap format image). gdImageCreateFromXbm() does not close the file.

You can use gdImageSX() and gdImageSY() to determine the size of the image. The image must eventually be destroyed by using gdImageDestroy().

EXAMPLE

... inside a function ...

```
gdImagePtr im;
FILE *in;
in = fopen("myxbm.xbm", "rb");
im = gdImageCreateFromXbm(in);
fclose(in);
```

```
/* ... Use the image ... */
gdImageDestroy(im);
```

Function: void gdImageDashedLine(
                   gdImagePtr im,
                   int x1,
                   int y1,
                   int x2,
                   int y2,
                   int color)

DESCRIPTION

gdImageDashedLine() is provided solely for backwards compatibility
with gd 1.0. New programs should draw dashed lines using the normal
gdImageLine() function and the new gdImageSetStyle() function.

gdImageDashedLine() is used to draw a dashed line between two
endpoints (x1, y1 and x2, y2). The line is drawn using the color index specified. The portions of the line that are not drawn are left alone so that the
background is visible.

EXAMPLE

... **inside a function ...**

```
gdImagePtr im;
int black;
int white;
im = gdImageCreate(100, 100);
/* Background color (first allocated) */
black = gdImageColorAllocate(im, 0, 0, 0);
/* Allocate the color white (red, green and blue all maximum). */
white = gdImageColorAllocate(im, 255, 255, 255);
/* Draw a dashed line from the upper left corner to the lower right
corner. */
gdImageDashedLine(im, 0, 0, 99, 99);
/* ... Do something with the image, such as saving it to a file... */
/* Destroy it */
gdImageDestroy(im);
```

Function: `void gdImageDestroy(`
                       `gdImagePtr im)`

DESCRIPTION

`gdImageDestroy()` is used to free the memory associated with an image. It is important to invoke `gdImageDestroy()` before exiting your program or assigning a new image to a `gdImagePtr` variable.

EXAMPLE

... inside a function ...

```
gdImagePtr im;
im = gdImageCreate(10, 10);
/* ... Use the image ... */
/* Now destroy it */
gdImageDestroy(im);
```

Function: `void gdImageFill(`
                       `gdImagePtr im,`
                       `int x,`
                       `int y,`
                       `int color)`

DESCRIPTION

`gdImageFill()` floods a portion of the image with the specified color, beginning at the specified point and flooding the surrounding region of the same color as the starting point. For a way to flood a region defined by a specific border color rather than by its interior color, see `gdImageFillToBorder()`.

The fill color can be `gdTiled`, thereby resulting in a tile fill using another image as the tile. However, the tile image cannot be transparent. If the image you wish to fill has a transparent color index, call `gdImageTransparent()` on the tile image and set the transparent color index to -1 to turn off its transparency.

Note that `gdImageFill()` is recursive. It is not the most naive implementation possible, and the implementation is expected to improve, but there will always be degenerate cases in which the stack can become very deep. This can be a problem in MSDOS and MS Windows environments. (Of course, in a Unix or NT environment with a proper stack, this is not a problem.)

EXAMPLE

... inside a function ...

```
gdImagePtr im;
int black;
int white;
int red;
im = gdImageCreate(100, 50);
/* Background color (first allocated) */
black = gdImageColorAllocate(im, 0, 0, 0);
/* Allocate the color white (red, green and blue all maximum). */
white = gdImageColorAllocate(im, 255, 255, 255);
/* Allocate the color red. */
red = gdImageColorAllocate(im, 255, 0, 0);
/* Inscribe an ellipse in the image. */
gdImageArc(im, 50, 25, 98, 48, 0, 360, white);
/* Flood-fill the ellipse. Fill color is red, and will replace the
        black interior of the ellipse. */
gdImageFill(im, 50, 50, red);
/* ... Do something with the image, such as saving it to a file... */
/* Destroy it */
gdImageDestroy(im);
```

Function: `void gdImageFilledPolygon(`
`                    gdImagePtr im,`
`                    gdPointPtr points,`
`                    int pointsTotal,`
`                    int color)`

DESCRIPTION

`gdImageFilledPolygon()` is used to fill a polygon with the verticies (at least 3) specified, using the color index specified. See also `gdImagePolygon()`.

EXAMPLE

... inside a function ...

```
gdImagePtr im;
int black;
int white;
int red;
/* Points of polygon */
gdPoint points[3];
```

```
im = gdImageCreate(100, 100);
/* Background color (first allocated) */
black = gdImageColorAllocate(im, 0, 0, 0);
/* Allocate the color white (red, green and blue all maximum). */
white = gdImageColorAllocate(im, 255, 255, 255);
/* Allocate the color red. */
red = gdImageColorAllocate(im, 255, 0, 0);
/* Draw a triangle. */
points[0].x = 50;
points[0].y = 0;
points[1].x = 99;
points[1].y = 99;
points[2].x = 0;
points[2].y = 99;
/* Paint it in white */
gdImageFilledPolygon(im, points, 3, white);
/* Outline it in red; must be done second */
gdImagePolygon(im, points, 3, red);
/* ... Do something with the image, such as saving it to a file... */
/* Destroy it */
gdImageDestroy(im);
```

Function: void gdImageFilledRectangle(
                gdImagePtr im,
                int x1,
                int y1,
                int x2,
                int y2,
                int color)

DESCRIPTION

gdImageFilledRectangle() is used to draw a solid rectangle with the two corners (upper left first, then lower right) specified, using the color index specified.

EXAMPLE

... inside a function ...

```
gdImagePtr im;
int black;
int white;
im = gdImageCreate(100, 100);
/* Background color (first allocated) */
```

```
black = gdImageColorAllocate(im, 0, 0, 0);
/* Allocate the color white (red, green and blue all maximum). */
white = gdImageColorAllocate(im, 255, 255, 255);
/* Draw a filled rectangle occupying the central area. */
gdImageFilledRectangle(im, 25, 25, 74, 74, white);
/* ... Do something with the image, such as saving it to a file... */
/* Destroy it */
gdImageDestroy(im);
```

Function: `void gdImageFillToBorder(`
        `gdImagePtr im,`
        `int x,`
        `int y,`
        `int border,`
        `int color)`

DESCRIPTION

gdImageFillToBorder() floods a portion of the image with the specified color, beginning at the specified point and stopping at the specified border color. For a way of flooding an area defined by the color of the starting point, see gdImageFill().

The border color cannot be a special color such as gdTiled; it must be a proper solid color. The fill color can be a special color, however.

Note that gdImageFillToBorder() is recursive. It is not the most naive implementation possible, and the implementation is expected to improve, but there will always be degenerate cases in which the stack can become very deep. This can be a problem in MSDOS and MS Windows environments. (Of course, in a Unix or NT environment with a proper stack, this is not a problem.)

EXAMPLE

... inside a function ...

```
gdImagePtr im;
int black;
int white;
int red;
im = gdImageCreate(100, 50);
/* Background color (first allocated) */
black = gdImageColorAllocate(im, 0, 0, 0);
```

```
/* Allocate the color white (red, green and blue all maximum). */
white = gdImageColorAllocate(im, 255, 255, 255);
/* Allocate the color red. */
red = gdImageColorAllocate(im, 255, 0, 0);
/* Inscribe an ellipse in the image. */
gdImageArc(im, 50, 25, 98, 48, 0, 360, white);
/* Flood-fill the ellipse. Fill color is red, border color is
        white (ellipse). */
gdImageFillToBorder(im, 50, 50, white, red);
/* ... Do something with the image, such as saving it to a file... */
/* Destroy it */
gdImageDestroy(im);
```

Function: `void gdImageGd(`
           `gdImagePtr im,`
           `FILE *out)`

DESCRIPTION

`gdImageGd` outputs the specified image to the specified file in the gd image format. The file must be open for writing. Under MSDOS, it is important to use "wb" as opposed to simply "w" as the mode when opening the file. Under Unix there is no penalty for doing so. `gdImageGd()` does not close the file; your code must do so.

The gd image format is intended for fast reads and writes of images your program will need frequently to build other images. It is not a compressed format and is not intended for general use. For external consumption, produce GIF images.

EXAMPLE

... inside a function ...

```
gdImagePtr im;
int black, white;
FILE *out;
/* Create the image */
im = gdImageCreate(100, 100);
/* Allocate background */
white = gdImageColorAllocate(im, 255, 255, 255);
/* Allocate drawing color */
black = gdImageColorAllocate(im, 0, 0, 0);
/* Draw rectangle */
gdImageRectangle(im, 0, 0, 99, 99, black);
```

```
/* Open output file in binary mode */
out = fopen("rect.gd", "wb");
/* Write gd format file */
gdImageGd(im, out);
/* Close file */
fclose(out);
/* Destroy image */
gdImageDestroy(im);
```

Function: `int gdImageGetInterlaced(`
                        `gdImagePtr im)`

DESCRIPTION

`gdImageGetInterlaced()` is a macro that returns true if the image is interlaced and false if not. Interlacing is used to permit Web browsers to display images progressively. Use this macro to obtain this information; do not access the structure directly. See `gdImageInterlace()` for a means of setting the interlace flag.

Function: `int gdImageGetPixel(`
                        `gdImagePtr im,`
                        `int x,`
                        `int y)`

DESCRIPTION

`gdImageGetPixel()` retrieves the color index of a particular pixel. Always use this function to query pixels; do not access the pixels of the `gdImage` structure directly.

EXAMPLE

... inside a function ...

```
FILE *in;
gdImagePtr im;
int c;
in = fopen("mygif.gif", "rb");
im = gdImageCreateFromGif(in);
fclose(in);
c = gdImageGetPixel(im, gdImageSX(im) / 2, gdImageSY(im) / 2);
printf("The value of the center pixel is %d; RGB values are
%d,%d,%d\n",
        c, im->red[c], im->green[c], im->blue[c]);
gdImageDestroy(im);
```

Function: `int gdImageGetTransparent(`
                         `gdImagePtr im)`

DESCRIPTION

`gdImageGetTransparent()` is a macro that returns the current transparent color index in the image. If there is no transparent color, `gdImageGetTransparent()` returns `-1`. Use this macro to obtain this information; do not access the structure directly.

Function: `void gdImageGif(`

                         `gdImagePtr im,`
                         `FILE *out);`

DESCRIPTION

`gdImageGif()` outputs the specified image to the specified file in GIF format. The file must be open for writing. Under MSDOS, it is important to use "wb" as opposed to simply "w" as the mode when opening the file. Under Unix there is no penalty for doing so. `gdImageGif()` does not close the file; your code must do so.

EXAMPLE

... inside a function ...

```
gdImagePtr im;
int black, white;
FILE *out;
/* Create the image */
im = gdImageCreate(100, 100);
/* Allocate background */
white = gdImageColorAllocate(im, 255, 255, 255);
/* Allocate drawing color */
black = gdImageColorAllocate(im, 0, 0, 0);
/* Draw rectangle */
gdImageRectangle(im, 0, 0, 99, 99, black);
/* Open output file in binary mode */
out = fopen("rect.gif", "wb");
/* Write GIF */
gdImageGif(im, out);
/* Close file */
fclose(out);
/* Destroy image */
gdImageDestroy(im);
```

Function: `int gdImageGreen(`
                          `gdImagePtr im,`
                          `int color)`

DESCRIPTION

`gdImageGreen()` is a macro that returns the green component of the specified color index. Use this macro rather than accessing the structure members directly.

Function: `void gdImageInterlace(`
                          `gdImagePtr im,`
                          `int interlace)`

DESCRIPTION

`gdImageInterlace()` is used to indicate whether an image should be stored in a linear fashion, in which lines will appear on the display from first to last, or in an interlaced fashion, in which the image will "fade in" over several passes. By default, images are not interlaced.

A nonzero value for the interlace argument turns on interlace; a zero value turns it off. Note that interlace has no effect on other functions or on image formats other than GIF.

When a GIF is loaded with `gdImageCreateFromGif()`, interlace will be set according to the setting in the GIF file.

Note that some GIF viewers and Web browsers do not support interlace. However, the interlaced GIF should still display; it will simply appear all at once, just as other images do.

EXAMPLE

... inside a function ...

```
gdImagePtr im;
FILE *out;
/* ... Create or load the image... */

/* Now turn on interlace */
gdImageInterlace(im, 1);
/* And open an output file */
out = fopen("test.gif", "wb");
/* And save the image */
gdImageGif(im, out);
```

```
fclose(out);
gdImageDestroy(im);
```

Function: void gdImageLine(
                    gdImagePtr im,
                    int x1,
                    int y1,
                    int x2,
                    int y2,
                    int color)

DESCRIPTION

gdImageLine() is used to draw a line between two endpoints (x1, y1 and x2, y2). The line is drawn using the color index specified. Note that the color index can be an actual color returned by gdImageColorAllocate() or one of gdStyled, gdBrushed, or gdStyledBrushed.

EXAMPLE

... inside a function ...

```
gdImagePtr im;
int black;
int white;
im = gdImageCreate(100, 100);
/* Background color (first allocated) */
black = gdImageColorAllocate(im, 0, 0, 0);
/* Allocate the color white (red, green and blue all maximum). */
white = gdImageColorAllocate(im, 255, 255, 255);
/* Draw a line from the upper left corner to the lower right corner.
*/
gdImageLine(im, 0, 0, 99, 99, white);
/* ... Do something with the image, such as saving it to a file... */
/* Destroy it */
gdImageDestroy(im);
```

Function: void gdImagePolygon(
                    gdImagePtr im,
                    gdPointPtr points,
                    int pointsTotal,
                    int color)

DESCRIPTION

gdImagePolygon() is used to draw a polygon with the vertices (at least 3)
specified by using the color index specified. See also
gdImageFilledPolygon().

EXAMPLE

... inside a function ...

```
gdImagePtr im;
int black;
int white;
/* Points of polygon */
gdPoint points[3];
im = gdImageCreate(100, 100);
/* Background color (first allocated) */
black = gdImageColorAllocate(im, 0, 0, 0);
/* Allocate the color white (red, green and blue all maximum). */
white = gdImageColorAllocate(im, 255, 255, 255);
/* Draw a triangle. */
points[0].x = 50;
points[0].y = 0;
points[1].x = 99;
points[1].y = 99;
points[2].x = 0;
points[2].y = 99;
gdImagePolygon(im, points, 3, white);
/* ... Do something with the image, such as saving it to a file... */
/* Destroy it */
gdImageDestroy(im);
```

Function: void gdImageRectangle(
                        gdImagePtr im,
                        int x1,
                        int y1,
                        int x2,
                        int y2,
                        int color)

DESCRIPTION

gdImageRectangle() is used to draw a rectangle with the two corners
(upper left first, then lower right) specified by using the color index
specified.

EXAMPLE

... inside a function ...

```
gdImagePtr im;
int black;
int white;
im = gdImageCreate(100, 100);
/* Background color (first allocated) */
black = gdImageColorAllocate(im, 0, 0, 0);
/* Allocate the color white (red, green and blue all maximum). */
white = gdImageColorAllocate(im, 255, 255, 255);
/* Draw a rectangle occupying the central area. */
gdImageRectangle(im, 25, 25, 74, 74, white);
/* ... Do something with the image, such as saving it to a file... */
/* Destroy it */
gdImageDestroy(im);
```

Function: `int gdImageRed(`
                          `gdImagePtr im,`
                          `int color)`

DESCRIPTION

gdImageRed() is a macro that returns the red component of the specified color index. Use this macro rather than accessing the structure members directly.

Function: `void gdImageSetBrush(`
                          `gdImagePtr im,`
                          `gdImagePtr brush)`

DESCRIPTION

A "brush" is an image used to draw wide, shaped strokes in another image. Just as a paintbrush is not a single point, a brush image need not be a single pixel. Any gd image can be used as a brush. By setting the transparent color index of the brush image with gdImageColorTransparent(), a brush of any shape can be created. All line-drawing functions, such as gdImageLine() and gdImagePolygon(), will use the current brush if the special "color" gdBrushed or gdStyledBrushed is used when calling them.

gdImageSetBrush() is used to specify the brush to be used in a particular image. You can set any image to be the brush. If the brush image does not have the same color map as the first image, any colors missing from the first image will be allocated. If not enough colors can be allocated, the closest colors already available will be used. This allows arbitrary GIFs to be used as brush images. It also means, however, that you should not set a brush unless you will actually use it. If you set a rapid succession of different brush images, you can quickly fill your color map, and the results will not be optimal.

You need not take any special action when you are finished with a brush. As for any other image, if you will not be using the brush image for any further purpose, you should call gdImageDestroy(). You must not use the color gdBrushed if the current brush has been destroyed. You can, of course, set a new brush to replace it.

EXAMPLE

... inside a function ...

```
gdImagePtr im, brush;
FILE *in;
int black;
im = gdImageCreate(100, 100);
/* Open the brush GIF. For best results, portions of the
        brush that should be transparent (ie, not part of the
        brush shape) should have the transparent color index. */
in = fopen("star.gif", "rb");
brush = gdImageCreateFromGif(in);
/* Background color (first allocated) */
black = gdImageColorAllocate(im, 0, 0, 0);
gdImageSetBrush(im, brush);
/* Draw a line from the upper left corner to the lower right corner
        using the brush. */
gdImageLine(im, 0, 0, 99, 99, gdBrushed);
/* ... Do something with the image, such as saving it to a file... */
/* Destroy it */
gdImageDestroy(im);
/* Destroy the brush image */
gdImageDestroy(brush);
```

Function: void gdImageSetPixel(
                    gdImagePtr im,
                    int x,
                    int y,
                    int color)

DESCRIPTION

gdImageSetPixel() sets a pixel to a particular color index. Always use this function or one of the other drawing functions to access pixels. Do not access the pixels of the gdImage structure directly.

EXAMPLE

... inside a function ...

```
gdImagePtr im;
int black;
int white;
im = gdImageCreate(100, 100);
/* Background color (first allocated) */
black = gdImageColorAllocate(im, 0, 0, 0);
/* Allocate the color white (red, green and blue all maximum). */
white = gdImageColorAllocate(im, 255, 255, 255);
/* Set a pixel near the center. */
gdImageSetPixel(im, 50, 50, white);
/* ... Do something with the image, such as saving it to a file... */
/* Destroy it */
gdImageDestroy(im);
```

Function: `void gdImageSetStyle(`
`                gdImagePtr im,`
`                int *style,`
`                int styleLength)`

DESCRIPTION

It is often desirable to draw dashed lines, dotted lines, and other variations on a broken line. gdImageSetStyle() can be used to set any desired series of colors, including a special color that leaves the background intact, to be repeated during the drawing of a line.

To use gdImageSetStyle(), create an array of integers and assign them the desired series of color values to be repeated. You can assign the special color value gdTransparent to indicate that the existing color should be left unchanged for that particular pixel (thus allowing a dashed line to be attractively drawn over an existing image).

Then, to draw a line using the style, use the normal gdImageLine() function with the special color value gdStyled.

As of version 1.1.1, the style array is copied when you set the style, so you need not be concerned with keeping the array around indefinitely. This should not break existing code that assumes styles are not copied.

You can also combine styles and brushes to draw the brush image at intervals instead of in a continuous stroke. When a style is created for use with a brush, the style values are interpreted differently: zero (0) indicates pixels at which the brush should not be drawn, while one (1) indicates pixels at which the brush should be drawn. To draw a styled, brushed line, you must use the special color value gdStyledBrushed. For an example of this feature in use, see gddemo.c (provided in the distribution).

EXAMPLE

... inside a function ...

```
gdImagePtr im;
int styleDotted[2], styleDashed[6];
FILE *in;
int black;
int red;
im = gdImageCreate(100, 100);
/* Background color (first allocated) */
black = gdImageColorAllocate(im, 0, 0, 0);
red = gdImageColorAllocate(im, 255, 0, 0);
/* Set up dotted style. Leave every other pixel alone. */
styleDotted[0] = red;
styleDotted[1] = gdTransparent;
/* Set up dashed style. Three on, three off. */
styleDashed[0] = red;
styleDashed[1] = red;
styleDashed[2] = red;
styleDashed[3] = gdTransparent;
styleDashed[4] = gdTransparent;
styleDashed[5] = gdTransparent;
/* Set dotted style. Note that we have to specify how many pixels are
        in the style! */
gdImageSetStyle(im, styleDotted, 2);
/* Draw a line from the upper left corner to the lower right corner. */
gdImageLine(im, 0, 0, 99, 99, gdStyled);
/* Now the dashed line. */
gdImageSetStyle(im, styleDashed, 6);
gdImageLine(im, 0, 99, 0, 99, gdStyled);
```

```
/* ... Do something with the image, such as saving it to a file ... */

/* Destroy it */
gdImageDestroy(im);
```

Function: `void gdImageSetTile(`
                                      `gdImagePtr im,`
                                        `gdImagePtr tile)`

DESCRIPTION

A "tile" is an image used to fill an area with a repeated pattern. Any gd image can be used as a tile. **For** `gdImageFilledRectangle()` **and** `gdImageFilledPolygon()` **only:** By setting the transparent color index of the tile image with `gdImageColorTransparent()`, you can create a tile that allows certain parts of the underlying area to shine through. All region-filling functions, such as `gdImageFill()` and `gdImageFilledPolygon()`, will use the current tile if the special "color" `gdTiled` is used when calling them.

`gdImageSetTile()` is used to specify the tile to be used in a particular image. You can set any image to be the tile. If the tile image does not have the same color map as the first image, any colors missing from the first image will be allocated. If not enough colors can be allocated, the closest colors already available will be used. This allows arbitrary GIFs to be used as tile images. It also means, however, that you should not set a tile unless you will actually use it. If you set a rapid succession of different tile images, you can quickly fill your color map, and the results will not be optimal.

You need not take any special action when you are finished with a tile. As for any other image, if you will not be using the tile image for any further purpose, you should call `gdImageDestroy()`. You must not use the color `gdTiled` if the current tile has been destroyed. You can, of course, set a new tile to replace it.

Again, if `gdImageFill()` or `gdImageFillToBorder()` is to be used, the tile image should not have a transparent color index. Transparent tiles may be used with `ImageFilledRectangle()` and `gdImageFilledPolygon()`.

EXAMPLE

... inside a function ...

```
gdImagePtr im, tile;
FILE *in;
int black;
im = gdImageCreate(100, 100);
/* Open the tile GIF. For best results, portions of the
        tile that should be transparent (ie, allowing the
        background to shine through) should have the transparent
        color index. */
in = fopen("star.gif", "rb");
tile = gdImageCreateFromGif(in);
/* Background color (first allocated) */
black = gdImageColorAllocate(im, 0, 0, 0);
gdImageSetTile(im, tile);
/* Fill an area using the tile. */
gdImageFilledRectangle(im, 25, 25, 75, 75, gdTiled);
/* ... Do something with the image, such as saving it to a file... */
/* Destroy it */
gdImageDestroy(im);
/* Destroy the tile image */
gdImageDestroy(tile);
```

Function: `void gdImageString(`
                    `gdImagePtr im,`
                    `gdFontPtr font,`
                    `int x,`
                    `int y,`
                    `char *s,`
                    `int color)`

DESCRIPTION

gdImageString() is used to draw multiple characters on the image. (To draw single characters, use gdImageChar().) The second argument is a pointer to a font definition structure. Five fonts are provided with gd: gdFontTiny, gdFontSmall, gdFontMediumBold, gdFontLarge, and gdFontGiant. You must #include the files gdfontt.h, gdfonts.h, gdfontmb.h, gdfontl.h, and gdfontg.h, respectively. The null-terminated C string specified by the fifth argument is drawn from left to right in the specified color. (See gdImageStringUp() for a way to draw vertical text.) Pixels not set by a particular character retain their previous color.

EXAMPLE

```
#include "gd.h"
#include "gdfontl.h"
#include <string.h>
... inside a function ...
gdImagePtr im;
int black;
int white;
/* String to draw. */
char *s = "Hello.";
im = gdImageCreate(100, 100);
/* Background color (first allocated) */
black = gdImageColorAllocate(im, 0, 0, 0);
/* Allocate the color white (red, green and blue all maximum). */
white = gdImageColorAllocate(im, 255, 255, 255);
/* Draw a centered string. */
gdImageString(im, gdFontLarge,
        im->w / 2 - (strlen(s) * gdFontLarge->w / 2),
        im->h / 2 - gdFontLarge->h / 2,
        s, white);
/* ... Do something with the image, such as saving it to a file... */
/* Destroy it */
gdImageDestroy(im);
```

Function: void gdImageStringUp(
                    gdImagePtr im,
                    gdFontPtr font,
                    int x,
                    int y,
                    char *s,
                    int color)

DESCRIPTION

gdImageStringUp() is used to draw multiple characters on the image, rotated 90 degrees. (To draw single characters, use gdImageCharUp().) The second argument is a pointer to a font definition structure. Five fonts are provided with gd: gdFontTiny, gdFontSmall, gdFontMediumBold, gdFontLarge, and gdFontGiant. You must #include the files gdfontt.h, gdfonts.h, gdfontmb.h, gdfontl.h, and gdfontg.h, respectively. The null-terminated C string specified by the fifth argument is drawn from bottom to top (rotated 90 degrees) in the specified color. (See gdImageString() for a way to draw horizontal text.) Pixels not set by a particular character retain their previous color.

EXAMPLE

```
#include "gd.h"
#include "gdfontl.h"
#include <string.h>
... inside a function ...
gdImagePtr im;
int black;
int white;
/* String to draw. */
char *s = "Hello.";
im = gdImageCreate(100, 100);
/* Background color (first allocated) */
black = gdImageColorAllocate(im, 0, 0, 0);
/* Allocate the color white (red, green and blue all maximum). */
white = gdImageColorAllocate(im, 255, 255, 255);
/* Draw a centered string going upwards. Axes are reversed,
        and Y axis is decreasing as the string is drawn. */
gdImageStringUp(im, gdFontLarge,
        im->w / 2 - gdFontLarge->h / 2,
        im->h / 2 + (strlen(s) * gdFontLarge->w / 2),
        s, white);
/* ... Do something with the image, such as saving it to a file... */
/* Destroy it */
gdImageDestroy(im);
```

Function: int gdImageSX(
                    gdImagePtr im)

DESCRIPTION

gdImageSX() is a macro that returns the width of the image in pixels. Use this macro rather than accessing the structure members directly.

Function: int gdImageSY(
                    gdImagePtr im)

DESCRIPTION

gdImageSY() is a macro that returns the height of the image in pixels. Use this macro rather than accessing the structure members directly.

CD Contents and Other Sources

This book includes a CD that contains the source code to all of the programs found in the book. In addition, the CD contains several useful libraries and other tools for CGI programmers. For those without convenient access to a CD-ROM drive, these materials are also available by anonymous ftp and via the Web HTTP protocol. The ftp and http sites will also receive occasional updates, when appropriate.

This appendix briefly explains the purpose of each major directory. It also reprints the Unix Makefile found on the CD. README.TXT files in each subdirectory provide up-to-date details.

Alternative Sources: Source Code Online

These materials are also available through the Web at

    [URL:http://www.boutell.com/cgibook/]

and by anonymous ftp from the machine ftp.boutell.com in the directory pub/boutell/cgibook.

Top-level Directory List

Following are the top-level directories of the CD:

Directory	Contents
source	All source code, libraries, and so on related to the book
mapedit	The author's Mapedit imagemap editing utility (evaluation copies)

The source Directory

Following are the subdirectories of the source directory:

Directory	Contents
c	C source code for all example programs in this book
cgic104	The author's cgic library for CGI programming in C
gd1_2	The author's gd library for GIF generation in C
perl	Perl source code for all example programs in this book
perllibs	Several Perl libraries useful to CGI programmers

> **IMPORTANT NOTE:** When you install these files to your working drive, you must install the gd1_2 and cgic104 directories as children of the same parent directory, just as on the CD. Alternatively, install them wherever you like and modify the Makefile in the c directory appropriately.

The c Directory

This directory contains C source code for all of the example programs found in this book.

Filename	Purpose
Makefile	A Unix Makefile for all examples; type make programname
bugrep.c	An e-mail form handler (Chapter 9)
cgicmnts.c	A comment handler, using cgic (Chapter 8)
cgictest.c	A demonstration program for advanced forms (Chapter 11)
cgipull.c	A client pull example (Chapter 12)
chart.c	A module for drawing bar charts (Chapter 10; see also chart.h)

`chart.h`	#include file for the `chart.c` module (Chapter 10)
`checkrej.c`	A function to reject unauthorized users (Chapter 6)
`comments.c`	A comment handler, not using cgic (Chapter 7)
`dimage.c`	A program that outputs an inline image (Chapter 10)
`gdshort.c`	A program that uses gd to draw an image (Chapter 10)
`hello.c`	A bare-bones CGI example (Chapter 3)
`mag.c`	An inline image "magnifying glass" (Chapter 12)
`nph-p2.c`	Server push, with fallbacks for older browsers (Chapter 12)
`nph-push.c`	A server push example (Chapter 12)
`nph-sss.c`	The Solar System Simulator (Chapter 13)
`parse.c`	Routines for reading a database in a text file (Chapter 14)
`parse.h`	#include file for the `parse.c` module (Chapter 14)
`refimage.c`	A program that references random inline images (Chapter 10)
`simtrade.c`	World Wide Web Wall Street, trading simulator (Chapter 14)
`testc.c`	A simple test program for the `chart.c` module (Chapter 10)
`trade.c`	World Wide Web Wall Street, main CGI program (Chapter 14)
`wbw1.c`	World Birthday Web, first version (Chapter 5)
`wbw2.c`	World Birthday Web, complete cgic version (Chapter 8)

The Unix Makefile in this directory is reprinted at the end of this appendix.

The Perl Directory

This directory contains Perl source code for all of the example programs found in this book.

Filename	Purpose
`bugrep`	An e-mail form handler (Chapter 9)
`clmnts`	A comment handler, using cgi-lib (Chapter 8)
`cgictest`	A demonstration program for advanced forms (Chapter 11)
`cgipull`	A client pull example (Chapter 12)
`cgi-lib.pl`	Steven Brenner's form processing library (Chapter 8)
`chart.pl`	A function to draw bar charts (Chapter 10)
`checkrej`	A function to reject unauthorized users (Chapter 6)
`comments`	A comment handler, not using cgi-lib (Chapter 7)
`dimage`	A program that outputs an inline image (Chapter 10)
`gdshort`	A program that uses gd to draw an image (Chapter 10)
`hello`	A bare-bones CGI example (Chapter 3)

Filename	Purpose
mag	An inline image "magnifying glass" (Chapter 12)
nph-p2	Server push, with fallbacks for older browsers (Chapter 12)
nph-push	A server push example (Chapter 12)
nph-sss	The Solar System Simulator (Chapter 13)
refimage	A program that references random inline images (Chapter 10)
simtrade	World Wide Web Wall Street, trading simulator (Chapter 14)
testc	A simple test program for the `chart.pl` code (Chapter 10)
trade	World Wide Web Wall Street, main CGI program (Chapter 14)
wbw1	World Birthday Web, first version (Chapter 5)
wbw2	World Birthday Web, complete cgi-lib version (Chapter 8)

Unix Makefile for the C Examples

The Unix Makefile included in the `source/c` directory of the CD is reprinted here. Note that indented lines must be indented with a tab.

This Makefile allows any of the C examples to be easily built, as long as the C, `gd1_2`, and `cgic104` subdirectories are installed as subdirectories of the same parent directory.

To compile a particular example, first be sure to change any #define directives at the beginning of the code to indicate reasonable paths and URLs on your system. Then type

```
make programname
```

to compile the desired program.

```
#Unix Makefile for the C example programs of
#"CGI Programming in C and Perl." Copyright 1995, 1996, Addison-
Wesley.

#For this to work, cgic104 and gd1_2 must be in adjacent
#directories. For best results cp -r the entire
#contents of the /source subdirectory of the CD
#to your drive.

#BE SURE TO MAKE ANY REQUIRED CHANGES TO THE SOURCE
#before compiling various programs.
```

```
#
#To compile a particular program, type "make programname".

#Change this to the ANSI C compiler on your system if you do not have
gcc.
#You must have an ANSI C compiler. gcc is freely available for most
systems.

CC=gcc

all:
        @echo Please type make programname to compile individual
programs.
        @echo Be sure to make any required changes to the source code
        @echo of each program before compiling.

#Ensure that libgd.a and libcgic.a are available.

libs: ../gd1_2/libgd.a ../cgic104/libcgic.a
        cd ../gd1_2; make libgd.a
        cd ../cgic104; make libcgic.a

#Ensure that there are no paths requiring modification
#in the source code of a program before agreeing to compile it.

checkpaths:
        @echo NOTE: this program contains paths and/or URLs which
        @echo must be set to reasonable paths and URLs on your system
        @echo before it will work properly. See the source code and
        @echo the relevant chapter of the book for details.

#Any additional directories in which libraries will be found
LIBDIRS=-L../gd1_2 -L../cgic104

#Any additional directories in which include files will be found
INCLUDEDIRS=-I../gd1_2 -I../cgic104

#Rule to create object files from C source files
.c.o: $<
        ${CC}  $< ${CFLAGS}  ${INCLUDEDIRS}  -c

#Libraries to be linked against: gd, cgic, and the standard math
library

LIBS=-lgd -lcgic -lm
```

```
#Rules to create each target from the object files that compose it

mag: checkpaths libs mag.o
        ${CC}  mag.o -o mag ${LIBDIRS}  ${LIBS}

cgipull: checkpaths libs cgipull.o
        ${CC}  cgipull.o -o cgipull ${LIBDIRS}  ${LIBS}

nph-push: checkpaths libs nph-push.o
        ${CC}  nph-push.o -o nph-push ${LIBDIRS}  ${LIBS}

nph-p2: checkpaths libs nph-p2.o
        ${CC}  nph-p2.o -o nph-p2 ${LIBDIRS}  ${LIBS}

nph-sss: checkpaths libs nph-sss.o
        ${CC}  nph-sss.o -o nph-sss ${LIBDIRS}  ${LIBS}

simtrade: checkpaths simtrade.o parse.o
        ${CC}  simtrade.o parse.o -o simtrade

trade: checkpaths libs trade.o parse.o chart.o
        ${CC}  trade.o parse.o chart.o -o trade ${LIBDIRS}  ${LIBS}

circle: libs circle.o
        ${CC}  circle.o -o circle ${LIBDIRS}  ${LIBS}

gdshort: libs gdshort.o
        ${CC}  gdshort.o -o gdshort ${LIBDIRS}  ${LIBS}

bugrep: checkpaths libs bugrep.o
        ${CC}  bugrep.o -o bugrep ${LIBDIRS}  ${LIBS}

wbw1: checkpaths wbw1.o
        ${CC}  wbw1.o -o wbw1

wbw2: checkpaths libs wbw2.o
        ${CC}  wbw2.o -o wbw2 ${LIBDIRS}  ${LIBS}

cgicmnts: checkpaths libs cgicmnts.o
        ${CC}  cgicmnts.o -o cgicmnts ${LIBDIRS}  ${LIBS}

hello: hello.o
        ${CC}  hello.o -o hello
```

```
testc: libs chart.o testc.o
      ${CC}  testc.o chart.o -o testc ${LIBDIRS}  ${LIBS}

cgictest: libs cgictest.o
      ${CC}  cgictest.o -o cgictest ${LIBDIRS}  ${LIBS}

comments: checkpaths comments.o
      ${CC}  comments.o -o comments

dimage: checkpaths dimage.o
      ${CC}  dimage.o -o dimage

refimage: checkpaths refimage.o
      ${CC}  refimage.o -o refimage
```

INDEX

Addison-Wesley Computer and Engineering Publishing Group

How to Interact with Us

1. Visit our Web site

http://www.awl.com/cseng

When you think you've read enough, there's always more content for you at Addison-Wesley's web site. Our web site contains a directory of complete product information including:

- Chapters
- Exclusive author interviews
- Links to authors' pages
- Tables of contents
- Source code

You can also discover what tradeshows and conferences Addison-Wesley will be attending, read what others are saying about our titles, and find out where and when you can meet our authors and have them sign your book.

2. Subscribe to Our Email Mailing Lists

Subscribe to our electronic mailing lists and be the first to know when new books are publishing. Here's how it works: Sign up for our electronic mailing at **http://www.awl.com/cseng/mailinglists.html**. Just select the subject areas that interest you and you will receive notification via email when we publish a book in that area.

3. Contact Us via Email

cepubprof@awl.com
Ask general questions about our books.
Sign up for our electronic mailing lists.
Submit corrections for our web site.

bexpress@awl.com
Request an Addison-Wesley catalog.
Get answers to questions regarding your order or our products.

innovations@awl.com
Request a current Innovations Newsletter.

webmaster@awl.com
Send comments about our web site.

mary.obrien@awl.com
Submit a book proposal.
Send errata for an Addison-Wesley book.

cepubpublicity@awl.com
Request a review copy for a member of the media interested in reviewing new Addison-Wesley titles.

We encourage you to patronize the many fine retailers who stock Addison-Wesley titles. Visit our online directory to find stores near you or visit our online store: **http://store.awl.com/** or call **800-824-7799**.

Addison Wesley Longman
Computer and Engineering Publishing Group
One Jacob Way, Reading, Massachusetts 01867 USA
TEL 781-944-3700 • FAX 781-942-3076

Effective Perl Programming
Writing Better Programs with Perl
Joseph N. Hall with Randal L. Schwartz

This book shows in sixty concise lessons how to tackle and solve common programming obstacles, and how to write effective Perl scripts. *Effective Perl Programming* explains idiomatic Perl, covering the latest release (Version 5), and includes information and useful examples about the structure, functions, and latest capabilities of the language, such as self-documenting object-oriented modules. You can also learn from Hall's answers to real-life questions and problems he receives from newsgroups and his Perl seminars.

0-201-41975-0 • Paperback • 288 Pages • ©1998

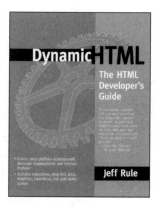

Dynamic HTML
The HTML Developer's Guide
Jeff Rule

This concise and readable tutorial and reference is just what you need to ease the learning curve of Dynamic HTML. This book helps you understand the principles behind DHTML and acquire techniques for effective DHTML scripting using a unique learn-by-example approach. Not only do the examples explain and illustrate theory they can be plugged into existing web pages to create instant dynamic effects such as pull-down menus, animations, pop-out menus, transitions, filters, and drag and drop. The book explains all of the key topics, including DOM (Document Object Model), CSS (Cascading Style Sheets), and XML (eXtensible Markup Language), essential technologies contributing to DHTML. It also offers comprehensive coverage of both Microsoft and Netscape implementations.

0-201-37961-9 • Paperback • 288 pages • ©1999

Drag 'n' Drop CGI
Enhance Your Web Site Without Programming
Bob Weil and Chris Baron

Drag 'n' Drop CGI enables webmasters and HTML coders who are not experienced programmers to add interactivity to their web sites. The CD-ROM includes pre-programmed scripts for forms, counters, search engines, imagemaps, and more. The book contains step-by-step instructions to configure and install a wide range of useful, industrial-strength, full-featured JavaScript and Perl scripts including: a complete online store with online secure credit card transactions, a search engine, and HTML form processing script, a floating web site directory panel, a programmable image display script, a scrolling browser message, and a visitor counter.

0-201-41966-1 • Paperback with CD-ROM • 384 pages • ©1997

Programming Applications for Netscape Servers
Kaveh Gh. Bassiri

With the infinite demand for information now available electronically, it is no surprise that the Web server market is growing rapidly. One of the more experienced, established players in this growing market is Netscape. Netscape's products have a proven track record of offering developers, programmers, and system administrators the tools they need to compete— proven accessibility to information electronically through the World Wide Web. *Programming Applications for Netscape Servers* covers the most recent release (3.5.1) as well as all past versions, providing you with the foundation of many programming options for extending the Netscape Server's capabilities. The CD-ROM includes code samples, utilities, and documentation for CGI, NSAPI, CORBA, and WAI—plus NSAPI extensions for Perl and Python and CGI libraries for C, C++, and Perl.

0-201-41970-X • Paperback with CD-ROM • 1008 pages • ©1999

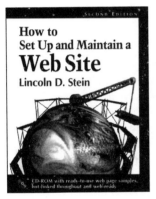

How to Set Up and Maintain a Web Site, Second Edition
Lincoln D. Stein

All aspects of WWW design, setup, and maintenance are covered, with chapters on unraveling the Web, installing and configuring a Web server, security, hypertext documents, tools for multimedia, server scripts, and Java applets. Included is a CD-ROM containing source code to all the examples in the book, HTML editors and syntax checkers, CGI, Perl 5 script libraries, and loads of applets.

0-201-63462-7 • Paperback with CD-ROM • 816 pages • ©1997

Tcl and the Tk Toolkit
John K. Ousterhout

This book introduces two systems, Tcl and Tk, that together provide a simple yet powerful programming environment for developing and using windowing applications under the X Window System. With these tools, it is possible for novices to create graphical applications, while providing experts with sophisticated features that go far beyond the capabilities of other toolkits. Written by the creator of Tcl and Tk, this book is the definitive guide to these systems. Specifically, you will learn about Tk's hypertext and hypergraphics widgets and Tcl's facilities for procedures, list management, and subprocess execution. And you will discover how Tk's windowing shell, wish, enables you to develop window-based applications with amazingly few lines of code.

0-201-63337-X • Paperback • 480 pages • ©1994